Modern Theory AND Method IN Group Training

NTL LEARNING RESOURCES SERIES

Modern Theory and Method in Group Training, Edited by William G. Dyer

NTL Learning Resources Series

Modern Theory AND Method IN Group Training

edited by
William G. Dyer

Brigham Young University

VAN NOSTRAND REINHOLD COMPANY

New York   Cincinnati   Toronto   London   Melbourne

Van Nostrand Reinhold Company Regional Offices:
New York Cincinnati Chicago Millbrae Dallas

Van Nostrand Reinhold Company International Offices:
London Toronto Melbourne

Copyright © 1972 by Litton Educational Publishing, Inc.

Library of Congress Catalog Card Number: 71-180158

Manufactured in the United States of America

Published by Van Nostrand Reinhold Company
450 West 33rd Street, New York, N. Y. 10001

Published simultaneously in Canada by Van Nostrand Reinhold Ltd.

15 14 13 12 11 10 9 8 7 6 5 4 3 2

Foreword

The spread of group training in individual and organizational behavior—sensitivity, laboratory, or T-group training—during the past twenty-five years has been phenomenal. Since the pioneering beginnings in the field at Bethel, Maine in 1947 carried out by the National Training Laboratories, interest and activity have taken root in every continent in the world. This growth has occurred in spite of excesses by inadequately trained and not always responsible persons, with corresponding adverse publicity, and with a wide proliferation of methods and approaches—a fact which underlines the need for and basic validity and effectiveness of this educational approach to many human and organizational problems.

The very flourishing of the field, however, has brought to the fore the crucial concern about the quality, background, experience, capability, personal motivation, and ethical responsibility of those who serve as trainers. In the highly sensitive area of human behavior, where damage can occur when fragile persons and inept or disturbed trainers conjoin, it is easily possible for a trainer to utilize the group to serve his own emotional needs to the detriment of the group.

The tasks confronting the trainer are complex. He must not only allow and assist the members to create and develop a group containing the necessary norms to encourage learning, but he must also assist them to discover and develop processes by which they learn from their individual and group experiences. At the same time, he must be sensitive to individual needs, defenses, and the extent of behavioral change so that he can help the group provide needed limits and protections. His own openness and authenticity must be used only to serve the group.

The role, skills, professional experience, and personal behavior of the trainer have become ever more crucial as the number of those attempting to serve as trainers multiplies and as the variety of theories or assumptions about training grows. It is increasingly clear that an effective trainer must possess a very careful blend of professional backgrounds, experience with individual and group behavior, awareness of organizational and cultural forces, sensitivity to others, personal awareness, security, and authenticity. At the same time, there has not yet been sufficient study or research given to this problem, even though isolated studies have been undertaken and such central organizations as the NTL Institute for Applied Behavioral Science and the European Institute for Transnational Studies in Group and Organizational Development have long been concerned and have developed standards for the acceptance of trainers and guides for their behavior. An emerging organization, the International Association of Applied Social Scientists, spun off from the NTL Institute, will be basically active in establishing standards for trainers.

The accreditation, however, is only part of the efforts that should be made. It is also necessary to provide help to those entering the field or developing in it. While the Trainer Development programs conducted by NTL, EIT, and several universities reach a few, there is need to provide literature of practical help to the trainer. Because this field is new and developing, the most effective help can come from the distillation of experiences of those long active in the field of applied behavioral science.

This is what this book attempts to do and why it is so important. Professor Dyer has brought together many experts in the field to provide a wide variety of chapters dealing with many aspects of trainer behavior. The chapters focus on helping the trainer in his role, and those dealing with ethical responsibility are particularly helpful in establishing standards. The breadth of this volume is excellent, ranging from the analyses of personal experiences to the conceptualization and development of models for trainer conduct.

A critical area in the important and growing educational field of behavioral training has been here opened up.

Leland P. Bradford

Former Executive Director,
NTL Institute for Applied
Behavioral Science

Preface

In the past few years, the group-training field has gained worldwide prominence—even notoriety. The mass media have spread wildly varying stories about the values and evils of sensitivity training, training groups, encounter groups, group marathons, nude groups, and so on. Yet even as the critics take up cudgels, group training is becoming entrenched as a major learning process. Increasing numbers of universities, public schools, counseling centers, hospitals, and business and government organizations are incorporating group methods into training and educational endeavors. A correspondingly large number of persons are making the field an important part of their professional careers.

People who come into contact with group training often ask, "How does one become a trainer?" They ask the trainer, "Have you changed any since you first started training?" "What differences do you see in groups now as compared with the first ones you handled?" The purposes of this book are to answer such questions—as well as those about the theories, research, and experience that add to the state of the science—and to give those who want to enter this complex and rapidly expanding field some understanding of its dimensions and developments.

ISSUES COVERED IN THIS VOLUME

Theory and method of trainer style. Every competent, mature trainer changes both in himself and in the ways he deals with persons and issues in groups. He continually integrates new experiences and information into his personal framework. Trainers find that they revise their goals, methods of training, and theories about learning and individual and group behavior. Although frequently trainers know that changes have taken place—gradual, subtle, dramatic, personal, or "public"—not many have thought through these changes as carefully or articulated them as precisely as William Golden has. His chapter may be, in fact, the most penetrating and revealing discussion of the personal development of a group trainer that I have found. Several experienced trainers who have previewed this chapter have remarked on the similarities between certain of their own experiences and those mentioned by Golden. It is hoped that while reading Golden other experiential trainers will feel this "shock of recognition" and be inspired to review their own values, theories, and personal behaviors, and that those entering the field will be better able to assess the progress of their own development.

In the following chapter, Jack Gibb also describes the changes that he has gone through as a person and a trainer. For him the areas are mutually interactive and virtually inseparable. After years of experience with groups, he has come to believe that the trainer must be as authentic a person as possible, using all his resources for the mutual learning of trainer and group. This leads him to describe his current style of training as "being with" a group.

One of the major issues in training questions whether the trainer enters the group as a person or as a competent professional filling a role. Fred Massarik explores this issue, viewing the "natural" trainer as one who uses his resources spontaneously to further group learnings. He develops the propositions that "a good trainer is natural" and that "not everyone who is natural is a good trainer." Massarik feels that the dual nature of trainership can be resolved; the trainer can legitimately combine naturalness with learned role resources to help effect maximum learning for clients.

Theory and method of trainer interventions. In his chapter, Gordon Lippit presents a summary of the conditions and forces he believes trainers should keep in mind when designing and conducting a training program. He deals with the multiple roles of the trainer in the group, the special problems of trainers, and the ethical dimensions of training and provides a list of guidelines useful in determining the timing of interventions.

Donald Klein describes first some major issues in the orientation or training style of the trainer. He distinguishes between the objective study of group patterns (rational-empirical), the emotional forces in a group (irrational-dynamic) and the orientation directed towards self-awareness (personal-reconstructional). Following this he points out the role of the trainer under different styles and relates this to the problem of training people for competence in working in today's community.

Arthur Cohen and Robert D. Smith tackle the very difficult problems of how, when, and why a trainer should intervene in a group. They identify two types of interventions which they call Planned Theory and Spontaneous Theory Interventions. They then examine the critical incidents that occur in groups and discuss the types of interventions that will be effective for particular incidents. Their model for analyzing a critical incident is useful in analyzing the group's actions and as a means of training new trainers to look at incidents and test the appropriateness of interventions.

Sherman Kingsbury also deals with the appropriateness of trainer interventions, stressing certain situations in groups which pose dilemmas for the trainer. In such cases, a choice of intervention is made even though the trainer cannot be sure it is right. Kingsbury isolates four areas where such dilemmas are likely and proposes methods of dealing with them.

Samuel Culbert presents a model for training interventions and, within its framework, elaborates on the moment-to-moment participation issues a trainer faces. He focuses on the unique responsibilities of the trainer, his opportunities for influencing others, and the human demands of participation as a group trainer. His chapter also becomes a statement of belief as he elaborates with humility—and often with humor—his thoughts about himself, about group members, and about situational components of groups.

Design developments in group training. Laboratory designs are modified and expanded just as individual trainers change and grow. Virtually every laboratory staff since the first one in 1946 has tried to develop unique features for its particular program. For most professionals, combining their talents to produce an improved program is very exciting, even though they run the risk (apparent, most often, to those new in the field) of "reinventing the wheel."

Because there is a lack of good evaluative research about laboratory design, it is impossible to know at this point if changes do in fact represent improvement and do provide maximum learning benefit to participants. Trainers often feel that the commitment of a staff to a particular design—not necessarily to changes in a design—results in better training.

This section of our book presents design features that we feel may signal advances in training.

The late Michael Blansfield describes an advanced laboratory design for those who have had previous training experience. It is an attempt to implement in training Eric Berne's theories of transactional analysis. It's design is structured and moves into deeper intrapersonal analysis than is characteristic of most designs for first-time participants. This is one of the last pieces written by Blansfield prior to his untimely death in 1971.

Goodwin Watson reviews the field of nonverbal activities in groups —probably one of the most controversial design elements to enter the training field in years. Nonverbal activities have been criticized by professionals as imposed experiences that deny group members the chance to experience psychological success in setting their own learning goals and working out their own ways of achieving them. Proponents argue that nonverbal activities release areas of emotionality and behavior that could not be tapped by ordinary methods. Moreover, they say, any group member can be helped to develop nonverbal techniques as part of his own repertoire and can initiate such actions in training groups. Watson deals thoroughly with situations in which he sees such activities as helpful or nonproductive and presents recommendations for their use.

Group methods and organization development. Many training-group participants have come from organization settings. Having sampled the trust, openness, authenticity of relationship, and collaborative effort that characterize a good group experience, a large number of the participants wanted to create the same conditions in their back-home organizations. To meet their needs, many organizations hired trainers to run training groups for employees. The results have varied. Some organizations seemed to benefit; others did not notice any significant improvement in the quality of work done. The operative words are "work done," for the organization of course expects to benefit by providing training.

Jerry Harvey and Sheldon Davis present an insightful comparison between the laboratory setting within which most group training is presented and the organization where development work takes place. They discuss the dimensions that are needed in the trainer's skills and theories if he is to be successful in transferring laboratory education to the organization setting. They also point out the danger that the trainer will try to duplicate the "culture island" laboratory in the organization; because this represents his area of greatest previous success, he may not try to understand the character of the new environment and will thus neglect the new skills and methods needed to bring about organizational change.

Robert Blake and Jane S. Mouton develop seven principles of organization development science and evaluate the training-group method against them. It is their conclusion that while the training-group method may be appropriate for individual learning and member development, it is inadequate by itself to accomplish organization change.

Ethical issues in group training.   As criticism of different forms of training develops, members of the profession have begun to examine carefully issues of ethics and and professional responsibility. These are not, of course, new concerns. Almost all of the founders of the process were ranking professionals guided by the professional standards of the other associations to which they belonged, such as the American Psychological Association. Many new trainers, however, are not oriented to the standards of a profession and lack a clear picture of the ethical issues involved in training.

Martin Lakin considers a number of serious concerns, among which are participant expectations. Training programs are sometimes inadequately, even falsely, advertised. This situation certainly has undesirable effects for participants, to which are added those generated by their own preconceptions about the therapeutic values of training and the actions of some inadequately prepared trainers who offer a kind of pseudo-therapy. Lakin also fears that, as groups move toward more expressive emotional forms, the traditional emphasis on democratic group process and cognitive as well as experiential learning will be lost, and that the trainer, by initiating a good deal of group activity, will unduly influence the group.

In my own chapter, I examine the rationales of two types of training groups: one which stays predominantly in the here-and-now and the other which moves into back-home, there-and-then concerns. I explore the shades of gray between the two orientations to see what ethical implications the trainer faces as he decides which focus of training should be used in the groups he conducts.

In a sense, no chapter in this volume can be read independently of any other. Ethical concerns, for instance, are at least implicit in virtually every chapter. Also, the nature of training interventions must be considered by the organization development consultant, and transfer of learning is of concern no matter what the trainer's learning and behavior theories. On almost every page there is a statement that can be compared or contrasted with a similar one on any other page. It is hoped that after concentrating on areas of his own particular interest, the reader will seek the generalizations that are suggested.

The group-training movement has had an exciting, rich, and influential history covering a relatively short period of not quite thirty years. During that time most trainers have expanded themselves as a result of their contacts with colleagues, associates, and participants in a wide variety of laboratory-training programs. None of these chapters could have been written without the growth experiences provided in the richness of these early laboratory programs. It is imperative that we acknowledge NTL Institute, an organization that pioneered so much in the early phases of group training.

We also give special recognition to John Lockhart of NTL Institute for his services in helping bring this volume to fruition.

W.G.D.

Contents

Modern Theory AND Method IN Group Training

Theory and Method of Trainer Style

On Becoming a Trainer

WILLIAM P. GOLDEN, JR.
San Francisco State College

WHATEVER I am as a trainer is the result of many forces. One is the kinds of roles I have been exposed to; another, the kinds of people who have had meaning for me—professors, fellow trainers, co-trainers, training-group delegates. Finally, my own mode of being has found increasing freedom within the framework of humanistic and existential psychology.

What am I doing in a training group and why? A number of peak experiences or encounters with significant others have greatly influenced my growth and development as a trainer. I have always been interested in the learning process. Starting a doctoral program in 1947 at the University of California at Berkeley, I concentrated on primary and secondary school curriculum change. My whole focus changed, however, with my exposure to the concepts of process-as-content and experience-based learning. My first training group experience was as a graduate student in 1948; it was at about the same time I became familiar with materials developed by the National Training Laboratory (now NTL Institute for Applied Behavioral Science) at Bethel, Maine.

When I first began training, the major purpose of a trainer or consultant was to help improve group process—that is, to help a group become aware of the fact that how the group operated was critically important. One of the first training roles I assumed was that of a group-process observer. I spent a considerable amount of time with school faculties trying to help on-going groups develop procedures for gathering process data. This role required training in demonstrating group-process observation, in helping groups clarify and practice leadership-membership roles, and in designing feedback instruments which enabled groups to secure immediate data about group process, leadership styles, atmosphere, communication, decision-making, and member-leader feelings and perceptions. The major training technique used in helping team leaders and members try out new behaviors was role-playing.

In 1952, I became associated with the Western Training Laboratory in Group Development. I was a group-process observer for a year and a junior member of a co-training team for three; I finally became a senior trainer and began to co-train with new professionals. An issue that frequently divided early NTL staffs centered on what Benne (Bradford, Gibb, and Benne 1964) has described as the differences in the conception of the trainer role as action-research or clinically oriented. I was constantly torn by this conflict. My own thinking was heavily action-research and group-process oriented, but I became increasingly aware that other trainers were focusing on the personal and interpersonal rather than on small group behavior as a target for change.

At this period I modeled my trainer style—my goals, rationales, and techniques—after trainers with whom I had a positive identification. At the time I was learning the role of group trainer, there were no written descriptions of it. Indeed, there was a good deal of mystique about the role. One had to learn it by observing another. In a way, there was a sort of guild system of operating. If one learned the secrets of the trade, he did not divulge them to others, and the novice tended to mimic the behavior of his master. There was always a very limited amount of time at a laboratory for senior and junior trainers to "clinic," and one had to learn on the fly. I had the feeling at times that even the senior trainer had no clear conception of what he was doing; and in a sense he did not, because he was exploring, risking, trying things out, and researching himself at the same time.

One did not really know what that role was until he was "flying solo." In 1953, I began to have opportunities to do this. Being alone in a group made co-training seem a beautiful luxury, and I became much more appreciative of the many reciprocal opportunities in the co-training relationship for both myself and group members. As I worked with a variety of different groups, I discovered that I could not develop a meaningful role if I were not free to behave naturally. I finally began to trust myself, to be flexible, and to stop defining my role on an either/or basis.

In 1956, I co-trained with a personal growth trainer. It took this experience to help me realize how dependent I was on a limited role concept. Training attention, I discovered, must be centered on both the "real" person and his life values as expressed in the here-and-now feelings and behaviors generated by interpersonal encounters in a group, on the various selves or roles which the individual acts out in a variety of back-home situations, and on the discrepancies and conflicts among those roles. Trainer strategy could thus legitimately be directed toward helping delegates to improve both personal and group functioning. A trainer thus needed to be flexible enough, and skillful enough, to deal with both kinds of process problems. Failure to attend to both personality and role relationships definitely could reduce the potential of a training-group experience.

In the period from 1955 to 1963, close working relationships with Carl Rogers and other existential psychologists such as Rollo May, Richard Farson, Abraham Maslow, and Hobart Thomas brought me still closer to the broader definition of the trainer role and to a personal awareness of my need to be what Rogers calls "that self which one truly is." The direct confrontations of Gestalt therapy have also furthered my redefinition of my role.

At this time too, I discovered that personal growth had to be concomitant with group growth. I learned that each group member had to be concerned first of all with intrapersonal and interpersonal relationships before he could become concerned with group phenomena. I began to experiment with my own behavior and to express myself with congruence. It was a great relief to be myself—to be free to behave existentially as a trainer, as a person, free of the restraints of some model, technique, or method. My experiences in several laboratories were now characterized by a number of what Martin Buber calls I-Thou relationships. I became aware of no longer being alone and was convinced that the training group was a primary means for helping human beings get in touch with their own feelings and those of others to reduce alienation and release human potential.

Since 1962 my own personal shift in orientation has been paralleled by a shift in delegate needs and expectations. Even NTL Institute changed from a "training laboratory in group development" to a "training laboratory in human relations." Delegates began to come to laboratories to learn more about themselves as persons, concerned increasingly with what Argyris (1968, p. 148) defines as "interpersonal competence." He says that interpersonal competence requires that individuals

> learn how to (a) communicate with one another in a manner that generates minimally distorted information; (b) give and receive feedback that can be directly validated and minimally evaluative; (c) perform these skills in such a way that self-acceptance and trust among individuals tend to increase; and (d) create effective groups in which problem-solving may occur.

A statement by NTL (1965) clearly indicates the emphasis on personal change. It outlines the outcomes of basic human relations laboratories, as summarized below.

1. "Introspectiveness" or "awareness"—the ability to reflect on feelings and ideas within themselves, including feelings and ideas about others.

2. Openness—the ability to be open to feelings and ideas within themselves and within others, reflected in the ability to be more expressive of themselves and more receptive to a wide range of expressive behavior from other people.

3. Awareness of feelings—developing a high regard for the importance of recognizing their feelings and the feelings of others.

4. Recognition and concern about feeling-behavior dissonances—developing an ability to diagnose the relation between their feelings and their behavior, and to move more toward consonance between these.

5. Flexibility—expanding the repertoire of behavior; developing skill in behaving in new and different ways from their accustomed behavior.

6. Integration among sub-identities—helping delegates move toward integrating their various sub-identities into a conception of a total self, rather than compartmentalizing them.

These are the ideas to which I now subscribe. Moreover, I have become increasingly free to be myself and not a role as I work with groups. Indeed, role-taking has for me become a form of gamesmanship, and I no longer feel comfortable in playing games with people.

THE TRAINING GROUP AS A MICROCOSM OF THE WORLD: AN EXISTENTIAL VIEW

Every trainer—every man—has a view of reality which helps him bring some semblance of order to his experience. Each trainer—each man—must attempt to answer the questions, "What is man, and what is his destiny in terms of his potential?" For me the most meaningful answers to such questions are those of the humanistic or existential psychologists and philosophers—such Europeans as Binswanger, Boss, Frankl, Marcel, and Sartre; and such Americans as May, Rogers, Maslow, Bugental, Jourard, Van Kaam, Fromm, and Moustakas.

I have come to see the training group as a crucible for existential learnings, as a microcosm of the world. Within the training group, the trainee faces existential issues. He becomes aware of personal existence and of the paradox of "being and nothingness." He feels anxiety that nothing is predictable and faces the absurdity that being has no built-in value. He confronts our ultimate aloneness and our ultimate relatedness. Above all, perhaps, he sees that freedom is choice, that choice is an impossible dilemma, and that responsibility is the experience of determining what happens—the affirmation of one's being as a doer.

Essentially, the training group is an experiment in freedom, that is, choice. The individual is confronted with an unstructured situation in which he is free "to be." The group seems to have no reason for being. Such a situation is absurd; it has no meaning. If the group is absurd, so is the member—an impossible predicament. But it is only when a person can start assigning to the group (or to life) his own reasons for its existence that the predicament becomes manageable. *The vacuum becomes the ground for human freedom.*

Choices of all types face the person. The more choices, the more freedom, the greater the possibility of conflict, anxiety, and frustration. He must choose between "I-Thou" or "I-It" relations, between a variety of conflicting choices about group membership, between varying feelings of authority and control. The questions of choice are faced by all group members, but the answers can never be generalized: they are always personal. The training group develops an increasing sensitivity in the individual to the necessity of choice, and it is this that is an act of creation. He realizes that his answers are the created values of his own life. His life will be authentic only if he decides to make it so. Existence includes contingencies, tension, alienation, and death; existence entails choice, choice entails risk, risk entails anxiety. Living authentically requires the courage "to be."

As a trainer, commitment to existential attitudes leads me to operate on the following assumptions in a group.

1. Every human being is a person of worth. I accept all human beings as equal at birth, in the sense that each possesses the potential for the development of those characteristics that distinguish him from others. The individual is a person and not a thing. As such his total self must be respected.

2. Nurturing and developing individual freedom and responsibility is a major responsibility of group training.

3. The entire environment of the training group should be strategically ordered so as to face the individual and the group with the constant necessity of making choices within limits and of experiencing the processes of becoming free and responsible.

4. A primary task of the training group is to help others become consciously aware of ever-wider sectors of experience. Allied to this is the task of helping individuals take the role of the other, thus coming to distinguish self from other selves.

5. Every person can learn, grow, change, and develop. Because he is *in process,* man learns new ways of behaving from new emotional-intellectual experiences.

6. Experience-based learning is the most effective way to change attitudes and behavior. Such learning occurs when the learner is emotionally involved in planning, carrying out, and evaluating learning experiences. For this to happen, the learner must be active, he must relate himself to his environment, and he must be involved with others. He must organize his own observations, gather his own data about the impact of behavior, both his own and that of others, and feed it back into the system.

7. The trainer is responsible for helping to establish a climate for experience-based learning and for building designs which encourage such learning. This means helping establish a nonthreatening psychological atmosphere in which one is free "to be" with minimal need for defenses. Such a climate is characterized by openness and freedom to experiment with new behavior. The learner must develop a sense of trust in himself and in others. Unless an individual can disclose himself, allow others to see him as he is, his learning will be limited and he will neither get adequate feedback nor benefit by it.

8. Data about feelings, emotions, and perceptions are critical for acting effectively and efficiently; facts are often less relevant. Each individual is *the* expert about his own perceptions, reactions, and feelings.

9. Here-and-now experiences afford the most effective means for studying both self and group process. The media for learning are the behaviors generated by the individuals in interaction with each other. Here-and-now experiences are immediate, public, first-hand, shared, and "gut-level." Everyone can participate meaningfully because he has shares in the data being analyzed.

Hampden-Turner (1966) has succinctly integrated these assumptions into a self-perpetuating "existential learning cycle" which fits well with my experience. In the training group the learner, with his unique cognitive map, risks acceptance or rejection. Through interaction, he becomes more authentic, reaches out to others, receives feedback, and is helped to find goals that satisfy him and others and thus resolve conflicts. Success breeds success; he invests and reinvests in the cycle. A major learning goal of the training group becomes that of helping the investor resolve difficulties he encounters at any point.

GOALS AND OUTCOMES OF GROUP TRAINING

When I accept an assignment as a trainer, I primarily accept a responsibility for helping others to learn, grow, develop, and change. I also accept a learning medium—the small, face-to-face group—and the interpersonal relationships which will occur among the staff and within the training group. It also becomes my responsibility to help develop a training design and to behave in a manner which will assist the group and its members to reach the goals of the laboratory.

Many of my goals have been defined by such authors as Bennis and Schein (1965) and Bradford, Gibb, and Benne (1964). Golembiewski (1967) adapted from those writers a table which I frequently use; it is an explicit statement of my goals for the training group. I think most trainers would agree with its precepts; differences arise because personal training styles and implementation choices differ.

My own training behavior depends on the goals of the laboratory and staff as I see them, the goals and needs of the trainees, and my learning theories and values (and those of other staff members). Goal-setting requires me to clarify the following issues.

What is the nature of the staff contract? I feel a professional obligation to develop a learning experience in accord with the purposes of the laboratory announced in its brochures. A trainer has a contract, implied or explicit, with the delegate. Failure to honor that contract is a violation of trust. Thus, in some instances I have found myself resisting attempts by some staff members to develop a program based on learning goals which meet primarily staff, not delegate, needs.

What is the target of change—the individual, the group, or a social system? The trainer cannot assume that a model based on personal growth will necessarily be useful where the target is organizational change. There seems to be a consensus among trainers that the first experience, whether a stranger (basic) or family (variant) training group, would have a very heavy emphasis on "sensitivity training" in self-and-

TABLE 1. Four Value-loaded Dimensions Relevant in Laboratory Approaches to Organization Change and Development

A Meta-Values of Lab Training	B Proximate Goals of Lab Training	C Desirable Means for Lab Training	D Organization Values Consistent with Lab Training
1. An attitude of inquiry reflecting (among others): a. a "hypothetical spirit" b. experimentalism	1. Increased insight, self-knowledge	1. Emphasis on "here-and-now" occurrences	1. Full and free communication
2. "Expanded consciousness and sense of choice"	2. Sharpened diagnostic skills at (ideally) all levels, that is, on the levels of the a. individual b. group c. organization d. society	2. Emphasis on the individual act rather than on the "total person" acting	2. Reliance on open consensus, in managing conflict, as opposed to using coercion or compromise
3. The value system of democracy, having as two core elements: a. a spirit of collaboration b. open resolution of conflict via a problem-solving orientation	3. Awareness of, and skill-practice in creating, conditions of effective functioning at (ideally) all levels	3. Emphasis on feedback that is nonevaluative in that it reports the impact on the self of other's behavior, rather than feedback that is judgmental or interpretive	3. Influence based on competence rather than on personal whim or formal power

4. An emphasis on mutual "helping relationships" as the best way to express man's interdependency with man

5. Increased capacity to be open, to accept feelings of self and others, to risk interpersonally in rewarding ways

4. Testing self-concepts and skills in interpersonal situations

4. Emphasis on "unfreezing" behaviors the trainee feels are undesirable, on practice of replacement behaviors, and on "refreezing" new behaviors

5. Emphasis on "trust in leveling," on psychological safety of the trainee

6. Emphasis on creating and maintaining an "organic community"

4. Expression of emotional as well as task-oriented behavior

5. Acceptance of conflict between the individual and his organization, to be coped with willingly, openly, and rationally

SOURCE: R. M. Golembiewski, "The 'Laboratory Approach' to Organization Change: Schema of a Method," *Public Administration Review* 27, no. 3 (1967): 217.

other awareness, authentic communication, and interpersonal feed-back. I am willing to accept this emphasis for the first experience; however, I feel that the person-centered and group-centered orientations are complementary. When feasible, my goals thus encompass both dimensions.

What are the expectations and needs of the trainees? Who determines trainee needs? Ideally, trainee needs are the result of collaboration between trainer and trainee. Currently, most descriptions of training laboratories contain statements of goals which include both personal learning and organizational development. While it is my experience that participants, particularly first-time participants, expect a highly personal experience, I feel I am remiss unless I point out that the training group may be limiting its learning by focusing on personal learning to the exclusion of group-process learning. A very real crisis can arise if group norms develop which allow no room for deviation in goals and methods or which seduce group members into believing that the only significant learning is that which is personal. (If trainees elect to avoid my interventions in this area, this creates more data for analysis.)

I allow the group the freedom to set its own goals and direction. My major responsibility in goal-setting is to involve the group in the decision-making process, to alert it to blind spots, to help it become aware of the options available, and to assist it in learning from the choices it makes in setting goals. In the final analysis, of course, the goals of group training must be cooperatively defined and should represent the needs of both trainer and trainee.

PRESENTATION OF SELF: TRAINER ATTITUDES

If I have learned anything during my experiences in training groups, it is that trainer attitudes have a greater impact on delegates than goals or techniques. The most important result of an interpersonal relationship is that of choice. Choice-making is encouraged in an atmosphere that encourages introspection, self-evaluation, openness, spontaneity, and self-direction. It seems increasingly clear to me that there are some core dimensions in interaction processes which facilitate growth and development. I really do not know whether or not I display the attitudes which I think I display. I do know that I try to espouse the following dimensions as part of my behavior as a trainer (they are suggested by Jourard [1968], Rogers [1961], Maslow [1962], May [1967]). For me these are the attitudes necessary and sufficient for learning in a training group.

Empathy. "Tuning in" on the delegate's wavelength; trying to see the situation as he sees it; adapting an "internal frame of reference"; being with the other; allowing myself to experience or merge in the experience of the delegate, reflecting on this experience while suspending my own judgment, and communicating this understanding to the delegate; being fully human and not reacting mechanically or merely intellectually understanding the delegate's problems; coexperiencing what people and things mean to the other.

Realness. Being honest, genuine, authentic, direct, congruent, open; reflecting my true feelings; "telling it like it is"; offering my truth and reality to the other; avoiding conscious or unconscious playing of the group trainer role; expressing feelings concretely; trusting that I am in no danger when I am unguarded, defenseless, open; being true to my own experience; not holding back; responding entirely and wholly.

Respect. Having a positive regard for the other; communicating warmth, care, understanding; accepting the other as of unconditional worth; respecting the other's feelings, experiences, and potentials; respecting my own feelings and experiences.

Commitment and presence. Being there; being fully present to the group and its members; being honest enough to let the group know when I am bored or my thoughts are elsewhere; seeing the individual and group "hang-ups" as a challenge; "hanging in there" during impasses and when I feel inadequate.

Confirming the other. Letting the other person be; standing back and allowing him to disclose himself; meeting the other; letting him know that he exists; recognizing the other person as a free agent who chooses his existence and is responsible for it.

Being transparent. Being transparent has two aspects: (1) Receiving the disclosure of the world; suspending my concepts and experiences of things and people and letting myself perceive their being; suspending my concept of my own being and letting my changing being present itself to my experience; letting structure collapse so new possibilities can present themselves to me; (2) Actively disclosing myself to the world and to others; letting myself—my aims, feelings, attitudes, beliefs, joys, sorrows—be known; letting myself be who I am; risking exposure of my vulnerabilities.

Each training group is for me like another combat flying mission, another encounter with the contingencies of the firing line. I sweat out each group because I am never really certain of myself. I do not know definitely whether my being present in a group serves any genuine purpose. Often during a group, I experience feelings of loneliness, uncertainty, and inadequacy. A training group in a sense is a happening, and so is flying at the critical moment. All the planning one has done, all the skill one has developed, all the conceptualization of strategies may or may not prove adequate to the situation one faces. Indeed there are times when I say to myself, "Why are you taking on this responsibility? Do you know what you are getting into? Who do you think you are? God?" And similarly, at other points in the process, I find myself asking, "What are you doing? Where is your blueprint? Are you aware that you are letting it happen and that you seem to have no plan or strategy? Come on, face it. Just what do you do in a group?"

I have asked myself these questions and others like them many times and can come up with no precise answers. It is my experience that my behavior in a group seems to help—that members do accomplish some of the goals that are important and critical in the experience.

A major role which I play in the training group is that of a change agent. The group can readily be regarded as a social-influence situation in which the members' relationships to the trainer, and to each other, are the primary vehicle for the production of change. The critical change process in group learning is attitudinal change. Such change is at the core of the learning process. Unless there is a change in attitude, there can be no change in behavior.

In helping to induce change, I must rely primarily on my interventions (or lack of them). In this regard I have shifted considerably. Early in my career, most of my interventions (as I see them now) were stilted, mechanical, and characterized by formula. I was a victim of the model of the time—nondirective, nonintervening, a "blank screen." I was only part of myself, for I deliberately restricted my interventions to "process" interventions. I avoided any direct answers to questions. I "appropriately" reflected feelings, tried to clarify perceptions, and never let members see me as a person. I denied expression of all the feelings, reactions, and ideas going on within me for fear that I might be trapped into the usual "telling role" of authority. In a sense, technique was my master.

I cannot function with such incongruence and no longer behave in this manner. I now feel free to intervene (or not intervene) on any level that makes sense to me of the moment, be it process or content.

The best, most trust-producing interventions I make are those which truly represent my own feelings of the moment.

TRAINER TASKS

In looking at my style and trying to define it more explicitly, I find that the concepts of Kelman (1963) make a great deal of sense. Even though his work is concerned primarily with the role of the group in the induction of therapeutic change, his concept of the therapist role clearly defines roles I find myself taking in the training group. Kelman sees behavior change in group therapy as the result of three kinds of social influence: compliance, identification, and internalization. Compliance occurs when an individual accepts influence from another person or group in order to gain favorable reaction from the other; that is, to gain approval or avoid disapproval from another. Identification occurs when an individual accepts influence from another person or group to establish or maintain a satisfying, self-defining relationship to the other. Internalization occurs when an individual or group accepts influence in order to maintain the congruence of his (its) actions and beliefs with his (its) value system.

Adapting Kelman's framework, I see myself as performing roles or influence attempts that center on the following tasks. (I will not here discuss the relationships of the group to the learning process—another issue altogether.)

Engagement in the learning process.   If the training group is to function, the delegates must be "trained" to produce some kinds of behavior and to bypass others. A basic ground rule is that the delegates will learn only if they allow themselves to experience and express their feelings in the here-and-now and to subject such data to study. Resistance to engaging in such process work is great. Even though I try to honestly communicate to the group my feeling that a training group is an experience in dealing with freedom (and allowing the group to struggle with defining freedom is a major personal problem for me), there is no such thing as absolute freedom, and I am sure that delegates begin to learn the rules of the game by trying to find out what I approve and disapprove. At this stage of the process, there is some degree of compliance. If and when I intervene, I respond to data generated by the group in such a way as to increase the probability that certain kinds of data will be generated. Of course, as I function this way, I also have to face the prospect that some delegates may become fixated at this level of compliance. They may learn to play the game—say all the right words, talk about feelings and process, but with no feeling for what they are doing.

I do mean what I say: the group is free. I do, however, also have to face the fact that I subtly influence the group in certain directions, even though I never tell them what to do. But such a response tells the group something: the responsibility for work is one that the group members must assume.

Commitment to the training-group process.   My behavior as a trainer may help the group become aware of certain norms or ground rules; if, however, the delegate becomes unduly threatened and anxious about the novelty of the experience, he may "go through the motions" or psychologically withdraw from the situation. For the training-group process to be helpful, the delegate must become committed to the experience and see benefits in it in spite of the pain, sacrifice, or anxiety it may produce.

Attitudes of trust and acceptance on the part of delegates will be induced primarily through the process of identification with me as a trainer. If I can be an accepting, permissive, caring listener; if I can help the delegate see himself as a person of worth; if I can build a reciprocal relationship that respects the delegate; then, to the extent that the delegate wishes to maintain this relationship, he will tend to adopt the attitude of trust expected of his role in the relationship. Consequently, my interventions, either verbal or nonverbal, are cues which, I hope, convey to the other that I understand and unconditionally accept him. Regardless of what self-disclosures are made, I do not make any judgments. I try to create a climate of safety.

Again I must face the fact that identification may become fixated and that establishing a self-defining relationship with me may be a means of avoiding change. At the risk of destroying the climate of trust I hope to create, I find at times that some of my interventions are directed at pointing out such avoidance patterns.

Occurrence of corrective emotional experiences.   In the training group, characteristic ways of relating to others are apparent. Indeed, this constitutes one of the great learning opportunities of the group. The very heterogeneity of most groups with regard to sex, age, education, occupation, and social status affords each member all sorts of opportunity to interact and display his feelings and behavior. The behavior generated in the here-and-now issues of group interaction provides rich data for self-examination, self-insight, and self-change.

The training group elicits all types of emotionality on the part of its members, and the beauty of the experience is that members get immediate feedback from each other which can lead to "corrective emotional experiences." As a trainer, my interventions (if any) at this phase of group experience are thus primarily in helping group members learn that it is safe to give authentic feedback and in modeling ways of giving feedback nonevaluatively.

Experimenting with new behavior. I intervene on occasion to suggest alternative behaviors for members to explore. Thus, if a person has had great difficulty expressing anger openly, I may suggest that he try expressing his anger (the next time he feels it) by standing up and telling off the person who evokes the anger. More often than not, fellow group members come up with both explicit and implicit suggestions for change. My interventions here are to encourage the risks involved—to let the person know that it does not make any difference if he fails. He can always try again or try another way.

Adopting a new frame of reference about himself and others. Individuals quite frequently need help in developing new frames of reference for viewing their behavior. Although the group member may model his behavior after mine, I do not try to communicate the message that this is the only model. I merely make available an image of behavior which may be new to most group members and which they can try out to see if it "fits" or needs to be adapted. The challenge here is to induce identification that contains the seeds of its own destruction. I encourage group members to adopt the concept of experience-based learning. What I hope remains from any identification with my role as a trainer are the processes of giving and receiving feedback, of being congruent and open in expression of feelings, of being supportive, committed, and concerned about others, of, indeed, seeing all interpersonal relations as in process of becoming, changing, and moving.

Generalizing training-group insights and behavior to back-home situations. If the group member internalizes what he has learned, his behavior when he gets back home should be characterized by his newer attitudes and values. Whether or not the individual applies his insights to new situations is perhaps the ultimate test of the validity of the training-group experience. Therefore, I encourage group members to evaluate their experience in the group and its implications for their lives. Such interventions are primarily directed at helping the group member reality-test new learning and subject any plans for change to the reactions of his fellow group members. The training group gives the member a chance to try out new behaviors in a dry run situation— a situation that is real, gut-level, but also psychologically safe.

STYLE, STRATEGY, PATTERNS: BEHAVIORS I SEE AS "ME"

My interventions are primarily directed at the development of an effective feedback system. I am certain that most other group trainers have similar strategies. What, then, is unique about my behavior in a group? Perhaps the best way to describe my style is to indicate the major themes around which I see my interventions centering.

Confronting, engaging, encountering.   To confront is to meet the other because I care. I take the risk of being seen as punitive or destructively aggressive because of my concern for and commitment to the other. By being direct, I endeavor to bring the person in touch with himself—to increase congruities in his experiencing and communication by pointing out incongruities, especially inconsistencies within his self (his ideal self versus his real self); between what he says and does (insight and behavior); and between illusion or fantasy and reality (my experience of the person versus the person's expression of his experience, himself, and me).

Sometimes my confrontations are also directed at the total group. Thus, if I feel that I have clearly indicated to the group that I do not intend to lead in a traditional way, and I continue to get dependency pleas from the members, I often confront them with how I feel about such pleas. My confronting also is directed at phoniness, game-playing, power plays, and pseudo-openness. Many times confrontation, too, is my way of openly displaying anger and of letting a group see what happens when anger is clearly directed at the person who evokes it. (And, if asked, I assure the group that my behavior is not a "put-on.")

Confrontation, of course, often creates a crisis for the person I am engaging, for me, and for the group. I open myself up to the hostile feelings of the other, while the prospect of conflict often appalls group members. There are instances when I am not sure whether I should confront. Often I fear that I will hurt someone who is fragile, or that I will make others anxious that their turn will be next. Confrontation is a risk, but it is a risk I feel I must take to communicate understanding. Then too, confronting fits me. I find that I grow as the result of crises, and so I intervene at times to provoke them, and thus impell the group and myself toward choice-making.

In short, I try to demonstrate that all of us can be more authentic, that we can "call the shots" as we see them, that we can respond directly without damaging others. It is true that there may be a loss of an illusion, a fantasy, a facade, a ritual, a defense, but in return for the loss one may receive the experience of being. I must take the responsibility for precipitating the crisis, but the person I encounter takes responsibility for his choice.

Silence.   Perhaps a major intervention in my style is silence. I really do not have a great need to talk. My verbal behavior in a training group is not significantly different from what it is elsewhere. Group members do not believe this at first and, in their anxiety, put pressure on me to become more visible verbally. To be helpful, to allow the group to be responsible for its own learning, and to respond to what is truly in me, I must, as Gendlin points out, spend a few moments of personal self-attention. I usually then find a great deal that I am willing to share.

I choose with care the interventions I do make. This is not to say that every input I make is calculated. It merely indicates that I am aware that my very silence can give more emphasis to the interventions I make. Surprisingly enough, I find that if I have the patience to wait, group members often do more effectively what I had hoped they would. The situation is paradoxical: as a trainer I do not want group members to feel that I am rejecting them (and my verbal nonparticipation may convey this to them), and I do not want them to become too dependent on me (which they might do if I were more active verbally). I want also to be free "to be." Accordingly, when I am confronted with my silence, I openly admit that I am aware of its impact, but I say that "this is me. I need time to tune in, to reflect, to see where I might help."

Being open, becoming real, disclosing myself.   Jourard (1968, p. 10) has beautifully and lucidly described the full meaning of self-disclosure; I hope my own self-disclosure—which has not come easily to me—may release such potential in myself and others.

But authentic disclosure is rare. More common is semblance, role-playing, impersonation of the other one wishes to *seem* to the other. Hence, the other person seldom truly encounters a person-in-process. He meets a pledge of consistency, a world of people who do not invite him into new possibilities. If I am in your world, and I do not grow and change, then you are in a world that obstructs and impedes your growth! In true encounter, there is a collapse of roles and self-concepts. No one emerges from an encounter the same as he entered. My willingness to disclose myself to you, to drop my mask, is a factor in your trusting me and daring then to disclose yourself to me. This disclosure of yourself to me aids the process of your disengagement from your previous way of being. And as I disclose myself to you, I am your world, and this world discloses new possibilities to you—it evokes new challenges and invitations that may stir you and enliven your imagination.

Struggling to develop trust. Fortunately, trust does not come packaged so that it can be bought like a commercial product. Trust must be earned, though I know of no formulas for earning it. For me, nonintervention during the early stages of a group is usually the way I test my own trust of myself and the group. I do not refuse to respond openly to questions and interactions directed toward me by participants. However, I do refuse to answer questions which require that I take over leadership of the group. I have come to realize that when I am "sweating it out" and "letting it happen," I am conveying my trust to the group even though my behavior may not be interpreted as trust initially. Whereas at one time I tended to hide my own concerns about membership and role, for instance, I now openly trust the group, and am free at any time to talk about my feelings, perceptions, and concerns about belonging.

Helping the group become sensitive to the "here-and-now." Without question, the major methodological strategy available to a group trainer is the development of procedures for using the immediate experience, the here-and-now, as a basis for learning. Such immediate experiential data has been publicly generated and shared, and it can be consensually validated so that distortions are checked. Furthermore, the here-and-now data become a basis for learnings which can be generalized to other situations. Perhaps the greatest bulk of my interventions are directed toward helping group members understand this. My interventions thus are subtle norm-sending messages. Because I am actively concerned with the process of training-group development, whatever I do or say suggests to group members, either directly or indirectly, that certain behavior should (or should not) be performed. Psalthas and Hardert (1966) have made a very helpful analysis and classification of trainer-intervention categories which develop normative patterns in a training group. Using their system of analysis as a guide, I have tried to rate myself. My own process interventions (as I see them on reflection and hear them in tape playbacks) emphasize the following norms (arranged in order of total frequency with the first category the most frequent).

Normative Patterns

Interventions

Feelings

Encouraging the natural and spontaneous expression and open acceptance of sentiments, emotions, and feelings on the part of group members, and the avoidance of intellectualization.

How do you feel about being cut off? What's it like for you as of the moment? Can you share your feeling?

Let's tell it like it is. Let's hear it from your guts, not your intellect.

I'm with you.

I feel you are afraid of anyone getting close to you.

I feel we're talking on Cloud Nine. Can we focus on what's happening in this room "here-and-now?"

I'm bored.

Feedback

Encouraging (and modeling) the process of exchanging reflections, observations, opinions, impressions, and evaluations regarding behavior of members, including selves.

How do you find out how others feel?

Did you hear what I was trying to tell you?

Would you like to check and find out how others see you? Could you help B out? Could you tell him how he comes across to you?

I've heard a great deal of evaluative feedback. I wonder if it is helpful. Could we take a look at what A just said to B?

Acceptance Concern

Helping in the formation of trust in other members, the reduction of fear of others and of self, and the encouragement

Are we blocking out A?

It seems to me we are putting pressure on J to change. What is this doing?

of the acceptance of self and others; the common acceptance among group members that each should have an equal chance to speak.

Are we facing the issue of trust? I sense that people are afraid to level, afraid to be open. We really don't trust each other, as I see it.

Why do you demand that P become active? Can you accept him as he is?

Analyzing Group Interaction or Process

The analysis of past and present member interaction in order to discover its significance as a learning experience.

What's happening now?

What does it mean?

This group just acted in terms of a decision. Could we look at how the decision was made?

Could we share impressions about what has been happening?

What was the meaning of the interchange between A, C, and D? What can we learn from it?

Does anyone feel that this group is operating with implicit norms? Check me, but one norm I see is that of "playing it safe."

If I am successful in establishing these norms, which are the heart and core of learning to learn, I work myself out of a job. I become unnecessary by producing delegates who no longer need "to be taught." They break loose and swing free of the trainer. Once out of this job, I can also swing free, and intervene more freely on either process or content levels.

Displaying care and affection. It is my experience that many persons, and especially men, have great difficulty in openly displaying feelings of care, concern, affection, and love. There seems to be a taboo against intimacy and a fear that the display of intimate feelings will over-commit the individual displaying them, or that such open-ness will lead to irrelevant sentimentality.

As I see it, one goal of a group experience is to help a person develop a dialogue with himself, become aware of his feelings, and share them with others, especially as they confirm or disconfirm others. To be present to another thus means that I must permit no screen to block off my concern. Being authentic for me is letting the other person clearly know that I have genuine empathy, love, and affection for him. As a trainer, I hope to encourage others, especially men, to take the risk of caring. If I, as a man, can let go, if I can respond as it is for me and not be concerned whether or not others see me as unmanly, perhaps I can help others express their feelings more spon-taneously.

Perhaps the most significant change I recognize in myself in this area is an increasing freedom to display my feelings nonverbally. I do not believe that physical contact with group members is unprofes-sional *per se*. It may be, I grant, if the trainer uses the touching relation-ship to meet his own needs and fails to recognize that touching always has erotic overtones. I used to be afraid to touch another, but I know now that one way to establish dialogue with another—and in some especially stressful situations, simply to be in contact with him—is by physical means.

Most of my attempts to show concern for another are gentle, even hesitant and fumbling, efforts to display love, affection, and warmth. Some of my touching is, however, not so gentle. In expressing affection for other men, I have found that direct physical contact is most im-portant. The camaraderie of the tumbling, wrestling, catch-as-catch-can rough-housing of boy's play carries an affection whose meaning is immediately known. Such play is a spontaneous release of the male need for physical contact with another man, a need which few men can express in a logical, rational, organization-man world. Thus, I frequently find myself engaging in tumbling and wrestling matches or free-for-alls with one or more men in a group. Such direct physical contact seems to establish a reawakening of human feelings between men.

I prefer to have such physical contact spring from the immediacy of experience. When it seems relevant, however, I use some of the non-verbal or sensory awareness "encounters" which are now part of the repertoire of most group leaders: the trust circle, the break-in or break-out of a circle, the body press, meditation, the blind walk, and so on. I make specific reference to such experiences as those described by Schutz (1968). Most nonverbal encounters are attempts to establish a dialogue through the senses, and essentially through touch, eye to eye, body to body. Such exercises should probably always be introduced with the proviso that delegates are free to participate or not. For me, there is nothing so inauthentic as phony intimacy; to employ nonverbal encounters in a stilted way is as meaningless and as regimented as GI calisthenics. If meaningful interactions are evolving naturally, I encourage them by my own behavior and refrain from introducing sensory awareness exercises.

TRANSCENDING TECHNIQUE

Looking back over what I have said, one thought becomes apparent to me. If I am real with myself and others, I do not need any technique or bag of tricks. Perhaps I am most helpful when I am not playing any role at all. I do not want to infer that it is not necessary to learn some of the skills related to the role. Training in some technique or theory is, however, primarily a way of proving the seriousness of one's intent to become a trainer; it means that I have tried to learn from my predecessors. I do want to say that the techniques I employ must be flexible and not stereotyped. Their intent must be to help group members understand and experience their mode of being and not to impersonate the style of another, as I did earlier in my career. I can only train in *my* way.

The need to transcend technique is particularly apparent when one faces crises and impasses, for there are no guidelines for responding to such situations. Recently one of my training groups had worked long and patiently to help a somewhat uninvolved, withdrawn, unemotional girl disclose her feelings. In spite of a number of direct encounters, she denied that she had any feelings about anything that happened. On impulse, I moved over to her, pulled her up from her chair, and asked her how she felt about my doing this. There was no reply. Suddenly, feeling that nothing but a direct action would put the girl in contact with her feelings, I slapped her lightly across the face. Before I could blink an eye, she struck back at me. Then as she held onto me, the tears began to flow, and she began to talk about her relationship with her father; she had never been allowed to express her feelings for fear of upsetting him.

I approach such encounters fully aware of the risks. If I expect others to trust their feelings, however, I must begin by trusting my own even if they are not always consistent with an ideal model. I felt that the only way to help this girl was to do something which could shock her into letting go. I have thus learned that a trainer can really be as free to respond as a respect for the growth, integrity, and dignity of another will permit.

UNFINISHED BUSINESS: TRAINER HANG-UPS AND DILEMMAS

Perhaps the most significant thing I am learning about myself in a group is that I continually seem to have to work through certain consistent "impossible" dilemmas.

Anxiety.   During the initial stages of group life, when the group is floundering and fearful because members see no structure, no agenda, no typical leadership, I too am anxious because I must "let it happen." However, there seem to be long periods (not so long, perhaps, when one looks back on them) when nothing seems to happen. Progress seems to occur in all groups except the one I am with. I begin to wonder if the lack of movement is because of the composition of the group, my inadequacies as a trainer, or my lack of trust in the learning process itself.

Trusting the group.   In spite of my intellectual acceptance of the concept that a climate of trust is generated by my trust, I find it difficult at times to really trust the group to decide its own destiny. Letting the group emerge is not easy. It takes real courage to hold back, to recognize and truly accept that the group exists so that it may learn by its own experience. I must genuinely accept the possibility that everything that occurs may be a source of learning, and that my goal is to help the group see possibilities for learning which the members may not otherwise perceive.

Confronting crises.   Each group experience presents members and trainer with a variety of crises—personal, interpersonal, and group. Although all crises are threatening, some are characteristic of group growth and development and are predictable; experience has taught one what to expect.

I have learned that I must be sensitive to the fact that what constitutes a crisis for some individuals may not be so for others. At the crisis point, I cannot rely on a set of answers or procedures, for there are none—no gimmicks, no techniques. All I can do is truly to be available to another. I can respond with my recognition that there is a crisis, a life and death situation in which all game-playing stops. I try to help the individual or group confront the crisis while overcoming my own tendency to want to "bail out."

MAKING THE EXPERIENCE MEANINGFUL FOR EVERYONE

I deeply feel an obligation to every member of the group not to add to the meaninglessness of existence. I hope to help others to see the meaning in any situation. In almost every group, a trainer becomes aware of the fact that he is not "touching" some persons, although he alone is not solely responsible for getting everyone "in." Failure to reach some members created a major crisis for me earlier in my career. My sense of adequacy as a trainer was at stake. Today I am able to accept the fact that this type of experience may not be meaningful for some persons.

Another side of this concern is my struggle to insure that a training group is more than just an "experience." How does one help members conceptualize without destroying the experience? How can one help them not to deny the rational, intellectual side of life?

A training group offers many persons a level of intimacy which may not be currently available in their own lives. Having experienced the authenticity of feelings and emotions in a group as contrasted with daily routines, it is most difficult for group members to want to return to the objective, the rational, the intellectual. Insuring that delegates have opportunities to develop cognitive maps is an increasing training problem. There is great resistance to the presentation of theory sessions in many laboratories. If a design does include theory sessions, the burden for conceptualization must be assumed, if at all, within the group experience. I am not personally comfortable giving "lecturettes" within the training-group experience; however, I presently find that I must force myself to talk about concepts toward the end if a more informal opportunity does not come up during the group experience.

I have finally come to accept the fact there will also be unfinished business. Although groups quite frequently get around to this clean-up process during the final hours of group life, there always seems so much that is undone. Still, as a trainer, I must place my faith in the process. If group members have "learned how to learn," they will be able to pick up the threads and continue to work on unfinished business in their own environments.

BEING VULNERABLE

Certainly a psychological armor seems to make it easier to relate, but encounters of humanness occur only in those all-too-few times when I am vulnerable and open to the possibility of change in myself. I recall very well an experience in which I was able to transcend my fears of seeming unmanly and weep freely with a girl whose feelings I shared. Another woman in the group then turned to me and said, "My God, you are a man after all. Why do you have to try so hard to be a man? What you just did took more courage than all your aggressive direct confrontations."

Such moments can be frightening, yet they are necessary to permit the total "me" to function—rational, adequate, tough, loving, happy, competent, alienated, responsible, and all the opposites to those words.

IS IT WORTH DOING?

I look forward to working in a training group because I am committed to helping human beings remain human. Our condition is such that it can only be comprehended if we can create relationships in which a person can experience himself as a human being. For me, a training group is first of all an opportunity for richer personal involvement than is available in my day-to-day professional role. It gives me a sense of intimacy that I need and a feeling that I am not alone in needing. As I relate to others and help them face existential contingencies, I too gain the strength necessary to confront my own anxieties and inadequacies. Finally, a training group is perhaps the only place where I can rebel against the meaninglessness of "systems" and their authorities and perhaps encourage others of the need to revolt against those conditions of society which reduce or ignore our humanness.

There is much joy to be found in being a trainer. One feels he is actually participating in life and shaping its course rather than drifting along and being propelled by the unknown "theys." He has the freedom to choose life, to be part of the world of others, to feel and taste and touch their hopes and joys, their despairs and sorrows. I have yet to see a group end without the resurgence of my faith that man can confront reality and learn from it. My experience in groups has, above all, taught me one thing: the major contribution I have to offer is myself as a person. My knowledge about what is happening to myself and others is always limited and is constantly changing. By serving as a model of authenticity, I come closest to helping others create moments from which we may all learn what it means "to be."

REFERENCES

Argyris, C. "Conditions for Competence Acquisition and Therapy." *Journal of Applied Behavioral Science* 4, no. 2 (1968): 147-177.

Bennis, W. G., and Schein, E. H. *Personal and Organizational Change through Group Methods.* New York: John Wiley & Sons, 1965.

Bradford, L. P.; Gibb, J. R.; and Benne, K. D. *T-Group Theory and Laboratory Method: Innovation in Re-Education.* New York: John Wiley & Sons, 1964.

Buber, M. *Between Man and Man.* New York: Macmillan Co., 1965.

Bugental, J. F. T. *The Search for Authenticity.* New York: Holt, Rinehart & Winston, 1965.

Burton, A. *Modern Humanistic Psychotherapy.* San Francisco: Jossey-Bass, 1967.

Coffey, H. S., and Golden, Jr., W. P. "Psychology of Change within an Institution." In *In-Service, Education* 56th Yearbook, pp. 67-102. Chicago: National Society for Study of Education, 1957.

Golembiewski, R. M. "The 'Laboratory Approach' to Organization Change: Schema of a Method." *Public Administration Review* 27, no. 3 (1967): 211-221.

Hampden-Turner, C. M. "An Existential 'Learning Theory' and the Integration of T-Group Research." *Journal of Applied Behavioral Science* 2, no. 4 (1966): 367-386.

Jourard, S. M. *The Transparent Self.* New York: Van Nostrand Reinhold Co., 1964.

————. *Disclosing Man to Himself.* New York: Van Nostrand Reinhold Co., 1968.

Kelman, H. C. "The Role of the Group in the Induction of Therapeutic Change." *International Journal of Group Psychotherapy* 13, no. 4 (1963): 399-432.

Maslow, A. *Toward a Psychology of Being.* New York: Van Nostrand Reinhold Co., 1962.

May, R.; Angel, E.; and Ellenberger, H. F.; eds. *Existence: A New Dimension in Psychiatry and Psychology.* New York: Simon & Schuster, 1967.

Moustakas, C. *Individuality and Encounter.* Cambridge, Mass.: Howard A. Doyle Publishing Co., 1968.

Parker, J. C., and Golden, Jr., W. P. "Democratic Group Processes." In *Group*

Processes in Supervision. Washington, D. C.: National Education Association, Association for Supervision and Curriculum Development, 1948.

Parker, J. C., and Rubin, L. J. *Process As Content: Curriculum Design and the Application of Knowledge*. Chicago: Rand McNally & Co., 1966.

Psalthas, G., and Hardert, R. "Trainer Interventions and Normative Patterns in the T Group." *Journal of Applied Behavioral Science* 2, no. 2 (1966): 149-169.

Rogers, C. *On Becoming a Person*. Boston: Houghton Mifflin Co., 1961.

Schutz, W. C. *Joy*. New York: Grove Press, 1968.

Van Kaam, A. *The Art of Existential Counseling*. Wilkes-Barre, Penn.: Dimension Books, 1966.

Weschler, I., Tannenbaum, R., and Massarik, F. *Issues in Human Relations Training*. NTL Selected Readings Series, no. 5. Washington, D.C.: NTL Institute for Applied Behavioral Science, 1962.

The Search
for With-ness
A New Look at Interdependence

JACK R. GIBB
Private Management Consultant
La Jolla, California

I grow when I am in *with-ness;* I contribute to the growth of others when I am deeply *with* them; the essential attribute of a growth experience is interdependence. I come into a training group with the intention of doing and being fully *with* people. When this effort is made evident, other significant conditions follow—the characteristics of with-ness.

Training groups are used variously to increase interpersonal competence, to foster personal growth, to build teams, to do therapy, and to develop climates in organizations. These goals are accomplished to the degree that members of the group, including the leader or trainer, are able to engage fully in *with-relationships* and to develop the capacity for taking on such relationships in other groups.

Moreover, the training-group leader is effective to the extent that he is able to be fully *with* other group members—to be interdependent.* This focus optimizes the conditions under which training-

---

* The more general theory of social systems from which this principle is derived is discussed at some length in J. R. Gibb, and L. M. Gibb, "Emergence Therapy: The TORI Process in an Emergent Group," in *Innovations to Group Psychotherapy,* ed. G. M. Gazda (Springfield, Ill.: Charles C. Thomas Publishers, 1968).

Discussions of implications of the theory for management, child rearing, and general social systems are found in J. R. Gibb, "Fear and Facade: Defensive Management," in *Science and Human Affairs,* ed. R. F. Farson (Palo Alto, Calif.: Science & Behavior Books, 1965).

group aims are accomplished. Experience with trainees indicates that they can internalize this principle relatively easily and that the use of this single guideline frees the trainee to contribute maximally to the training group.

Table 1 lists in abbreviated form some characteristics of with-ness I have observed in effective trainers and members of training groups. The *Being with* behaviors and internal states are inevitable if a person has internalized the theory of with-ness and has learned from with-directed experience the satisfactions of such an orientation. (Research is under way to determine the characteristics most definitive of the concept.) Behaviors and internal states designated as *Being under, over, or away* are incommensurate with, and sometimes antithetical to, interdependence and include various forms of interpersonal distancing.

TABLE 1. The Nature of With-ness

Being with	*Being under, over, or away*
1. Spontaneity; relative freedom from inner programming; doing what feels good at the moment.	1. Programming, planning, building expectations, using methods or techniques.
2. Being personal; being free from seeing self or other in role; taking responsibility for my own growth.	2. Being in role; seeing self and other in role; placing responsibility for my growth upon others; observing.
3. Intrinsic pushes; relative freedom from external pressures; emergent relationship.	3. Extrinsic pulls from external expectations, obligations and responsibilities; prescribed relationship.
4. Available; opened up; feeling with; "having soul."	4. Closed; tuned out; filtering; unresponsive; analytical.
5. Being in the here-and-now; in touch with the present moment.	5. Being in the there-and-then; responding to the past or future; out of touch with the moment.
6. Giving clean messages; telling it like it is.	6. Giving cluttered messages; dissonance and distortion in expressing behavior and words; covering up the message.
7. Focusing on interactive and interdependent behavior; synergistic action; doing with.	7. Non-interactive; dominant or submissive; dependent or independent; unilateral.
8. Physical and psychological closeness and intimacy.	8. Withdrawal; aloofness; separateness.
9. Inner peace, comfort, joy.	9. Stress, discomfort, tension.
10. Allowing self and others to be; comfort with diversity and unpredictability.	10. Controlling self and others; making demands; grasping.

SPONTANEITY

The person who is set toward letting things happen *with* others moves toward opening himself to deeper, richer, more diverse experiences.

There is evidence that training groups are valuable in helping a participant identify and change the expectations—the internal programs—that limit his freedom, spontaneity, and receptivity to new experience.

At various times in my career, my expectations upon entering a group included the following: "I will not intervene at the content level." "I will participate less than others." "I will focus my remarks on group norms." "I will attempt to provide missing roles in the group." "I will try to keep the group at the process level." "I will try to protect and support members who need help." I no longer place such advance restrictions on my behavior; instead, I come into the group expecting to do whatever feels good to me at the moment. I do not feel now that it is especially helpful either to study advance information about participants or to plan methods or strategies, by myself or with associates, before or between sessions. I may participate in in-group planning if I feel at the time that it is useful or if the other group members and I have decided to do some planning.

A training group is anything the group wants it to be and can create it to be at any given moment. I thus have no definition of a training group and no special training-group technology. I do not use terms like nonverbals, sensitivity training, role-playing, or process observing for group activities. Such labels tend to be restrictive and to limit the group's vision of what is possible. I have no arbitrary advance restrictions on former taboos, such as acting out, content focus, "getting into therapy," and escape to the there-and-then. I express my preferences or feelings for or against an activity depending upon my reactions at the time a decision is being made by the group.

BEING PERSONAL *

In the early days of grouping, each trainer assimilated specific patterns of behavior that came to define "the trainer role." This role was then carried on by later generations of trainers. They modified the

* The meaning of being "personal" is discussed more fully in J. R. Gibb, "The Counselor as a Role-Free Person," in *Counseling Theories and Counselor Education*, ed. C. A. Parker (New York: Houghton Mifflin Co., 1968).

patterns in some ways but usually attempted to "do what a trainer must do" to create an effective training group. For a long time, I (and many others) tried to construct a role that would be most helpful, constructive, confronting, and facilitative.

I now make no effort to "take a role," model behavior, demonstrate effective action, help others, build a group climate, be an effective participant-observer, teach interpersonal skills, or fulfill any of the role prescriptions that I, or others, have constructed as theoretical models. I simply make an effort to be whatever I am, to become whatever I become. I am never completely sure of my feelings at a given moment, never completely certain of who I am, and always somewhat puzzled—and a bit incredulous—when I hear people say that they know exactly who they are or precisely how they feel at any particular moment. I look upon the process of seeking personal identity and the determination and communication of inner states as a continual, never-ending search, a movement through an uncharted, idiographic, and delightfully unpredictable life flow. This is very different, phenomeno-logically, from attempting to take a role—that is, consciously or un-consciously taking on a particular pattern or constellation of behaviors and attitudes.

Being *with* another person is somehow to establish, in the moment, a person-to-person contact. A concrete and unique self is in touch with another concrete and unique self in a never-to-be-replicated interaction. A role is a construct, a generalization, a logical entity, a useful tool for analysis and prediction, and a linguistic manipulation. A role cannot be *with* a role. It is at best an image and at worst a mask of the person underneath.

At the beginning of the life of a training group, I make it clear that I intend to enter the group as a person, to do what I can to help myself grow and have a rich learning experience, to participate fully as a member with no special responsibilities or privileges, to initiate and interact, to show my full being as much as I am able, and to experience myself more deeply as a growing person. I make clear my assumption that whatever responsibilities or obligations are embodied in the posi-tion of trainer are best met by my entry into the group as a person rather than in a role.

To be personal is to be and show my uniqueness. I am being personal (and most helpful) when I show or tell my feelings impulsively without consideration of the consequences. I am being in role (and, I believe, least helpful) when I filter out feelings that I believe to be unconstruc-tive, unhelpful, irrelevant, impolite, too revealing, dangerous to me or others, or untimely. I often do such filtering, of course, but I am learning to show and tell a much wider range of feelings and attitudes as I become more personal and have greater with-ness.

Another way of stressing this point is to say that I refuse to take any special responsibilities different from those of other members in the group. I accept full responsibility for myself, for my relationships, and for the success of the group experience; I assume that each of the other members will also come to feel that he is fully responsible for himself, his relationships, and for the group experience. Such responsibility is an essential for personal growth, not to be assigned to fate, previous experiences, parents, trainers, or therapists. Research and observation (Gibb and Gibb 1969) lead me to conclude that a relatively role-free training group is the most effective medium for the development of growth-critical and life-giving feelings of responsibility and freedom. For me this is highly significant.

INTRINSIC EMERGENCE

When a person is *with* another person, the relationship is intrinsically rewarding and free from external pressures; the relationship flows, emerges, happens. The quality may ebb and flow, but there is a touching of two people. The feelings—love, anger, sadness, euphoria, despair, tenderness—arise solely from with-ness. Interdependence is self-fulfilling.

The glue in an interdependent relationship comes from the good feelings that emerge from enjoying closeness, not from external pressures. These pressures—responsibilities, expectations, obligations, sacrifices, loyalties, commitments, bonds, role prescriptions—always truncate the experience of with-ness and diminish the relationship. With-ness is a condition that is relatively free of restraint. Each party is free to move toward or away from the other.

When I am *with* another, I experience the joy of sharing, the exhilaration in a common search or zest in a fight, the pain of a problem. There is always a diminution, a "put-down" when I come to another or another comes to me to help, to get help, to apologize, to fill an obligation, to render a service, to act out a role, or to make a sacrifice. Being truly together is something else.

AVAILABILITY

A person who is *with* another person is available, open to the flow of depth communication, empathic, "tuned in." Some pairs seem to tune in with each other rather quickly; others take time, effort, or change.

Some relationships start with role relations: reactions to hearsay, reputation, role perceptions, physical appearance, clothing, stereotypes, projected fears, and irrelevant aspects of the situation. When I am aware of such reactions in myself I have to fight through them, "listen to my stomach," or pull myself into the immediate present.

As I make an attempt in the group to show what is going on in me, I am increasingly able to let myself go and to let what happens happen. Sometimes this is impossible for me, and the best I can do is to tell in words what is going on. Thus I may say, "I'm feeling that I ought to come over to you to show my affection, but I don't like the feeling of doing what I 'ought to do,' and I'm struggling with what is going on inside me." "I'm terribly confused by what you are saying and by what is going on in me." "I'm happy for no reason that is apparent to me." I feel best when I am able to show how I feel, quite good when I can tell what I feel, and least good when I am unable, because of some kind of fear, to do either.

When I am available to others, I am "there." I feel with and am open to the feelings of others. I make an effort to hear and to see what others are saying, feeling, and doing. I am close to primitive feelings, minimally contaminated by interpretations, evaluations, and cognitive elements. I can cut through these impure elements and be close to, available to, the unmasked core of the inner person.

BEING IN THE MOMENT

It is impossible to be *with* another person without being in the here-and-now. Since the most relevant and powerful aspects of the present moment are usually the persons with whom one shares the moment, to be in the moment one must be *with* the person who shares it.

There are many occasions when it is important to depart from the here-and-now: to exchange ideas, plan for the future, share experiences of the past, construct a theory, observe oneself introspectively, create a fantasy, or perform a task. When it seems meaningful or interesting to me, I share in these activities as they occur in the group and I may also initiate some of them. More and more I find myself, in training groups and in other life situations, enjoying the moment, and finding enrichment and meaning in with-ness. I greatly value my capacity to be deeply *with* others and prize the opportunities to enjoy this.

It is impossible to be genuinely *with* another person without responding fully to his current feelings. One is not in the moment when he is analyzing, observing, rationalizing, planning, evaluating, introspecting (watching himself), remembering, role-playing, controlling, or using a method. One can be in the present moment when he is fully involved in laughing, crying, hurting, loving, hating, enjoying, fighting, touching, exploring, knowing, being.

GIVING CLEAN MESSAGES

In thinking about training groups, I often focus upon the giving of uncluttered messages as a critical aspect of with-ness. I find that as people begin to lose fears and to be more personal, they increase the clarity of their outgoing messages; this clarity improves their capacity for being *with* others.

Each of us has learned many ways of cluttering the message: smiling to cover up fears, hinting to soften the message, hiding negative or positive feelings, trying to conceal our loneliness, or trying to avoid hurting others. A person is seldom as inventive as he is in avoiding speaking the plain truth about feelings.

It is impossible to deepen rapport and put ourselves in deep communion with another without continually showing our true feelings. Those who build trust quickly are those who can show inner feelings quickly. Words and actions must be relatively consistent. Verbal and nonverbal cues must be consonant for with-ness to develop quickly and to grow in depth.

DOING WITH

Doing things together, in a fully interdependent way, is a rare event in our competitive culture. People usually work under someone or over someone. The symphony has a conductor. The football team has a quarterback. It *is* rare, but possible for conductors and quarterbacks to work in participative ways and to generate with-ness feelings. Most people, however, work *for* someone else rather than *with* them. People cannot be truly interdependent when they feel inferior or superior to others.

The training group is a place where people try things out. Most groups learn to do things together, synergistically, in an emerging and flowing way and with high interdependence.

A total group with-ness is a unique event. It is clear to me that genuine group activities transcend the activities of individual members or pairs of members. I have vivid memories of a group, its members tuned in to one another's moods and needs, moving in a lovely and emergent way to pick up and cradle a man who showed signs of despair and loneliness. Individuals seemed to move as one. Positions were taken, shoulders touched, the man's head was tenderly cradled, the group invented new and tender ways of expressing care and concern. It was clear that everyone enjoyed the caring, the lifting, the doing-it-together, the interdependence. Two or three could not have done the lifting alone. No one led the group. We could not remember who first started toward the man.

In recent years, I have come to appreciate anew the significance of physical behavior in the learning process. I think now that the deepest and most permanent learning in the training group comes from doing things of one's own initiation—preferably doing things *with* others. Little significant learning comes from observing, analyzing motivations or past history, or "getting" insight, understanding or sensitivity. A person learns by carrying out impulses to show his anger, to walk over and touch another lovingly, to express himself in clear ways in the heat of interaction, or to ask for help when he wants it. He does not learn by resolving to be a better listener, intending to be more loving, or promising himself to go home and love his children. He does not learn by understanding why he does not express his love for his children or by observing others who express affection well. He learns by repeatedly trying things in physical ways, thus creating new and observable effects in himself and others, and then, after integrating these effects, trying again in new ways. The way to change behavior is to *do something now* that begins to build new physical patterns of behavior.

When persons are doing things *with* each other, the enjoyment of the doing transcends the extrinsic rewards of winning, praise, or pay. Physical with-ness is its own reward. "Win-win" actions—social dancing, sexual relations, cooperative team efforts, being with—generate self-fulfilling and emergent processes.

PHYSICAL AND PSYCHOLOGICAL INTIMACY

Physical and psychological intimacy are highly correlated. It is possible to use hugging and kissing to avoid intimacy; it is possible for persons to be deeply in tune without physical contact. It is usually obvious in a group, however, that those who have difficulty expressing feelings have difficulty in physical expressions of affection, hostility, trust, and competition. They even have difficulty in role-playing these states.

Physical patterns of relating are usually direct manifestations of inner attitudes. Persons can learn to enjoy, even to welcome, physical expression of affection in hugging, deep eye contact, sitting close, and lifting. Often distancing relationships are changed by direct efforts to work things out in physical confrontation. Learning to overcome fears of physical intimacy is an important step in learning to make deeper contact at psychological levels. Physical closeness, under most conditions, leads to psychological closeness.

Since learning to be more free in my own physical expressions of fighting and loving, I have reached deeper levels in relationships with people. It is much easier now for me to show my affection and my anger, and I have less need to express these feelings verbally. I find, too, that there is an increasing congruence in my nonverbal and verbal messages. My anger or my love shows in voice tones, facial expressions, bodily postures, and other forms of expressive behavior. With-ness is impossible without communicable expression of feelings, which are the fabric of being and doing *with*.

INNER PEACE

Apparently some kinds of inner tension and discomfort lead to deeper feelings, greater learning, and growth. Other kinds, in different circumstances, oppose growth forces, produce defensive behavior, and are unproductive. I have some working hypotheses about these relationships but am not confident of their validity.

I do not believe in deliberately producing ambiguity and discomfort to produce learning and growth. Individuals must take responsibility for producing their own discomforts and learn for themselves how to handle their own tension and pain. The training group is a productive ground for such learning.

I do believe that learning and growth can occur without discomfort and tension. Internal forces move us toward the four definitive signs of growth: greater personhood, openness, self-determination, and with-ness.* These states are self-rewarding.

* This four-factor theory of personal and organizational growth is discussed at length in J. R. Gibb, and L. M. Gibb, "Humanistic Elements in Group Growth," in *Challenges of Humanistic Psychology*, ed. J. F. T. Bugental (New York: McGraw-Hill, 1967).

ALLOWING SELF AND OTHERS TO BE

A person cannot be deeply *with* another person when he is trying to teach him a lesson, change his behavior, revise his life style, remedy or correct his deficiencies, train him in new skills, or help him to become. With-ness implies allowing the other to be himself, reaching out to establish contact and empathy, sharing joy or pain, giving love without expectation of reward or feeling of sacrifice, moving with the other toward the uncharted and unpredictable, trusting self-and-other-and-the-universe to produce something good, and having a willingness to risk. Indeed, there is no feeling of risk in genuine with-ness. With-ness contains no danger.

I often experience a wish to change someone else. I sometimes verbalize this wish or this fantasy and sometimes invite others to share their wishes for me, although as I get less defensive I have less urge to change others. Hopefully we create a climate in which expressed concerns have a less coercive quality.

As a person and as a leader, I come into the group with the intent to learn and not to teach, to grow and not to control or guide the growth of others, to seek companions on a quest and not to lead the venture, and to be deeply *with* these companions.*

A depth experience of being *with* another person is rewarding in and of itself. The state of with-ness is growth-promoting, healing, and team-building. "People problems" are the primary forces that produce anxiety, organizational sickness, alienation, and the other major ills of our time. For me, the lack of with-ness is the critical factor in these problems.

With-ness, as defined here, is the crucial ingredient of inner peace, enduring comfort, and deep joy. The *essential* dynamic of the training group is the search for with-ness.

REFERENCE

Gibb, J. R., and Gibb, L. M. "Role Freedom in a TORI Group." In *Encounter: A Primer on Sensitivity Training and Encounter Groups,* edited by A. Burton. San Francisco: Jossey-Bass Publishers, 1969.

*Some training implications of this theoretical position are discussed in J. R. Gibb, and L. M. Gibb, "Leaderless Groups: Growth-Centered Values and Potentials," in *Ways of Growth: Approaches to Expanding Awareness,* ed. H. A. Otto and J. Mann (New York: Grossman Publishers, 1968).

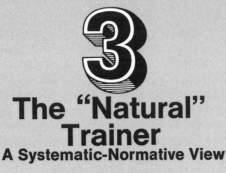

The "Natural" Trainer
A Systematic-Normative View

FRED MASSARIK
University of California
Los Angeles, California

WHOEVER coined the phrase "the age of complexity" must have had in mind the state of human relations training in the 1960s. Since its creative and cautious beginnings, the training-group concept (whatever the synonym) has come to encompass widely differing program concepts and designs. Whether at Esalen or Aureon, TRW or Standard Oil, UCLA or Boston U, NTL or anywhere else, training offerings present a nearly infinite variety. No matter what the approach, some brochure is bound to offer it.

The trainer is at a crossroads. Should he develop "his own thing," with a rather specialized procedure that becomes his personal trademark? Should he identify with a particular school or method—Gestalt, for instance, or "personal growth?" Or should he strive for an enveloping generalism, with the nagging fear that thus he may be trying to be all things to all men?

There are, of course, no firm answers to these questions. Each trainer works out his own solution to complex dilemmas. This, then, is the present situation and also this chapter's central thesis (an old one redefined): The man is the style. It may be a good or bad thesis in a normative sense. It may make for more or less effective training outcomes. Whatever the nature of the forces at work, however, I submit that a good trainer is natural—he is himself—and that not everyone who is natural is necessarily a good trainer. Hopefully, these propositions provide an opportunity for the systematic conceptualization of some aspects of trainer behavior and group process as they relate to the trainer role.

THE FIRST CIRCLE: THE TRAINER-AS-PERSON

As the trainer faces the group, he is perceived by all concerned as a person who is doing something and being somebody. This is true, of course, for group members as well, but for the trainer his presence as a person is the existential reality. He cannot avoid it. It is the most basic fact of his and the group's life.

This reality of the trainer-as-person is essentially holistic, although studies of person perception may focus on salient sub-elements.* He comes to the group as a whole person, not as a blank slate to be inscribed with a neatly catalogued set of role behaviors. As his impact increases, he willingly or otherwise reveals to others the pattern of his personhood.† No set of role behaviors in and of themselves, regardless of how thoroughly studied, makes a person a "good" trainer unless one all-important question can be answered affirmatively: Does he shape up well as a human being, specifically in his relationships with people in the group?

This query can open the Pandora's box of "good guy-bad guy" labels. This is not the intent. Various writers have addressed themselves to concepts of self, at least in part, considering such aspects as authenticity, positive mental health, and simply freedom from neurotic hang-ups.‡ However, such concepts, while important, are not purely individual; they must be judged in the context of the norms of the broader culture and in terms óf the group's expectations at a given stage of development. At any rate, a total "sense of the person" comes

---

* For a comprehensive statement of relevant variables see R. Tagiuri, The Handbook of Social Psychology, 2nd ed., vol. 3 (Reading, Mass.: Addison-Wesley Publishing Co., 1968), pp. 395-449.

† For a humanistic view of the life-cycle concept, a relevant backdrop to any ahistorical view of person (trainer) behavior, see C. Bühler and F. Massarik, eds., The Course of Human Life (New York: Springer Publishing Co., 1968), pp. 12-26.

‡ An excellent down-to-earth statement of a "healthy" view of self is C. R. Rogers, On Becoming a Person (Boston: Houghton Mifflin Co., 1961), pp. 15-27.

across to the group and establishes a basis for the continuing relationships between trainer and group.

In addition, the trainer's specific personal needs, as they operate in his interpersonal interactions, are crucial determinants of his total effectiveness. A number of need theories, including those of Bühler (1968, pp. 92-101), Maslow (1954, pp. 63-154), Schutz (1958, pp. 13-56), and Rokeach (1960), among others, may be appropriately advanced. Selectively, we note three need configurations that may be of special relevance in determining trainer effectiveness.

- *Structure flexibility.* Is the trainer capable of proceeding without elaborate structure in group relationships? Can he, on the other hand, function within structural conditions and indeed initiate structure, if required to do so?
- *Affect flexibility.* Is the trainer able to give and to receive affection in a balanced way? Is he comfortable in close relationships while having the ability to terminate relationships when appropriate?
- *Need satisfaction/self-limiting adaptation balance.* Is the trainer's search for personal satisfaction integrated with a capacity for accepting interpersonal limitations and for adapting his behavior to situational constraints?

Other necessary conditions for effectiveness, treated in detail elsewhere, are variables such as trainer self-knowledge; capacity for understanding other individuals, groups, and organizations; and cognitive knowledge of behavioral science concepts.*

Conceptually, we may now postulate the trainer's presence in the group as a person doing what comes naturally to him. We denote this by the first circle in figure 1.

THE SECOND CIRCLE: THE GROUP'S LEARNING NEEDS

Almost without exception, the trainer faces a fundamental dilemma, which may be called the "you can't please all the people all the time" bind. Even under conditions of apparent homogeneity, group members' learning needs differ enough to create conflicting demands. For instance, the trainer may strive for "distributive justice," seeing to it that all (or most) members eventually have the opportunity for self-exploration and social learning. This process is sometimes articulated

---

*See, for example, lists of criteria variously employed by the NTL Institute for Applied Behavioral Science, Washington, D.C. in selection of trainer network members.

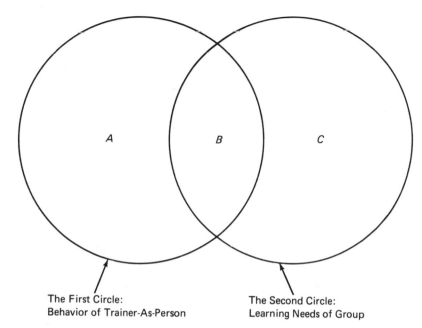

The First Circle:
Behavior of Trainer-As-Person

The Second Circle:
Learning Needs of Group

Fig. 1 Behavior of Trainer-As-Person and Learning Needs of Group. *A,* trainer's needs met; *B,* area of primary trainer effectiveness; *C,* group's learning needs unmet.

by group members in expressions like, "Today it's my turn to be on the 'hot seat,' " or "When are we going to let Joe off the hook so that someone else can become the focus?" It may also be felt in concern about silent members who do not seem to be giving or receiving their fair share of attention.

The trainer, then, confronts various member and group-process needs by trade-offs, by meeting some, and by ignoring others for the moment. We may also think of the totality of member learning needs at a given time—a kind of momentary joint vector of the multiplicity of such needs. In turn, we may conceive of the accumulation of these joint vectors in their unfolding throughout the group experience as specifying the extent to which, by and large, relevant member or group needs were met. (While we have used the terms *member needs* and *group needs,* we do not preclude needs which have to do with the learning of organizational roles, team-building, and other personal processes related to larger social systems.)

The learning needs of the group—colloquially described perhaps as "what people ought to get out of training"—is denoted by the second circle of figure 1.

THE UTOPIAN OVERLAP

Ideally, the trainer will be optimally effective if he functions naturally; if he is insightful about self, individuals, groups, and organizations; if he is comfortable with or without structure; if he can give and receive affection in balance; and if he reconciles the striving for personal need satisfaction with the realities of situational constraints.

Figure 2 shows this "utopian overlap": perfect harmony between the natural behavior of the trainer-as-person and the group's learning needs. It should be noted that "pseudoutopian overlap" is an occasional occurrence. While superficially resembling the ideal, it is actually a situation in which the trainer's neurotic patterns satisfy the group and vice versa. (Perhaps this set of circumstances accounts for the extreme and phantasmal euphoria, devoid of long-range learning, encountered in particular growth center and guru-led training experiences.)

But what about the more common reality of the good fostered by a humanly imperfect trainer? What logic governs his actions?

THE BASIC GAP: GROUP'S LEARNING NEEDS UNMET

The trainer may indeed come to the group naturally and spontaneously, but, given his particular pattern of needs and characteristics, this somehow is not enough to satisfy all of the group's learning re-

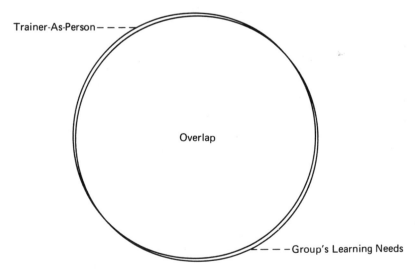

Fig. 2   The "Utopian Overlap."

quirements. A gap remains. Whether at a specific moment or as the cumulative interaction of trainer and group, this gap represents the extent to which the trainer's presence as a person is not fully responsive to the group's needs.

The trainer may be aware or unaware of the gap. In the latter case, he will do nothing to deal with it, and his effectiveness as trainer will be reduced. If he is aware of it, what can he do to bridge it? Primarily, he can reach into his repertoire of learned trainer-role behaviors,* applying these with conscious intent to fill in where his personal spontaneity leaves off.

Some role behaviors may have become so thoroughly internalized as to be indistinguishable from spontaneous, integrated personality structure. There are two additional kinds, whose use is based on cognitive analysis or advance planning.

First is the purposeful intervention. The trainer develops a way of training that includes, for instance, intentional, nondirective echoing of member comments; redirecting group process to the here-and-now; and inserting brief, consciously interpretive statements. In each case, he has in mind (rather than "in gut") an objective that he believes (rather than feels) to be appropriate, given his assessment of the group's learning needs.

Second is the training construction, a generic heading for such procedures as exercises, theory sessions, role-playing, feedback forms, and the use of film and video tape. The training construction is intended to meet a learning need of one or more group members or of the group as a whole. It serves thereby as a necessary and, hopefully, appropriate adjunct to the trainer's natural, interpersonal behavior.

The use of purposeful interventions and training constructions does not, of course, automatically assure that all will be well, either with the group or the trainer. On occasion, the latter may find himself responding artificially and woodenly. As he misses the mark, one or more group members feel growing dissatisfaction and confusion. Such disenchantments, however, must be distinguished from those induced more naturally and functionally in the early stages of the group experience. For instance, frustrations brought about by the usual lack of structure at the beginning of the laboratory have beneficial effects on

---

* For examples of trainer role behavior, generically viewed, and its interplay with group process, see L. P. Bradford, "Trainer-Intervention: Case Episodes," in *T-Group Theory and Laboratory Method: Innovation in Re-Education,* ed. L. P. Bradford, J. R. Gibb, and K. D. Benne (New York: John Wiley & Sons, 1964), pp. 136-167; and R. Tannenbaum, I. R. Weschler, and F. Massarik, "Observations on the Trainer Role," in *Leadership and Organization* (New York: McGraw-Hill, 1961), pp. 188-205.

"getting the juices flowing" and on establishing fluidity as the basis for the emergence of novel procedural patterns.

The basic gap may thus be closed but imperfectly. As figure 3 shows, this gap may be regarded as shading into two segments: group needs effectively met by learned trainer-role behaviors and those not met by these means nor by the trainer's natural spontaneity. As necessary, but only as necessary, the trainer develops somewhat artifactual skills—techniques, if you will—to reach beyond the limitation of his authentic self. He strives to aid group members by such intentional interventions to augment the impact of his natural presence.

In reducing the basic gap, the trainer needs cognitive and emotional insights of the kind customarily emphasized for trainer selection and evaluation—insights focused on group and personal variables. For example, he must understand personality dynamics, interpersonal patterns, and group functioning. Further, he is expected to act on the basis of this knowledge to facilitate learning. (Incidentally, the unintentional double meaning of the term "act" is significant, suggesting the purposeful, "not quite himself" actor's overlay in the trainer's behavior.)

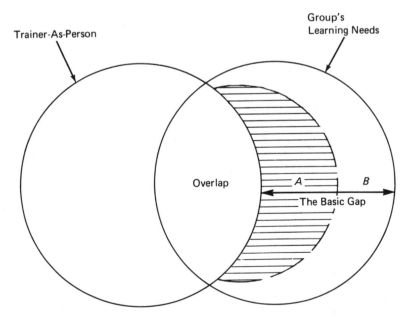

Fig. 3 The Basic Gap: Extent to which trainer-as-person does not meet group's learning needs. *A*, group's learning needs met by learned trainer-role behaviors; *B*, group's learning needs unmet.

THE "NEUROTIC TRAINER": ONLY TRAINER'S NEEDS MET

There is a corollary aspect to the basic gap: the trainer's natural and spontaneous behavior may serve in some measure to meet his personal needs alone and not those of any substantial number of group members. If this is the case, the trainer will fail to perceive correctly his connection with the group's requirements and/or he will fail to respond appropriately. He does what fits him, but it is not what fits the group. In (hopefully) rare instances, he may be characterized as self-centered or exploitative, using the group consciously or un-consciously as a vehicle for self-gratification and ignoring the implications for the learning outcomes or for the elementary welfare of group members. Even if his motives are the best, under these conditions the trainer's behavior is neurotic, particularly from the group's viewpoint. A vicious circle is created: the trainer's ineffective actions cause members' resistances and hostilities; these in turn force the trainer farther from the group's need and into a defensive shell of maladaptive self-orientation. This is the trainer's road to hell, par excellence.

An extreme remedy for this situation may be for him to withdraw from the trainer's role altogether. Some people (including, alas, certain trainers now practicing) plainly are not cut out to be trainers. Whatever technique they may learn, whatever their intellectual grasp of psychological and social phenomena, their development as persons is such that there is little possibility of their ever becoming truly effective trainers.

In less serious circumstances, other alternatives are possible. The use of learned, trainer-role behaviors is, of course, the manifestation of the trainer's effort to respond suitably to group needs that may not otherwise be met. On occasion, however, he may employ such devices neurotically for self-gratification, with no concern for group consequences. Here, the trainer may need to suppress his less healthy impulses to prepare the way for those more appropriate (learned, trainer-role) interventions that do come naturally to him. These functional suppressions are indicated by the shaded section in figure 4.

Finally, the trainer may, within the constraints of his existing pattern, modify his own need configurations; this may mean psychotherapy or intensive involvement as a participant or client in trainer groups. If deeply-rooted learning takes place as a result of the retraining, an area of enlarged overlap may result between the first circle, the trainer-as-person, and the second circle, the learning needs of the group (see figure 5). (These modifications should positively affect the trainer's personal as well as his professional life.)

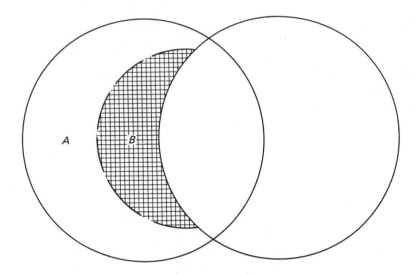

Fig. 4 Needs of Trainer-As-Person. *A*, only trainer needs met; *B*, functional suppression of "inappropriate" trainer needs.

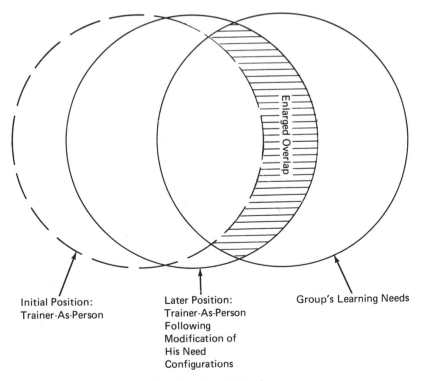

Initial Position:
Trainer-As-Person

Later Position:
Trainer-As-Person
Following
Modification of
His Need
Configurations

Group's Learning Needs

Fig. 5 Enlarged Overlap.

In general, lessening of the neurotic elements in trainer behavior hinges on increasing the trainer's knowledge of himself—hardly a novel view, but basic just the same. Instead of expressing self-serving needs, he must be aware of his impact on the group so that he can judge when to suppress a need and determine what interventions are in order. And surely he requires at least rudimentary insight to make decisions respecting his future as a trainer.

THE AREA OF PRIMARY TRAINER EFFECTIVENESS

We now approach the full circle, recognizing that the utopian overlap is indeed an ideal not often encountered in everyday reality. The good trainer, however, has a personality structure that provides a substantial coincidence of his needs and those of the group. His total and genuine self is in some measure truly responsive to the group's learning needs. Under these conditions, what is good for the trainer is good for the group. This happy state (or better, happy process) is the area of primary trainer effectiveness (see figure 6).

Here we encounter the apparently effortless aspect of the training experience. Nothing is contrived. The laboratory is often pleasant fun (though pleasure is not valued for its own sake). This is not to say that

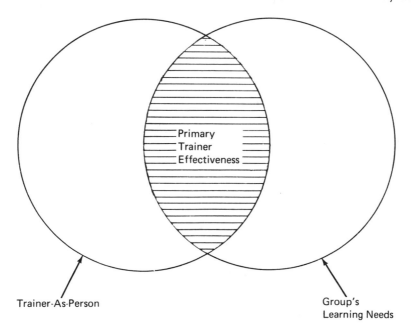

Fig. 6   Primary Trainer Effectiveness.

all group members must, or will, feel happy at every stage of learning. Silence, intense confrontation, or lack of structure may all be elicited naturally by the trainer, although the purpose of these experiences may not be immediately apparent to the participants. In the long run, we may posit primary trainer effectiveness by the extent to which group needs are met—operationally definable by some later systematic outcome assessment—as a consequence of natural, spontaneous trainer behavior.

From a research standpoint, the problem is complex. It becomes necessary to examine causal and quasi-causal links between trainer behavior and member learning without losing sight of a sometimes Medusa-like tangle of interacting variables such as the confluence of internal and contextual forces.* Still, the idea of primary trainer effectiveness may give focus to the inquiry.

* What is intended to be a fairly comprehensive framework of the interacting variables appears in F. Massarik, "A Sensitivity Training Impact Model: Some First (and Second) Thoughts on the Evaluation of Sensitivity Training," *Explorations in Human Relations Training and Research*, no. 3 (Washington, D.C.: NTL Institute for Applied Behavioral Science—National Education Association, 1965.)

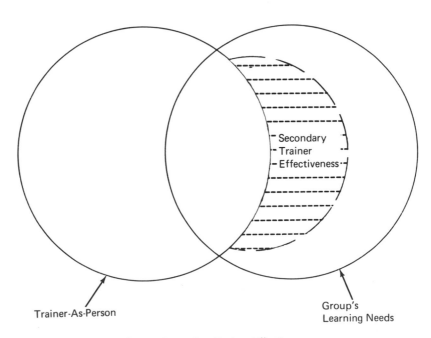

Fig. 7   Secondary Trainer Effectiveness.

THE AREA OF SECONDARY TRAINER EFFECTIVENESS

In moving beyond the "doing what comes naturally" level of effectiveness, the trainer of course seeks to meet member needs by engaging in specific, learned role behaviors. These may be regarded as supplements to the trainer-as-person, particularly helpful in areas affected by his personal and interactive limitations. To the extent to which he succeeds in these augmentations, the trainer broadens the area of secondary effectiveness (see figure 7).

The key to distinguishing secondary from primary effectiveness is the degree of internalization of the intervention. If the intervention is part and parcel of the trainer's personality and emerges genuinely, even ingenuously, in the group context, it falls at the "primary" end of the continuum. If it is planned or preplanned as a device deemed suitable to the circumstances and is not well-integrated into the trainer's behavioral repertoire, the intervention is to a greater or lesser degree secondary (see figure 8).

SOME NORMATIVE REFLECTIONS: A REPRISE

Charles Maher of the *Los Angeles Times* writes, "In football, there is a theory (some consider it a law) that the first thing a team must do on offense is to establish its running game." "But," Maher continues, "Roman Gabriel no longer buys it." Maher quotes Gabriel, the Los Angeles Rams' top 1969 quarterback, as suggesting that instead of adhering to any "law" about running, no matter how seemingly persuasive, one just passes or runs when the situation seems right. Surely this assumes the availability of well-developed skills—those carefully drilled pass plays, for instance. But most of all it underlines the benefits

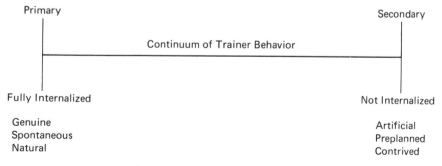

Fig. 8 Continuum of Trainer Behavior.

of knowing, deep-down, what to do, and the spontaneous capacity to act when the situation is in fact right. Mechanical, by-the-book interventions are to be avoided by professional football players—and by professional group trainers.

In Gabriel's game, the philosophy pays off on the scoreboard. In the trainer's world, the outcomes of primary and secondary effectiveness are not so readily posted. They are part of a life history of events; they emerge, not with lights flashing at a training group's end, but as the products of many forces.

The man *is* the style, and the starting point for all training is necessarily the trainer-as-person vis-à-vis the group. If there is little available in him-as-himself that makes learning sense for those involved, chances are slight that he will be able to close the gap between himself and the group by mechanical trainer role behaviors. This implies that conventional professional credentials (including the Ph.D. in psychology) are as such no assurance that an individual will prove to be an effective trainer, particularly if the learning they represent is centered principally on technique. To paraphrase a saying of another era, there is no substitute for humanness. And the trainer's human uniqueness in the context of his total professional self is the basic ingredient of any trainer "role." Accept no substitutes.

REFERENCES

Bühler, C., and Massarik, F., eds. *The Course of Human Life.* New York: Springer Publishing Co., 1968.

Maslow, A. H. *Motivation and Personality.* New York: Harper Brothers, 1954.

Rokeach, M. *The Open and Closed Mind.* New York: Basic Books, 1960.

Schutz, W. C. *FIRO, A Three-Dimensional Theory of Interpersonal Behavior.* New York: Rinehart & Co., 1958.

2

Theory and Method of Trainer Interventions

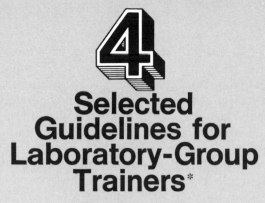

Selected Guidelines for Laboratory-Group Trainers*

GORDON LIPPITT
The George Washington University
Washington, D.C.

NO two sensitivity-training groups or laboratory programs are identical. Dissimilarity results from variations in the purpose, objectives, and nature of the overall program of which the group-learning experience is a part; such differences as those in group composition, size, sophistication, motivation, training facilities, and leaders bring into sharp focus each group's awareness of a unique learning experience.

Any training program, with its specific learning opportunities, is the result of background events; trainer and participant backgrounds and needs, training location, and program all make impact on a given session and moment to produce a training event. Whether this event (silence, leadership struggle, conflict between two members, hostility, subgroupings, and so forth) will be used for appropriate learning will in large part be determined by the skill and sophistication of the trainer.

* This article is an extension of an earlier article co-authored with Leslie This in 1967 and later adapted for the author's book *Organization Renewal* (New York: Appleton-Century-Crofts, 1969).

Schein and Bennis (1965), among others, feel that trainer intervention, style, and values are the major influences on laboratory-group learnings. While each group may be unique and trainer style may vary, certain problems, group phenomena sequential phases, and group behavior patterns can be predicted with a fairly high degree of accuracy. This predictability has enabled the laboratory method to evolve into a useful training technique. After twenty-five years of intensive use and study, a significant body of process knowledge has emerged and some desirable trainer behaviors have been codified.

Consideration of significant roles, problems, and trainer qualifications are requirements for professional performance in sensitivity-training situations. The dynamic group and individual processes with which the trainer is concerned are sufficiently known and predictable to be described and explained. Some useful guidelines can be established.

FACTORS AFFECTING THE TRAINER'S ROLE

Whether he works in a sensitivity-training group, or in a three-day or a four-week laboratory, the trainer will be called upon to assume several roles that demand professional competence and responsibility. His response to these role demands and subsequent performance in the group will vary and will be conditioned by the following ten factors.

Purposes and design of the training.   The way a trainer carries out his role is partially affected by the overall purposes of the training program. If the laboratory method is being used in a development program for supervisors, the trainer is not so much concerned with intragroup relationships as with developing skills to enable participants to work with employees. On the other hand, if a trainer is dealing with a homogeneous organization staff unit, he will be concerned with such matters as the personal risk felt by members of the group.

Length of training programs.   In a three-day program, the trainer normally needs to provide more learning stimulus than in a two-week program. He must create more rapidly experiences which will aid the participants in the learning process. In the shorter time, the trainer may also find it desirable to be more directive in opening the group to speed entrance into various learning processes.

Group composition.   If a developmental group experience is being conducted for the first time in an organization and participants know little about its purpose or methods, the trainer may need to provide additional support in initiating the diagnostic concept and process. If, however, the concepts of laboratory training are known to and practiced by group members, the trainer has little need to dwell on purposes, objectives, and methodologies.

The factor of status will also condition the trainer's role. The higher the status of the individual members, the less free such individuals are to let down their hair. It frequently occurs to the top man in an organization that the organization may be ready to develop a system of communication characterized by openness, but his immediate subordinates are reluctant and fearful. Disparity in ages, the proportions of men to women and of superiors to subordinates, and similar aspects of group composition should be carefully considered if not actually planned by the trainer. All such factors have a real significance for the trainer's behavior and style.

The practicing philosophy of the trainer.   Trainer approaches to laboratories vary, mostly because trainers interpret differently the relation of the trainer role to the learning process (although all interpretations are based on similar learning philosophies). This can be seen in the widely debated differences in regard to the directive versus the nondirective training role; the continuum from one to the other obviously presents many opportunities for differing trainer practices.

Even the most nondirective trainer, however—one, for example, who believes that the group should set its own standards and who protects those standards completely—will recognize the need for alertness to any group standard (or behavior) which in any way hurts an individual or subgroup. The area of standard-setting is but one of many where such differences may arise. Generally, however, we can say that those kinds of learning experiences which honestly confront the reality of the group situation are healthy if they are seen as helpful by the group members and if they take place in a supportive climate of "caring about each other."

Expectations of participants.   The whole field of laboratory and sensitivity training has received national publicity recently. Some stories emphasize the more experimental types of training; in some, training is improperly called laboratory or sensitivity training. Many conceptual distortions have arisen as a result. A participant seldom is without preconceptions, and those range from valid to distorted. The trainer will want to assure himself that an adequate explanation of laboratory education has been or is provided. If the group has received a valid orientation to the training, the trainer can proceed more quickly to the diagnostic learning process.

Expectations of program sponsors. Generally speaking, the trainer is responsible for establishing a connection between the way in which the group training is designed and conducted and the goals of the sponsoring organization. The sponsor may expect the group learning process to relate to the back-home situation of the trainees. In other cases, the expectation will be that the process be divorced as much as possible from the job situation. In some instances, the desired training will be oriented to personal growth, and in others, it will focus on team-building. Such factors will condition the style and method of the trainer.

Background organizational needs. A training design normally tries to meet the needs of an organization or of persons attending the program, as Blake and Mouton (1965) have pointed out. If the design evolves from an organization's desire to improve employees' interpersonal competence because of a poor record of labor-management relations, the trainer must be fully aware of the background circumstances. Similarly, the trainer should know if training is intended to improve interpersonal communications skills of, for example, salesmen.

Personal needs. In some cases, the trainer will find the personal needs of participants very evident. A person may have come to the training program with expectations that the laboratory group process will solve one or more of his personal problems. Assessing such expectations on the part of the individual or the organization is of paramount importance to the trainer.

Influence of trainer's peers and profession. The trainer's style will be conditioned by the actions of his peers in a training situation and by his own concept of his professional role. In most situations where more than one trainer is involved, a norm of trainer behavior emerges which influences the methods and style of each. If such a norm dictates that an "effective" trainer is one who uses a highly nondirective approach, the trainers are likely to operate in that fashion. Not enough importance has been attributed to peer influence factors among laboratory staff personnel.

The trainer's professional background will also affect his style. A clinical psychologist may focus on the learning experiences for individuals, a social psychologist, on the group learning aspects of the situation. A consultant in business or public administration may try to direct the group-learning experience to administrative or organizational factors. The effects of these professional learnings need to be examined honestly by trainers.

Current state of research and experience. Since the first laboratory-group training in 1946, numerous books and articles have explored the behavior of people in groups. Knowledge about individuals and the learning process has increased rapidly. The effects of feedback on group learning, the use of dyads, the value of instrumentation, the use of nonverbal experiences, and numerous other methodologies are now available for review and assessment. Research on the effects of laboratory education in sensitivity training has been reported. A well-informed group trainer will avail himself of these resources in assessing his approach, style, and intervention techniques. Each trainer will need to base his conduct of training on his own skills and abilities, but these can be based on validated principles and guidelines.

Needs of the trainer. Every individual brings his own needs to a learning process, and this is no less true of the group trainer. A trainer may feel he must meet certain status needs, or he may wish to carry out experiments relative to his research interests. Whatever his needs, it is imperative that the trainer be as insightful as possible in assessing both needs and their possible influence on his style and behavior. A professional trainer will not permit his own needs to interfere with the learning of others but will recognize their reality and share them, when appropriate, so the group can diagnose their effects on the group process.

The trainer's personal needs, conscious or subconscious, tend to make him a special group member. Certainly, membership of some kind is essential to his being himself, rather than some artificial person. If the group sees him as a fellow human being trying to learn, share, and care, he can be most helpful to others. His role is perceived by the group as different, and yet it is desirable for him to relate to the group in such a way that his own needs are recognized and openly shared.

MULTIPLE ROLES OF THE TRAINER IN THE GROUP

The laboratory trainer has several roles, but there is no fixed characterization of each. Six, however, are readily identifiable.

Initiator of diagnostic training concepts. The trainer is responsible for helping the group see that its own processes and problems
provide much of the curriculum for the learning experience. In various
ways, he initiates the concept of the diagnostic process in the learning
of the group. Initiating diagnostic procedures can be done in a nondirective fashion, as suggested by Roy Whitman (1964, pp. 310-335),
and/or can proceed on a continuum at the other end of which the
trainer may spell out his responsibility in a short introduction.

In the latter case, for example, at the beginning of a developmental
group session, the trainer might begin:

> This is the development group. We will be meeting in this room for five,
> two-hour sessions during the next three days. The purpose of this group
> is to provide an opportunity for group members to interact with one
> another in developing a group life and to use our development stages as
> material for analysis, observations, and learning about human relation-
> ships.
>
> As was indicated in the orientation session, four things are missing from
> this group that are usually typical of an everyday group.
>
> This group does not have a stated agenda, a designated leader, agreed-
> upon procedures, or a common history. If this group finds these things
> necessary, it should provide them as it sees fit.
>
> As the trainer, I see my function as helping the group to use its experiences
> to learn more about human relations. I do not see my function as that of
> a leader and will resist being put into that role. To do so would handicap
> me in performing my trainer function—and would prevent you from dis-
> covering emerging needs and processes.

Even this more directive beginning is obviously insufficient to cause
the group to accept group diagnosis as its curriculum. No matter how
a trainer begins the meeting, he must continue to initiate the diagnostic
observation concept to "prod" the group until such observation becomes a norm and the trainer no longer needs to focus on it. One of
the most effective ways to initiate the group diagnosis process is to
get each member of the group to share his own feelings, concerns, and
goals in the here-and-now situation.

Diagnostic observer at appropriate time and level. One goal of
all laboratory trainers should be to advance the skill of learning how to
learn so that group members become their own diagnosticians.

The trainer is not responsible for all diagnosis. He may find it desirable, however, to initiate such an observation at a number of points
for one or a combination of reasons: the observation might not be

appropriately made by a group member; the group is not yet sufficiently sophisticated to make it; or the group is unwittingly neglecting this aspect of the learning process. When the training groups are "family groups," or the training is taking place "on company site," additional demands, sensitivities, and expertise are required. At all times, the trainer must balance his own insight and feeling of the moment against the readiness of the group to "hear" the data and its ability to internalize the existing experience.

Innovator of learning experiences. As a group progresses, the trainer can, and should, use his training resources in a number of ways. This does not mean that the trainer should assume responsibility for the tasks of the group. The difference between innovating a particular experience and becoming involved in "teaching" is a fine distinction that requires astute judgment.

If the group does not know how to use a particular area of interest for its own learning, the trainer may set up a testing situation. This might be in the area of procedure, such as role-playing to test out different approaches. It might be a suggestion that the group select alternating group observers so that everyone has a chance to experiment with the role or situation being analyzed. It might even be developing a proposal to utilize a nonverbal experience to enhance personal relationships and trust.

Arbiter of group standards. The training environment and the laboratory work itself lead to the emergence of group standards such as diagnosing the here-and-now rather than the there-and-then life of individuals or the "looking at behavior rather than at motivations" of other group members. If the group departs from these yardsticks, however, the trainer must sensitively decide if his function is to protect them for the good of the learning experience.

A group will usually develop its own standards. The trainer will find others related to establishing a learning climate, forestalling behavior which may really "hurt" another, and developing methods appropriate to the training objectives. These may not be necessary. Nevertheless, at times the trainer may want to suggest standards to govern the level of diagnosis or of personal attack; at other times he may want to protect (in a sense) the group or an individual from unproductive self-punishment, especially if he sees some long-range consequences of such an attack. The vulnerability of individuals and subgroups varies widely. It behooves the trainer (and emphasizes the need for professionalism) to be sensitive to these differences.

Arbiter of group-member function. Some writers on laboratory training hold that the trainer never becomes a group member. This is an unrealistic interpretation of the psychology of group life. Not only the fact that the trainer's needs necessarily bring him into the group but also the fact that the training group is a cultural unit imply that it has all the potential aspects of group identification, cohesion, and growth. The group builds expectations for all persons in the training situation, and this includes the trainer.

Each individual exerts and is subject to influence. The trainer meets, exceeds, falls short, changes, and frustrates the expectations of different group members. In doing this, he becomes a "member," someone whom the group must handle. The trainer may be a unique member, but as the laboratory group matures, so each member becomes unique.

When a group has begun to take over its own diagnostic function and to see the differing contributions of its members, it reaches a point when it overtly indicates that the trainer "is now a member." The trainer may have covertly accepted this status long before the group recognized it as a fact. Thus, while the trainer will never be the same kind of member as the others, his group identification and membership eventually gives the group its feeling of "wholeness."

SPECIAL PROBLEMS AND PITFALLS OF TRAINERS

The laboratory trainer is vulnerable to problems and traps that do not usually confront other kinds of trainers. As laboratory trainers share their experiences, five problems seem to occur frequently.

Trainer becomes too directive. Acting more like a teacher than a trainer is one of the major problems in leading a laboratory group. The teaching process is a seductive one, and frequently a trainer may find himself elaborating a diagnostic observation when in reality the group itself could analyze the observation with greater learning impact. Self-discipline and commitment to the professional aspects of the sensitivity-training process can help trainers avoid this problem.

Trainer and group become too clinical. The purposes of the training group—improving interpersonal sensitivity, increasing insight, developing membership skills, and other related knowledge in human and organizational relations—make it very easy for the emphasis to become overly clinical and therapeutically-centered in its diagnosing and learning. Diagnosing or judging early-life motivational factors can be the focus rather than the behavior in the here-and-now. The trainer must examine his own motivation and that of the group to prevent such personal and clinical emphasis from becoming dominant. The balance between using all the data appropriate to group members and overdoing immersion into unhelpful exploration of individual life experiences is not always easy to determine.

Trainer becomes too involved personally. The trainer will become involved in the life of the group, but unless he guards against his personal agenda's becoming dominant in the group agenda, he loses much of his ability to contribute to its purposes. Obviously, the trainer will be a part of the group in its discussions, and group members will deal with the trainer in terms of their dependency and leadership needs. The group will also want to give and receive feedback about the trainer's behavior. This does not mean, however, that the trainer becomes so involved personally that he neglects his special role as a professional serving the learning needs of a group. Retaining an awareness of responsibility does not necessarily mean remoteness.

Training group is used in an inappropriate way. Unless a group has adequate time, training which focuses on interpersonal group learning and growth should not be used. Appropriate learning is unlikely in the short time available.

The laboratory group is also inappropriate when there is no back-home organizational or personal support for participants in using their learning and insights. The use of the laboratory group should always be related to specific organizational or trainee development purposes, and these should be kept in mind in designing the total learning experience. In addition, the established conditions for effective learning should be maintained to realize results, as This and Lippitt (1966) have pointed out.

Frustration and floundering mistaken for learning. Floundering and frustration are often a part of the group growth process and are appropriate when clearly a part of group diagnosis and learning. However, if the group does not or cannot learn from such experience, it is inappropriate training. Some persons have incorrectly interpreted exposure of behavior as synonymous with emotional disequilibrium. Such disequilibrium is not an end in itself, but sometimes occurs in some individuals as a step toward learning. It should not be allowed to persist unless it is intricately related to the curriculum of the group.

COMMENTS ON TRAINER INTERVENTION

The trainer's role in laboratory training frequently involves him directly in the learning experiences. He may be involved in a role play, or he may be a part of a here-and-now experience, a member of a discussion or diagnosis session, the leader of a role play or group exercise, or an observer of the group and its processes.

At such times, the trainer frequently is faced with the question, "Should I intervene in the group discussion or activity, or should I let the group find its own way?" The following guidelines have been useful.

- For the most part, the purpose of trainer intervention is for the group to learn about its processes.
- Trainer interventions may be helpful to both the individual and the group in making possible the exposure of behavior for analysis.
- Intervention by the trainer is helpful in encouraging the use of feedback among members of the group for both individual and group learning.
- Trainer intervention may be necessary if, in the professional judgment of the trainer, a particular individual or subgroup is too threatened by group analysis. Individuals and groups vary widely in their ability to tolerate such feedback.
- As the group takes over the various diagnostic functions, the interventions of the trainer can become less frequent and can be made at a different level from the group's observations.
- Training interventions may be procedural in nature, so as to maximize learnings within a group experience.
- Group members frequently expect not only that they share their feelings about one another and the ways they have seen one another but also that the trainer will share with them his feelings and observations about the group's growth, learning, and effectiveness. At any stage in the group's experience, such sharing is a legitimate aspect of the intervention and "member-role" responsibility of the trainer.

Trainer interventions are closely related to the learning process. Although interventions are basically conditioned by the goals of the training process, they are constantly affected by situation, time, and member and trainer needs. It is also to be expected that trainer interventions will be affected by the group's concept of the trainer's role as experienced and redefined at various points in the life of the group.

ETHICAL DIMENSIONS OF BEING A SENSITIVITY TRAINER

As trainers improve their ability to further human growth, it is well for them to examine the ideas and beliefs that are fundamental to their efforts, the ethical principles that should guide group trainers and group actions.

Individual worth.   A belief in the individual is an imperative in the development of group trainer skills. We see the individual as an end in himself, not as a means to an end, or a pawn to be moved about.

It is essential that a group leader be sensitive to the motivations and needs of individuals, including his own. To understand individual needs is to be aware of the complexity of personality, its structure and capacity for growth toward selfhood. As Rollo May (1952, p. 42) has said:

> It [selfhood] means achieving a dynamic unity which is manifested chiefly in the potentialities in productive work and the expanding meaningfulness of one's relations with one's fellow men.

An effective trainer will want each member of the group to be involved, to take part, and to contribute to the achievement of the common goals.

Authenticity of group relationships.   Of the many reasons for the formation of groups—to secure representation, support, knowledge, or experience or to focus responsibility—perhaps the most basic is to provide personal satisfaction. Kenneth Berrien (1951, p. 132) has indicated that people search for social satisfactions through "the development of close relationships which anchor the individual securely in some stablizing continuing group."

The great challenge to sensitivity for group trainers is to develop honest, nondefensive, and authentic fellowship for the life of the group. Ross Snyder (1959, p. 14) has paraphrased Martin Buber in describing the authentic relationship:

> Authentic existence is meeting each fresh situation with a spontaneous wholeness: responding out of the depths rather than in terms of previously decided rules or images, or from compulsive emotion.

Influence of members on group learning.   Research in human behavior verifies our supposition that people tend to support what they themselves create. When people feel that they can really influence the group as it carries out its growth experiences, they will back up its activities, its feedback, and its learning. To tap the potential of individuals, encouraging them toward common goals, is a key role of the group trainer.

The search for truth. Trainer behavior must be based not upon friendship, not upon likes or dislikes, hunches or intuition, but rather upon the objective search for the truth of the meaning and feelings of the group situation.

Trainers who believe in the search for truth will encourage full play of members' minds in solving the problems of the group. A good mind, encouraged to work, will penetrate half-truths and expand the incomplete view to a broad perspective. Effective group behavior depends upon reality confrontation, sensible process of search, and coping—all part of the problem-solving process.

Toleration of diverse behavior. A prime tenet of Western culture is the toleration of diversity: many beliefs, attitudes, and personalities form the web of mankind. Christian values caution that we judge not lest we be judged.

While a group trainer will develop his own perceptions of feelings towards others in the group, he must not *judge* a member's contribution—or individual worth. Hostility, aggression, and personal ill will are to be expected in group activity as well as love, affection, trust, and openness. The trainer must be as tolerant as any other.

The group trainer must try to understand the other person in order to communicate and learn. It is only as the trainer understands the feelings and actions of others—however embarrassing, negative, and even frightening they may appear—that he will feel free to discuss and explore them. This freedom is an essential of group growth and learning.

CONCLUSION

As an important innovation in the field of learning, the laboratory philosophy, theory, and methods demand trainers of the highest professional competence and personal integrity.

These guidelines have been found meaningful in working with laboratory groups; they have emerged out of failure and mistakes. They are shared, not as a final statement, nor as standards anywhere yet consistently achieved, but as guideposts to be re-examined by other practitioners—those assuming the awesome responsibility of furthering human growth.

REFERENCES

Berrien, F. K. *Comments and Cases of Human Relations.* New York: Harper & Brothers, 1951.

Blake, R. S., and Mouton, J. S. "Initiating Organization Development." *Training Director's Journal* 19, no. 10 (1965):18-26.

May, R. "Religion, Psychotherapy, and the Achievement of Selfhood." *Pastoral Psychology* 2, no. 1 (1952):42

Schein, E. E., and Bennis, W. G. *Personal and Organizational Change through Group Method: The Laboratory Approach.* New York: John Wiley & Sons, 1965.

Snyder, R. *The Authentic Life: Its Theory and Practice.* Philadelphia: Friends Central Conference, Religious Education Committee, 1959.

This, L. E., and Lippitt, G. L. "Learning Theories and Training Trends." *Training and Development Journal* 20, no. 5 (1966).

Whitman, R. M. "Psychodynamic Principles Underlying T-Group Process." In *T-Group Theory and Laboratory Method: Innovation in Re-Education,* edited by L. P. Bradford, J. R. Gibb, and K. D. Benne. New York: John Wiley & Sons, 1964.

Training for Community Competence

DONALD C. KLEIN
NTL Institute for Applied Behavioral Science
Washington, D.C.

MY experiences with the training group and laboratory training have taken place over a period of fifteen years. In 1954, a recent graduate in clinical psychology of the doctoral program at the University of California at Berkeley where I had some exposure to group dynamics *, I went as a participant to Bethel. I had just assumed the executive directorship of the Human Relations Service of Wellesley in Massachusetts, an early and innovative attempt to exemplify what might be done if clinical psychiatry, public health, and the behavioral sciences turned their combined attention to preventive, community-wide efforts in mental health.

THE INDIVIDUAL AND THE COMMUNITY

One theme, in retrospect, seems to have guided my development within laboratory training. That theme already was well delineated

* Under Hugh Coffey

within the Wellesley mental health experience. It involves the individual, on the one hand, and the community, on the other. It is
concerned with the growth and development of the person through
the entire course of a lifetime; it is equally concerned with the community as the predominant context or shaping environment within
which the key personal issues (of security and inclusion, identity and
control, self-esteem and significance) are managed for better or
worse.*

As a participant in the Human Relations Laboratory at Bethel in the
summer of 1954 and three summers in the late 1950s when I returned
as a staff member, my major professional preoccupation was with dif-
ferentiating the training group from the therapy group. I knew how to
behave as a group therapist of that day—detached, interpretive, observing, and minimally interactive with participants. It was a protective
mantle that as a participant I wore with some success—despite the
efforts of the group trainer †—for the first week of the three-week
lab. As a trainer in those early years, I gradually learned how to preside
over a learning setting (the training group) in which the task was to
somehow combine the involvement in the irrational, profoundly unconscious dynamics of group life with the rational analysis of manifest
group processes (such as decision-making and communication) and
of interpersonal events (via feedback). It proved to be an exciting and
deeply meaningful challenge, personally and socially.

Training groups and human relations laboratories were then an
ambitious and often awkward mix of coexisting themes and intellectual
streams that frequently clashed and boiled against one another and
only rarely merged into harmonious fusions. Prelaboratory staff gather-
ings were the places where the alien and mysterious powders were
mixed—almost always with excitement, apprehension, and struggle;
on occasion with a sense of creation, mystery, and breakthrough;
periodically with pyrotechnics, passion, and even panic.

ORIENTATION TO LABORATORY TRAINING

Three main streams of sensitivity training were feeding into laboratory design at that time. They still exist powerfully today. These streams
as I have labeled them are: (1) the rational/empirical; (2) the irra-
tional/dynamic; and (3) the personal/reconstructional.

* This basically ecological viewpoint is more fully developed in D. C. Klein, *Community Dynamics and Mental Health* (New York: John Wiley & Sons, 1968).
† Herb Thelen.

The *rational/empirical orientation* is concerned largely with the identification and study of group-level interaction patterns. These are the observable phenomena of face-to-face groups that exist virtually apart from the psychological characteristics of the individuals composing them. They arise out of the ecology of the group situation and the uses (psyche or socio) to which groups are put. In this category I am inclined to lump the laboratory studies of small group behavior in the tradition of Kurt Lewin, the interaction analyses of Bales and others, and the naturalistic observations that have led to various conceptualizations of stages in group growth and development. This level of group analysis is concerned with such matters as patterns of leadership and followership, essential functions of task and maintenance, approaches to decision-making and their consequences, standard-setting, and communication flow.

Much training-group time was devoted then to painstaking reconstruction and analysis of group-level phenomena. The group was its own laboratory; the individual participant was trained to be both participant and observer; the trainer was responsible within this context to help the group organize a collective inquiry of its own experience.

Adjunctively related to the training-group's effort were carefully thought out theory presentations and skill practice sessions. There was something comfortably reassuring and mysterious about the fact that over and over again participants could recognize in the conceptual offerings made in the early morning of one day the eventful struggles of their training groups the day before. There was also an incentive for theory presenters to engage in creation of new conceptual frameworks, some of which proved to be quite powerful. They have helped to organize and give meaning to data and experience that had previously eluded understanding. Some of these ideas (such as hidden agenda) have entered the everyday world of common sense. Others continue to be the main ingredient of laboratory reading books, articles by practitioners, and the training handbooks that from time to time are developed for such groups as Peace Corps, antipoverty agencies, overseas training programs, and voluntary national organizations.

Comparatively little energy is devoted these days to the engineering of new, integrative ideas in the application of group theory and research to real life problems. Theory sessions at training laboratories have gone out of style for the very good reason that as acts of communication they leave so much to be desired. Little has taken their place and it may well be that, however imperceptibly, the rational/

empirical orientation to group training is today in danger of withering because its tap root is no longer being cultivated.

It is noteworthy that skill practice sessions in 1954 were totally separated from the training-group experience. They were even planned and conducted by a separate staff—a state of affairs which may have reflected and certainly contributed to a sense of conflict and competitiveness between the staffs that was communicated to the participants.

In subsequent years, skill practice sessions were carried out by total laboratory staffs and finally the training group itself became the vehicle for staff designed and conducted sessions.

The 1950s also featured repeated attempts to develop theory and skill sessions devoted to the role of the change agent in the community. Regional City simulations, based on Floyd Hunter's (1953) analysis of the dynamics of power in a medium-sized city, formed a major slice of the middle period of most three-week laboratories. Participants were assigned to community groups (extending from voluntary associations, to planners, political bodies, and economic interests) which interacted with each other in attempts to influence one or more critical community decisions. The action, which typically took place in a large space afforded by a gymnasium and adjacent rooms, was brisk and for most people highly involving. Regional City exercises usually generated far more experience than anyone was capable of analyzing and using for learning. The problem was two-fold: first, our idea systems were inadequate to the task of understanding large system dynamics; second, our analytic tools were not capable of processing and making the data available rapidly and in usable form.

I include the Regional City simulations under the rational/empirical rubric because they represent an early effort to get at community-level phenomena (such as conflict, collaboration, power allocation, action strategies) which are observable in all communities regardless of the unique psychological and ideological qualities of the individuals, groups, and organizations involved. A later section of this chapter returns to the matter of training in community dynamics as it has engaged my attention in the 1960s within NTL's Center for Community Affairs in association with a subgroup of network members and central office staff.

The *irrational/dynamic orientation* is concerned largely with what Bill Schutz (1958) has called the "underworld" of group life. It focuses on the deeply irrational and often demonically powerful forces that determine whether individuals are ennobled or destroyed by their participation with others, whether group work is vigorously creative or grayly mediocre, and whether groups maintain cohesion and member loyalty on the basis of coercion or genuine freedom. Training groups in the 1950s were powerfully influenced by the psychoanalytic study of group development, especially by the work of Bion. A major early issue that characterized every training group concerned the authority of the trainer, the group's ways of coping with that authority, and the members' own feelings of dependence. These issues were able to surface for discussion and analysis because of the trainer's commitment to a style of impersonality and partial detachment that encouraged rapid projection of members' fears and hopes. It was possible to highlight the passionate and opposed demands which groups make on authority figures as a means of reducing member risk and avoiding individuals' confrontation of themselves and each other. Fight, flight, pairing, and dependency became demonstrable reactions to the anxieties engendered by and about the authority of the trainer.

Many trainers today (and I include myself among them) remain concerned with helping participants learn from the training group about the irrational/dynamic components of group experience. A growing body of experience in this country is being developed by the Tavistock Institute and the Washington School of Psychiatry in annual programs offered in Western Massachusetts and the Washington, D.C. area. Meanwhile some of us are struggling to find new and better ways of furthering learning than the earlier clinically derived, therapist-like stance described above. I say "better" because it has been pretty well demonstrated by research and experience that participants find it difficult, if not impossible, to apply back home what they have learned about authority and dependence because the entire learning experience itself has been so dependent on the strength of the trainer and his ability not to be destroyed by the powerful irrationality that he has helped unleash.

I dwell on only one aspect of the underworld of group life that can be explored within the training group—that of authority and dependence—because it has always seemed to me the central theme from which all others flow. These other aspects include the pervasive and powerful predilections of groups to project that which is unacceptable about themselves on the enemy without or the scapegoat within. They also encompass the often troubling and frequently sexualized peer relationships among members that are interwoven with the shame and guilt evoked by the internalized taboos of the society.

It is also clear that interreligious and interracial attitudes and feelings are approachable primarily within the framework of training group or other laboratory experience that probes the irrational/dynamic underpinnings. Max Birnbaum is one of the early people who pioneered in the modification of group and laboratory training to focus on interreligious prejudice and individual racism. It is noteworthy that the trainer cannot help the group get at deeply held prejudices by maintaining the traditional detached stance of the earlier model. It appears that he must become bulldog-like in his readiness to confront and challenge the group to get past the barriers of shame in order to do the necessary work of exposing the vomit and excrescence of primitive prejudices. Here the strength of the trainer at times must become committed to a direct struggle against denial, rationalization, and suppression. It is his capacity to accept and confront his own and others' violations of deeply held values that enables others to follow suit.

There is more than a little overlap between the trainer role recommended for intergroup training and the trainer style used by many workers in the third orientation discussed next.

The *personal/reconstructional orientation* is concerned largely with an existential experiencing by individuals to the fullest extent possible of the essence of their humanity. It seeks to help individuals know themselves through their encountering of others in the face-to-face group situation. It explores the problems and possibilities of interpersonal phenomena in a variety of nonverbal as well as verbal ways, through the use of fantasy and artistic expression, through movement and music, and through techniques drawn from Gestalt therapy and other approaches that help individuals confront and work through crippling barriers to their experiencing of themselves and others. The personal/reconstructional orientation is movingly expressed in Bill Schutz's book *Joy* (1967), a book that has, by the way, irritated and otherwise turned off some more traditional trainers and therapists (judging from certain reviews).

I have dubbed this orientation "reconstructional" because, in my opinion, it helps individuals rediscover and cultivate intimations of their humanness which they had once experienced, perhaps as infants and young children, perhaps even as adults in occasional peak experiences. I am not sure whether Schutz and other proponents would accept this analysis. For some, like Carl Rogers and Abe Maslow, it is training for intimacy that allows individuals to abandon and be liberated from the interpersonal defenses and the interpersonal role constraints that stand as barriers to the realization of human potential. I think this view is consistent with the reconstructional idea, for I suspect that the power of intimacy training lies in the fact that it demonstrates that adults do not have to purchase either sanity or task effectiveness by sacrificing potentials they once possessed. It is certainly in keeping with Bernes' (1961) conceptual scheme and therapeutic approach which seek to help people become reconciled with their child as well as adult selves, with their expressive, playful qualities as well as their responsible, care-taking parental selves.

The rational/empirical training-group experience, interestingly enough, also has intimations of the personal/reconstructional experience, as does the irrational/dynamic. For it is almost always the case that once the training group has worked on the structural and processual material of its development (either at the rational group level or at the level of the more primitive underworld), members discover that the laboratory norms of openness and risk-taking have led them to discover a sense of intimacy, we-feeling, and caring that few members had ever before experienced in their adult lives. Many people have returned home from "traditional" training laboratories seeking to reconstruct in their families and work settings the openness and intimacy of the latter stages of their training groups. Most of them have failed.

People returning from the more deeply encountering marathons, personal growth groups, and advanced human relations laboratories have tended to solve the problem of back-home change by seeking to establish and support social institutions that are supportive of the personal/reconstructional norms. Esalen and the growing number of similar growth centers (over eighty at last count) represent a promising new social invention that may help our society be more promotive of humaneness. The development of the existentially oriented American Association of Humanistic Psychologists is a further instance of a possible diffusion of the personal/reconstructional orientation well beyond the confines of training groups, training laboratories, and similar learning institutions.

THE ROLE OF TRAINER

I have been fascinated by the problem of distinguishing between the role and functions of the personal/reconstructional trainer and the trainers involved in the other two orientations. The following analysis is probably guilty of oversimplifying and doing violence to many of the shades of difference within each of the three orientations. It should also be emphasized that some trainers, including myself, attempt to use all three selectively with different groups for different overall goals or with the same group for different purposes.

The major difference appears to lie in the implicit contract which the trainer establishes with the participants. In the personal/reconstructional orientation, the trainer is seeking to help the individuals use the group experience to explore and develop new capacities to use themselves in a variety of human interactions. If the new capacities are relevant for the achievement of work, all well and good. If they are relevant for the individual's participation in back-home committees, work teams, and other small group settings, also good. However, the personal/reconstructional trainer is not undertaking to help participants gain more understanding of and ability to work with face-to-face groups. In fact, the face-to-face, training-group interactions serve only as a vehicle for the individual's exploration of himself and the world of intraperson.

By contrast, in the other two orientations—especially in the case of the rational/empirical—the contract is for the trainer to help participants learn as much as possible about those aspects of group life that will help them function in and make use of groups more effectively back home. If the individual learns more about his own humanity and that of others in the process, all well and good. If he becomes more able to be open and caring at the same time, also good. But the rational/empirical and irrational/dynamic trainer is not undertaking to help participants gain new competencies in risking themselves with others or in setting aside those innerpersonal barriers or role constraints that interfere with intimacy. The face-to-face training group for both orientations is approached as the basic unit for study and learning; the individual's exploration of himself and the world of intraperson are primarily in support of group-level analysis and understanding.

MARINER TRAINING OR AN "OUTWARD BOUND" EXPERIENCE

Perhaps an analogy will help sharpen the difference which seems so meaningful to me. Consider a group of young people embarking on a training cruise in a sailing vessel under the tutelage of a master mariner. The captain of the vessel is analogous to the trainer. It is his job to help the trainees learn from the cruise. But what are they supposed to learn and what is he supposed to teach?

If the vessel is taking its cruise as part of the curriculum of a merchant marine academy or of the U. S. Naval Academy, the job of the captain is to help the trainees become better mariners. He must make it possible for them to learn the rudiments of a trade in which he is an established expert. He can best do this by a combination of didactic sessions, such as demonstrations of knot-tying, chart-reading, navigation, and the like, and supervised experience in performing the various aspects of seamanship required to take the vessel successfully through a wide range of conditions. He probably tries to put the trainees through a graded series of experiences that are designed to add to their knowledge, to build their individual competence, and to bring them into shape as a well-functioning crew. At the end of a cruise, he can mark his success by the extent to which the crew is capable of handling the vessel without him. Basically, then, the training cruise is designed to help learners develop skills of seamanship. In the process, no doubt there are some opportunities to work on character development and, under the best of circumstances, the trainees are affected in ways which will shape their handling of interpersonal situations, teamwork, and life challenges on dry land as well as at sea.

By contrast, let us look at the teaching-learning contract if the vessel is taking its cruise as part of an Outward Bound experience. Here the job of the captain is not primarily to help the trainees become better mariners. Outward Bound's major mission is character training. It can achieve these objectives by means of several kinds of experiences—including mountain climbing, sailing, or anything else which requires team effort in coping with real danger and physical challenge. The captain of the Outward Bound vessel also must make it possible for the trainees to learn enough about seamanship to be able to help run the vessel. It is not necessary, however, for them to learn enough seamanship to assume full responsibility for the training craft or other vessels in the future. The captain probably also tries to put the trainees through a graded series of experiences, but for different purposes. He uses all his skills as a mariner to put the trainees through challenges that will demonstrate to them that they are capable of taking responsibility, of over-coming fear, of taking risks. It is his job to see that each individual trainee, as well as the total training crew, is challenged sufficiently, but not past his ability to stretch in order to cope. At the end of a cruise, the Outward Bound captain can mark his success by the extent to which the trainees individually indicate character growth in their ability to view themselves as effective, problem-solving, risk-taking individuals with high self-regard and an ability to function as part of a team.

Basically then, the Outward Bound cruise is designed to help learners develop personal skills. In the process no doubt there are many opportunities to work on seamanship skills and most, if not all, must return with increased ability to understand and manage sailing vessels. The Outward Bound trainer, however, is concerned primarily with personal growth; the merchant trainer is concerned primarily with skill development in a task area.

Though many of the daily activities of the two captains are probably very similar, there are apt to be some significant differences in their handling of their roles and in their "training design." The merchant marine trainer will be more concerned with theory, knowledge transmission, and specific skill development in task areas. He will have a clear idea of what is required of any individual if he is to be considered a competent seaman. He will have few doubts about his own responsibility to evaluate the growing competence of trainees.

The Outward Bound trainer will be more concerned with role-modeling the character traits, attitudes, and values that he hopes the trainees can emulate during this phase of their growth and development. He will be alert to the particular growth needs of individual trainees and will attempt to support the individual in his own unique quest. He will have few doubts about his responsibility to help each trainee evaluate his own strengths and potential growth areas.

Returning to the different orientations in group and laboratory training, the merchant marine training situation seems analogous to the group-oriented rational/empirical and irrational/dynamic orientations where the emphasis is on learning more about the area of group life in which the trainer is an expert. The Outward Bound training situation seems analogous to the personal/reconstructional orientation where the emphasis is on using the trainer's expertise with group interaction as a resource to help the trainees grow as human beings. The personal/reconstructional trainer is a guru-like figure who uses his own competence to prescribe, model, coach, and challenge individuals to use more of themselves. The other trainers are technical experts in a field of competence who are helping individuals gain increased skills in that field. Once again, as stated earlier, I am drawing the differences more sharply than they exist in real situations partly in order to clarify real distinctions and partly in order to help those who wish to get some perspectives on how to use the range of approaches for different purposes if they wish to do so.

PERSONAL GROWTH AND MACRO-SYSTEM TRAINING

Two developments have occurred in recent years that open up important new possibilities "beyond the training group" in laboratory training. The first is the invention of training approaches that focus on the development of the individual as a continuously learning and changing being. The second is the reemergence, at a more sophisticated level, of training approaches designed to help people learn about large-system dynamics.

Though at first these two developments—one focussed on the individual, the other on macro-systems—appear to be thrusting in quite different directions, I am hopeful that they may represent crucially important breakthroughs bearing on competence in community change that are highly supportive of one another. I will discuss each of the developments briefly and then suggest their interrelationship.

Experience-based training approaches focusing on individual growth encompass much of the work described earlier under the heading of the personal/reconstructional. The latter also encompasses some other training methodologies not usually associated with the personal growth field. Two of them have gained wide currency in recent years.

The first, known as risk-taking or "nongroup" training, was developed by Richard Byrd and colleagues. It presents the individual with the task of identifying his own personal learning goals and of determining the approaches he may need to take toward others in the training laboratory in order to achieve his goals. Individuals are free to function alone, to pair, or to engage in joint learning activities with larger groups. People are not expected to remain in a single learning group; nor are they expected necessarily to acquiesce to others' attempts to involve them in others' learning efforts. The trainers function under the same guidelines. Periodically, participants come together to pool their observations about the risk-taking experiences involved in reaching out to and responding to others' learning efforts.

The second approach, known as personal life planning, was developed by Herbert Shepherd. It presents the individual with the task of achieving perspective on his future by considering where he is and who he is along his own "life line" and by determining what he wishes to become and be in that part of the life line that lies in his future. Personal life planning is typically done in a group and can be carried out in the course of a training-group's development. The observations by others who know the individual from the group often help to clarify aspects of the life planning. Similarly, each individual's own way of handling his analysis of his past, present, and future typically opens up new potentials for others engaged in their own personal effort. Individual participants, as well as the trainer, interview one another and offer feedback. Techniques drawn from personal/reconstructional group training also help individuals with in-depth analysis and exploration.

Experience-based training approaches focusing on large-system phenomena draw in part from the kind of large-system role-playing involved in the Regional City design mentioned above. Community-oriented games of varying degrees of complexity have been designed by planners, political scientists, and economists, as well as by laboratory-oriented trainers. A highly effective, simple game for training purposes (SITTE) was invented by Hall Sprague and colleagues at the Western Behavioral Sciences Institute. We have used it in community-change specialist laboratories and community leadership programs and have found that it opens up for discussion and analysis important issues bearing on intergroup influence, coalitions, use of power, and the like. Far more complicated games based on complex computer analysis of economic and political information also exist. Like Regional City, however, they seem to be so complex that it is virtually impossible for players to comprehend and build personal skills on an analysis of the intricacies of the play.

Another approach to large-system training involves the laboratory participants in the design and analysis of their own complex learning organization or community. To my knowledge, this approach was initially spawned by an interchange between Barry Oshry and myself en route to Harriman, New York and was tried out at the Arden House Management Work Conference staff of which we were a part in the early 1960s. The approach was subsequently refined by Barry in ways which made it less threatening to participants and which built in more effective means for interrupting and analyzing action.

After the first use of the emerging large-system design at Arden House, we began experimenting with this approach within a community framework. In 1968 at the Boston University program in Community Psychology, for example, we designed a one-day planning community experience at which students and faculty had the task of determining planning tasks and structures that would facilitate the design of the next year's program. The experience was staged in three large adjoining spaces in a nearby hotel. Individuals began by establishing "home bases" in separate locations. There was a publicly visible planning and decision area and several newsprint pads for "mass" communication. It was the task of each individual to determine what he needed to know about his own and others' learning needs and resources and to begin to develop coalitions and action strategies required to help the "community" arrive at a curriculum design.

A design committee for the NTL Community Laboratories at Bethel and Cedar City in 1968 developed a comparative design of two emerging community approaches. The first was based on a totally unstructured situation in which participants and staff members began as individual citizens responsible equally for helping build the laboratory learning community. The second began with a series of more structured pre-community experiences in small groups and other combinations designed to give participants the design and analysis skills that might be useful in learning from the subsequent attempt at community building. A three man team of participant observers conducted a comparative evaluation of the two experiences. The conclusion was that the more structured approach was more satisfying and provided more learning potential for participants; the unstructured approach, on the other hand, was more exciting to staff members because it illuminated some more subtle aspects of community dynamics which they were better prepared to analyze than were the participants.

For the past two years, I have been involved in designing and testing a simulation approach to community analysis and training known as the Community Action Laboratory. The method is especially applicable for use as a training approach with a specific client group that is seeking to achieve a definable action objective in the community. An example was a Spanish-American group wishing to influence the local school committee to push bilingual education in the public schools. The simulation builds in measures of trust, power, and social connectedness among participating groups. It also enables periodic data collection concerning goal achievement and provides frequent stop action sessions at which all those involved meet in an analysis room for discussion and critique of the experience.

All the large system community training approaches have in common the fact that they involve participants in interactions that do not concentrate on face-to-face communication in a stable, small group. Individuals may begin in "home base" locations analogous to the individual residence space in the back-home community, or they may begin as members of special interest groups found in the typical community situation. Their tasks are to diagnose the crucial factors and forces in the larger system and to determine action strategies and tactics designed to influence and bring about change at the community level.

THE CURIOUS CONVERGENCE: AN ECOLOGICAL VIEW

The point at which the individual must function in the training situation outside of a stable, small group setting seems to be the point at which the individually oriented and the large-system training approaches converge. Face-to-face group interactions entail a relatively small part of the nonfamily lives of most individuals. As people move out into communities, their own capacities as experiencing, relating individuals are important determinants of their success in (1) finding or developing a sense of community or communalness, and in (2) becoming effective users of resources, solvers of problems, and shapers of change in the complexities of today's community. In either case, the individual is more apt to be effective if he "comes on" as a sensitive, caring person who understands how he is affecting those with whom he interacts.

To understand this convergence better it may be helpful to return at this point to the guiding theme mentioned in the second paragraph of this chapter: the individual, on the one hand, the community on the other. This is really an ecological perspective that is concerned not only with man and not only with the environment but rather with man-in-environment. From a training point of view, we tended to concentrate primarily in the early years on man-in-small group. We saw that it was not the psychology of the individual alone that counted but also the basic dynamics that occurred when individuals placed themselves in relation to one another so that simultaneous communication and interaction could occur among all those involved. The basic configuration was the closed circle and typically the training group has been arranged so that eye and voice contact was possible between members.

Somewhat later it became apparent that many participants, especially those from industry, returned to working environments in which the basic ecology included man in environments other than the simple circle. Individuals in organizations were located in comparatively fixed positions which determined with whom they could ordinarily interact and for what purposes. Their "positions"—spatially and organizationally—often determined if and how they could put their small group skills to use. Therefore, training approaches bearing on man-in-organization have tended to move increasingly towards organizational simulation and towards organizational development programs extending over several years and including a variety of consulting and training efforts. Part of the effort has been to examine existing organizational configurations (the pyramid being the most pervasive) to determine whether more functionally adaptive ones could be invented.

TERRITORIALITY AND RISK-TAKING

To some extent, the training of individuals for competent community leadership must include skills in both the above man-in-environment configurations—the face-to-face group and the structured organization that positions the individual according to role and func- tion. I am equally certain, however, that community-oriented training must also pay attention to another and in many ways more complex man-in-environment configuration that for present purposes I will call *territorial.*

In the community-as-environment, each individual exists in one or more domains or territories. These may be physically located, such as a house in a neighborhood, or they may be functional in nature and involve such factors as socioeconomic status, family history, and the like. The training of individuals for community competence must provide territorial experience, by which I mean that it must require individuals to function out of one or more territorial bases, to interact with other individuals outside his territory, to make choices among an indeterminate number of alternative movements, and above all to *move out from* and enter into contact with individuals, groups, and organizations which are not part of existing, stabilized social environ- ments of which he is already an accepted member. In short, the individual in the community as environment has the opportunity to function outside of enduring group and organizational contexts. To be an effective change agent, he must understand the complexities of the various contexts operating in the community and he must be capable of taking the risks required to move beyond his own home bases or established territories. It is here that the training of individuals for their own personal development and their training as competent community change agents seem now to converge. For it is the individual as risk- taker who appears to be the most flexible and effective agent of community change, provided, of course, that he also understands and functions effectively in the face-to-face and organizational environments.

The "individual as risk-taker" no doubt requires far more definition and the kind of clarification that further years of experimentation with community training may provide. Now I can only suggest certain attributes that seem to be worth striving for in our training efforts: (1) As Warren Bennis (1968) has emphasized, he should be capable of entering readily and fully into temporary systems of relationship; (2) He must be capable of accepting and caring about the humanness of himself and others; (3) He must be able to integrate the immediacy of direct experience and the abstract complexities of a cognitive map that understands the various systems involved in community; (4) He must be able to reach out as well as respond to others in order to be proactive in creating suitable contexts for problem-solving and pleasure. Why do I term these four qualities "risk-taking?" In each instance the person takes a chance of losing as well as gaining, of being rejected rather than accepted, of arousing anger and incurring guilt rather than of arousing pleasure and incurring joy.

By now it has become reasonably clear that in community-oriented training, just as in the organizational field, it is important to develop continuing, long-range efforts within individual localities. Already we have been able to establish working relationships with several training and consulting centers located in individual communities as locally supported and auspiced applied behavioral science centers. Through NTL Institute we are in the process of developing a national Community Research and Action Laboratory that will help to link the individual community-based training locations, conduct comparative studies of methods, disseminate promising approaches, and carry out the training of trainers capable of helping others gain the group, organizational, and territorial competencies required for effective risk-taking in the community.

In many respects I feel that today in our efforts to apply behavioral science for community improvement, we are at about the same place the mental health team was when it first entered Wellesley in 1948. Much has happened in the community mental health field since then, including massive federal legislation to establish comprehensive community mental health facilities in so-called catchment areas in every major population area. Perhaps we are just beginning to see the potential for group and laboratory-training approaches for community improvement. If so, I think it will be because we are clearer than we were fifteen years ago that training for community competence cannot choose between individual growth and an understanding of environmental complexity. In any case, I for one am prepared to pursue the matter.

REFERENCES

Bennis, W. G., and Slater, P. E. *Temporary Society*. New York: Harper & Row, Publishers, 1968.

Bernes, E. *Transactional Analysis*. New York: Grove Press, 1961.

Hunter, F. *Community Power Structure*. Chapel Hill: University of North Carolina Press, 1953.

Schutz, W. C. *FIRO, A Three-Dimensional Theory of Interpersonal Behavior*. New York: Rinehart & Co., 1958.

———. *Joy*. New York: Grove Press, 1967.

6

The Critical-Incident Approach to Leadership Intervention in Training Groups

ARTHUR MARTIN COHEN
ROBERT DOUGLAS SMITH
Georgia State University
Atlanta, Georgia

INTRODUCTION

THE problem of effectively shaping group growth and development through verbal intervention has been a continuing source of concern to both researchers and practitioners. There is little argument that the essence of the process by which any group develops its potential is the progressive modification of ideas and behavior through verbal interaction. When an idea is introduced spontaneously by one of the participants in a group, other members may suggest an extension, a different emphasis, or perhaps the approval or rejection of the point. Thus, there is an idea in the making, a preliminary statement changed by the work of the group through verbal modification until it represents, more or less adequately, their cumulative, developing, mutual point of view.

A vital cornerstone in the acceptance, rejection, or clarification of an idea is the group leader. It should be pointed out, as Bonner (1959) has done, that the leader alone does not bring about changes in the group or in its members, but that these changes are the results of a multitude of attempted leadership acts. However, while the group leader does not primarily control others, he does initiate verbal and behavioral responses that strongly influence others to perform certain acts that shape the group as a whole. Personality variables—intelligence, physical characteristics, and the like—which have played a very prominent role in studies of leadership in the past do not by themselves account for leadership impact in human groups (Bonner 1959). We believe that these characteristics induce desired behavior in others when the member or trainer who possesses them shares the values of the group and is *able to respond with leadership acts at the appropriate moment.*

All things being equal, the group leader stimulates growth and development through appropriate responses to certain vital situations. This is a field-dynamic view in which the leader is seen as a center of high potential in a social field at a particular critical period of time. At some point during the development or culmination of an idea, the group leader is faced with critical situations or incidents and has to choose a method of responding. Some of the incidents may be trivial; others are crucial to the development of group solidarity, productivity, and direction of movement. The productive group leader must have at his fingertips an effective means of dealing with these "critical incidents" and must choose a good intervention response. This prescription would apply to both task-oriented and process-oriented groups.

Many investigators dealing with the issue of trainer interventions have assumed that maximum group progress is somehow a function of consistency in trainer behavior-attitude, or a function of "sensitivity" judgment (Bach 1966, Berzon and Solomon 1966). Frequently the present authors have referred to books ostensibly devoted to aiding the beginning group leader in identifying and handling the issues that arise in group interactions, only to have them fall short of providing helpful technological training. While each of these books offers many intelligent and well thought-out conceptualizations about the small group, few are of much help in the concrete here-and-now, give-and-take of group interaction. It is not only important to know, for example, that "maintenance and building problems, as they emerge, exercise a prepotent demand upon the energies of the T-Group" (Bradford, Gibb, and Benne 1964, p. 226), but it is also of equal importance to know how to respond concretely at a particular point to a hostile, confused, or otherwise involved group member.

We disagree with the view that "simply being oneself" is both necessary and sufficient for effective group leadership. First, there are many instances when being spontaneous in the group may conflict with what is best for the group. Secondly, as Fiebert (1968, p. 835) has stated, "To the leader himself the group process is an involving challenge, one in which *he attempts to respond selectively to a myriad of interpersonal* [italics added] cues in his effort to crystallize the basic themes of the group and its members." Even if the trainer acts "naturally," he may not be able to choose an appropriate response to appropriate cues. There are many situations, it is granted, when it would be wise *not* to respond; but in each of these instances the choice should be based on a rational decision, and not result from a lack of knowledge concerning the appropriate response to make. Fiebert (ibid., p. 837) discusses this point:

> It seems to this author that with either rationale of group leadership, directive or spontaneous, the leader presents a value orientation which may be contrary to participants' expectations. The critical question, then, is not which value orientation one offers but rather the pragmatic issue of which class of trainer interventions is more effective in group development. At this point it seems a philosophical question dissolves into an empirical one.

BACKGROUND RESEARCH

Research studies relating group experiences to the behavior of training-group leaders were given a firm base by Bradford, Gibb, and Benne (1964, pp. 136-137). They discuss "crucial situations which test the trainer's diagnostic skill, his ability to integrate his own actions into the group process, the extent to which his own personality presents problems to the group, his ability to make intervention decisions, the consistency of his behavior, and its congruence with his beliefs." The above authors then present six episodes which reveal a number of "crucial situations" to which the group leader replies and notes the effect on the group. These six episodes would be more instructive if embedded in a systematic technological approach to leader intervention, with a focus upon specific outcomes and the probabilities of certain desired outcomes of specific interventions. The beginning group leader would find the episodes more helpful if leader responses could be related to one another more specifically, with discussions and evaluation of the alternatives available to the leader.

An approach of a more engineering nature in a related area is the "leaderless" or instrumented training group described by Berzon and Solomon (1966). In their studies, each intervention is programmed for introduction at an appropriate moment and, most importantly, the effects of that intervention upon the group are evaluated. Other researchers (Miles 1960, p. 303) have defined the problem areas as "action skills: the ability to intervene effectively in ongoing situations in such a way as to maximize personal and group effectiveness and satisfactions." Yet another study (French, Sherwood, and Bradford 1966, p. 218) has mentioned such important findings as "a person's self-identity is influenced by the opinions that others have of him which they communicate to him and that the more that is communicated, the more change there is in self-identity." This last study may be taken as representative of many such studies in the group area in which feedback and leader interventions are spoken of in general terms as being important. However, there is no systematic presentation of what feedback specifically entails. Such studies offer inadequate help to the beginning group leader who, when faced with a critical situation, needs to know more than that he must now deal with a "maintenance issue" or a "counter-dependency" problem.

Although other very good reviews of the literature on small group work have appeared (Buchanan 1965, House 1967, Stock 1964), the most recent work by Campbell and Dunnette (1968) has special relevance to this chapter. In their comprehensive review (p. 97), they point out that

> research concerning the relative contributions of specific technological features of the T-Group is also sparse. For example, there are no systematic studies examining the influence of differences in trainer personality and/or style on the outcomes achieved by participants. Case reports and anecdotal evidence are all that exist.

In indicating needed research approaches, these same authors single out seven major research deficits (ibid., p. 100), one of which is especially important in our discussion:

> It is imperative that the relative contributions of various technological elements in the T-Group method be more fully understood. It is surprising indeed that essentially no research has been done on the differential effects of changes in the trainer role in spite of frequent allusions in the crucial role played in a T-Goup by the trainer's behavior. Questions concerning the optimal procedures for giving feedback, for enhancing feelings of psychological safety, and for stimulating individuals to try new behaviors should also be investigated. This chapter specifically addresses itself to this last point.

Extensive narrative accounts of what happens in a training group are given in Klaw (1961), Weschler (1959), and Kuriloff and Atkins (1966). The important fact is that there are certain basic problems or issues invariably common to all these groups. While we recognize the uniqueness of each group, we are also impressed with the emergence of recurrent and consistent critical situations. In essence, we are proposing a conceptual model of group growth and development based upon the evolution of critical incidents, and with both descriptive and prescriptive properties. Descriptively, this model provides a framework for recognizing the salient features of an ongoing group process and places important events in an ordered perspective. Prescriptively, the model presents a systematic approach to effective group leadership through appropriate and effective interventions. The utilization of a model which offers both of these advantages would seem to be a step nearer to the prediction and control of behavior toward a desired group goal.

If the assumption is valid that the majority of groups have to deal at one time or another with certain basic common problems (that is, critical incidents), then an attempt should be made to systematize and deal with these issues to promote effective group development. Within each of these critical situations, a number of alternative intervention responses should be at the group leader's fingertips. Which one he utilizes—or whether he chooses to respond at all—is his decision, based upon his particular leadership style and the needs of the group.

In this chapter we attempt to: (1) present the concept of a critical incident as a way of describing and ordering group phenomena, (2) propose a critical incident model in outline form, and (3) present three critical incidents, in their entirety, to illustrate the model. In each critical incident example we present critical situations commonly found in training groups and offer several alternatives to the beginning group leader. In addition, we ask the reader to look at the nature of interventions as a three-dimensional "intervention cube," which is discussed in some detail later in this chapter. Finally, we offer an overview of this "technological" approach, summarizing the significant points and indicating some important future research areas.

THE CONCEPT OF CRITICAL INCIDENT

A *critical incident* is defined as the confrontation of a group leader with one or more members, in which an explicit or implicit opinion, decision, or action is demanded of that leader. It may also be observed conversation, a confrontation among members, an event taking place, or a period of silence. The essential property of a critical incident is that the phenomenon is judged important enough by a group leader to consider, consciously and explicitly, a decision to act in a way assumed to have an important impact on the group. This implies that the group leader is faced with a number of "choice points" or alternatives in both the content and style of possible responses. If the final choice of response is appropriate and effective, group growth and development may be facilitated. On the other hand, if the choice of response is inappropriate the group may move into nonproductive areas or be unable to perform. With each choice of response, the group leader simultaneously constructs alternate universes and opens new paths of group movement while inhibiting others. *The fact that certain effects are likely to follow each intervention choice should motivate an attempt to systematize intervention decisions and study their consequences.*

The evolution of the critical incident concept began with the observation that there are critical situations that, with variations, emerge and repeat themselves in different groups as they develop. Examples of critical incidents were collected from two years of direct observation and recording, especially from tapes of training groups. These incidents were then examined to determine the most general, relevant, and problematical situations faced by the beginning group leader. The situations were fitted into a general framework that specified such parameters as *climate of group, number of sessions, specific events that led up to the group leader's response,* as well as *level, type,* and *intensity of response intervention.* As a final step, nearly sixty critical incidents were checked for frequency of occurrence by advanced graduate students beginning their first experience as training-group leaders. Each of these graduate students reported the occurrence of specific critical incidents as they emerged, as well as the frequency with which certain specific critical incidents clustered together. In this manner, the critical incident approach was used both as a research tool and as a teaching and training device.*

THE PROPOSED MODEL

After a great deal of evaluation, a general framework for reporting critical incidents was constructed. The brief, overall outline of this

---

* The final refinement of techniques of effective leader interventions in groups using the critical incident model is found in A. M. Cohen and R. D. Smith, *The Critical Incident Approach: Leadership Intervention in Small Groups* (Philadelphia: F. A. Davis Co., 1971). In this book, the critical incident model, using some sixty critical incidents, is integrated with a theory of interventions and a theory of group growth and development. In addition, the critical incidents used are cross-indexed with those reported by over eighty other authors representing an extensive variety of approaches to interventions in groups. Comprehensive and annotated surveys and analyses are presented of the literature on interventions in groups and on the works of over eighty theorists of group growth and development.

model will be presented first, followed by a detailed discussion of each of its parts. In conjunction with the model, we propose several conceptual frameworks to strengthen our technological approach to interventions.

The proposed critical incident model is a way of arranging events in sequence, from those that led up to and immediately preceded some critical incident to those that identify the consequences of certain interventions. It is an attempt to identify and understand the important influence of each of these parts upon group members for their growth and development as a group. In essence, we are asking the group leader to organize his perceptual framework around a model that observes events as they occur, evaluates them appropriately, and decides upon one or more specific interventions. *Thus, group movement becomes a series of critical incident sequences, not just a group of isolated or unrelated occurrences.*

The proper use of this model will allow the group leader to identify his particular style of intervention and the patterns of response characteristic of different theoretical approaches and should permit direct comparisons as to the effectiveness of various types of interventions.

CRITICAL INCIDENT MODEL

   I. **Specify the context within which the event occurs.**
       A. Approximate stage of the group: Specify session number and phase of the group, such as beginning, middle, end.
       B. Climate of the group as it relates to the critical incident: Specify whether dependent, counter-dependent, unified, silent, hostile, etc.
       C. Brief description of person(s) involved with each other and/or the group leader: Specify quiet, loud, passive, etc.
  II. **Specify the behavior and/or conversation that led up to and immediately preceded the choice point.**
       Group Member A: "I think . . . should answer me."
       Group Member B: "I agree, and furthermore . . ."
 III. **Describe the critical incident choice-point situation as you perceive it. Specify both the surface issue and the underlying issue.**
       A. Surface issues.
       B. Underlying issues.
  IV. **Specify the level, type, and intensity of the intervention responses.**
       A. Level of intervention: group, interpersonal, individual.

     B.   Type of intervention: conceptual, experiential, structural.
     C.   Intensity of intervention: low, medium, high.
  V. Specify the results of the intervention on the group.
     A.   The intended directional movement of the group by the
         group leader.
     B.   Immediate group response to interventions such as
         silence, agreement, further developing incidents, etc.

Each of the sections of the critical incident model will now be considered in greater detail. Sections one through three are concerned with identifying the elements involved in the emergence of a specific critical incident. They require little explanation. Section three specifies the desirability of the group leader recognizing both the surface issue and the underlying issue. Often what is being said by group members may be masking other more important underlying cognitive or emotional issues. For example, an "intellectual" argument about man's "rationality" may actually mask a struggle for power and possibly on a deeper level an attempt to control sexual impulses.

GENERAL NATURE OF INTERVENTIONS

We distinquish between two basic types of theory interventions: the Planned Theory Intervention (PTI) and the Spontaneous Theory Intervention (STI). A PTI may be carried out at any time in a group session. At the beginning, it usually has two main functions. First, it provides continuity between sessions which enables the group leader to shape at least the initial action of the group. Second, it facilitates and enhances the mood setting when a particular group climate is judged to be desirable. A PTI introduced appropriately in the middle of a group session usually centers on "what is going on right now" and brings theoretical concepts to bear upon the phenomena to underscore, emphasize, or direct attention to them. When a PTI is used at the end of a group session, its purpose is to provide a framework for the events that have taken place, to compare and contrast regularities between groups, and/or, most importantly, to direct thinking toward important future issues.

Some caution must be exercised, however, in that excessive PTI during the closing period of a group may create a situation in which the trainer does too much work for the group or brings premature closure of issues still needing examination. This may cause the leader to acquire the role of a "professional summarizer." At its worst, such paternalism would give group members the feeling that the leader starts them and ends them, and that all that is necessary for the group is to perform in some active way. Independent choice and responsibility would be restricted. Some examples of PTI topics are trust, group decision-making, leadership, deviance, and feedback.

A spontaneous theory intervention (STI) is often referred to as "on-the-spot theory" and is a reaction to immediate ongoing events in the group. It is generally quite short in duration since any intervention that becomes extensive tends to effectively stop the action of the group. An STI usually has two basic parts: 1) a brief observation of ongoing events, and 2) a brief tie-in between the observation and theory. The STI is effective in a number of areas among which are communicating the trainer's awareness of and involvement with the group, sharpening and defining the role of the trainer as a capable resource, putting the current problem in focus, and/or pointing the way to a larger question to which the group may need to be sensitized. The STI may involve any of the topics identified under PTI. An STI example is illustrated by the following situation: The group leader may note that member "X" frequently speaks up immediately following a statement by member "Y." These statements by "X" are invariably critical of "Y" and his suggestions. The group leader may observe this ongoing process and give a brief STI on the problems of a struggle for leadership and on the individual need for influence in the group.

Both the PTI and STI are part of a matrix consisting of the *level of intervention*—whether the focus is group, interpersonal, or individual; the *type of intervention*—whether the intervention is conceptual, experiential, or structural; and the *intensity of intervention*—the degree to which choice of response is directed at the emotional center of the target issue on a continuum from low to high. The three response dimensions of level, type, and intensity are conceptualized as an Intervention Cube.

The *level of intervention* is the target to which the group leader directs his intervention. He may choose to direct his remarks to the group as a whole, to a relationship in the group that has an interpersonal focus, or to one member on an individual one-to-one basis.

The *type* of intervention requires that the group leader choose between three major modes, or a combination of them, in which to express his intervention. In the conceptual mode, the group leader might simply say, "We've had a number of ideas tonight, and all of them seem directly concerned with ways to reach an agreement." He thereby pulls together major concepts and trends. The experiential mode is usually a reporting of direct experience concerning current, ongoing behavior, as in "I'm feeling pretty tense and angry over what

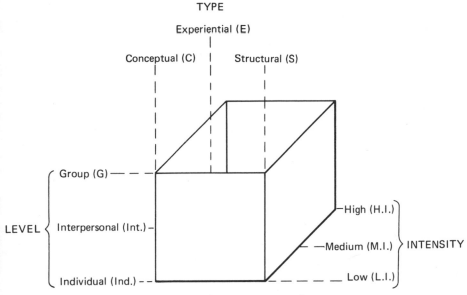

Fig. 1   The Intervention Cube.

just occurred." The structural mode is the deliberate use of planned structured activities, such as sensitivity skill exercises, which focus attention upon surface or underlying issues and the related emotional involvement.

The above framework can be useful in investigating and categorizing the different styles of leadership intervention. An inexperienced group leader might prefer to make "C-G" interventions, composed of conceptual inputs at the group level in the form of a PTI, while avoiding the "E-Ind." or direct experiential confrontation with individual members. Further research might reveal that this hypothetical group leader emphasizes primarily the cognitive elements of group growth and development, as revealed in a progressive step-pattern of "C-G," "C-Int.," "C-Ind." with only a few "C-G" interventions. *Awareness of an "intervention style" may lead the group leader to adopt a more healthy mix of interventions as well as allow him to experiment with new styles and to chart his progress.*

We assume that the effective group leader does not operate primarily on a session-to-session spontaneity basis, but rather employs some concept of group growth and development and acts in accordance with his beliefs that some group directions are more productive than others. Presumably the group leader functions within a framework that includes one or more theoretical models of group development.

Thus the importance of appropriate design strategy cannot be stressed too highly, since the impact of certain knowledge, skills, and values depends largely upon both how and when the interventions are introduced. A wide variety of possible techniques, tools, structural and instrumental approaches may be used by the trainer to introduce topics. Feedback, for example, can be introduced by modeling, through a PTI, through skill exercises, and so on. A design strategy may be thought of as a describable and consistent posture, orientation, or "set" with which to respond using the appropriate skills and tools. While design is acknowledged as important by a number of investigators (Berzon and Solomon 1966, Bradford, Gibb, and Benne 1964, Miles 1960), little attempt has been made to systematize design factors as they affect intervention decisions in groups.

IDENTIFYING AND RESPONDING TO CRITICAL INCIDENTS

The primary requirement is that the group leader be aware of the existence of critical incidents and be able to recognize their appearance, for his behavior is most crucial to the group at the point when critical incidents occur. A group leader functions most effectively when he asks himself the following questions: (1) *When should I intervene?* (2) *What are the surface and underlying issues involved?* (3) *What level, type, and intensity of interventions are appropriate?* (4) *What are the probable effects upon thĕ group of a chosen intervention?*

The appropriate time for intervention would seem to be whenever a critical incident is occurring. Other than this, there is no specific time. Many interventions may be made during one session, and few, or none at all in others. In our prescriptive approach, no generally applicable guideline exists regarding a decrease or increase in the number of trainer interventions which should take place. Individual member participation will increase over a period of time and different members will assume some of the functions of the trainer, summarizing, clarifying, and so on. Thus the leader should be active primarily in those areas that are not handled well by the group members at that specific time. The leader's role will acquire different qualitative functions as the group moves to greater depths of expression and relationship and as the interactional competence of members increases.

Our theoretical orientation toward group development is that interventions made in the beginning stages of group life will tend, and generally ought to be, more superficial and general. Often group members report they recall little that was said by the group leader during the initial sessions. They may distort or confuse what they do recall.

As the group progresses and as a climate of trust and sharing begins to build, interventions should be on a more interpersonal level and deal increasingly with underlying motivations and the recognition of feelings. During the latter part of this middle phase there will probably be a noticeable increase in the number of experiential one-to-one encounters among individuals, and significant learnings will tend to take place at the interpersonal level. Interventions at the end of a group life should tend once more to deal with topics at the group level but in a manner that uses intrapersonal expressions of feelings to blend both task and maintenance issues.

Obviously not all group leaders would invariably follow this pattern, and there are certainly many ways in which different group movements may achieve the same ends. We are suggesting, however, that *interventions have differential consequences and effectiveness depending upon the stage of the group*. It would seem awkward and ineffective, for example, to begin a group with a progressive series of interventions oriented toward one-to-one encounters, especially with a group of strangers who have had no prior group experience. This might well "freeze" or immobilize the group. Yet this very same approach may be highly effective in motivating a group when appropriately introduced at a later time.

A point often overlooked in the choice and use of an appropriate intervention is the fact that the trainer sets the standard for the level and type of responses by group members. If the expression of feelings is encouraged by the trainer's direct example, there will be an expectation of shift in the group in the same direction. If this is attempted inappropriately or prematurely, however, the group may react by rejecting this level of response and moving to a less threatening (frequently a conceptual) level. In reality, there is usually a mixture of reactions to a shift in level and type of leader interventions. Some members welcome the movement; others prefer to remain for a time at some other level, usually one less demanding or threatening. The group must be allowed to discover a means of using all its resources regardless of their varied levels of responding. Trying out different levels and member roles is a part of the self-exploration process and should be encouraged.

It is important for the group leader to attempt to understand and clarify group issues and the motivations of group members if he is to recognize the "role-pressure" being put upon him. The beginning trainer may be especially influenced and his effectiveness decreased by the expression of negative feelings or aggressively critical statements directed at him. The inability to recognize or the refusal to deal with certain underlying issues may lead to an implicit assumption on the part of the group that certain criticisms are "correct." On the other hand, to react to criticism with defensiveness toward the group may lessen the group leader's effectiveness. Using relevant critical incidents of a stressful nature in a role-playing situation would help prepare the beginning group leader for such experiences.

APPLICATIONS OF THE CRITICAL INCIDENT MODEL

Three critical incidents have been chosen for their relevance to the beginning, middle, and end phases of group growth and development. Each critical incident is preceded by direct references from the training-group literature in order to illustrate the generality and frequent appearance of these issues. These three critical incidents follow the critical incident model introduced earlier. The presentations include discussions of the primary issues involved, the level, type, and intensity of possible interventions, the optional use of an appropriate sensitivity exercise as a structural intervention, and a consideration of the implications for the group. For learning purposes, we usually provide at least two relevant response alternatives for any given critical incident. Space limitations, however, prevent a consideration of more than one class of response alternatives for the purpose of this chapter.

CRITICAL INCIDENT I

The following type of critical incident is very likely to occur during the first group session. This has been noted in the literature (Bradford, Gibb, and Benne 1964, pp. 138-139) as follows:

> After a few seconds of silence someone else very mildly suggested that perhaps they might introduce themselves, adding that this seemed customary in groups of his experience.
>
> A number of members said that they wanted to know who others were —their names and where they came from, where they worked, and what their titles or job descriptions were. . . .
>
> 'When we did accomplish something, even though it was only introducing ourselves, you've indicated you didn't like what we did. If you don't like what we do, tell us what to do; otherwise you have no right to criticize us.'

I. Specify the context within which the event occurs.   This is the first group session. The general climate of the group is a mixture of awkwardness and anxiety. Members are unsure of their direction and unfamiliar with one another. Dependency statements have been made to the group by particularly anxious members, but there has been little interaction. One group member (A) who appears aggressive has apparently decided to initiate some action, as he begins speaking in a loud, authoritative voice.

II. Specify the behavior and/or conversation that led up to, and immediately proceded, the choice point.

Group Member A: "Well, I think we should know something about ourselves. Let's go around the room and tell something about ourselves. You know, introduce ourselves, and tell where we are from."

Group Member B: "That's a great idea. Why don't you start?"

The group picks up this idea and continues until everyone is finished. It is now the leader's turn and everyone is watching him expectantly. What are the issues involved and the response alternatives available to him as a leader?

III. Specify the level, type, and intensity of intervention response. The level of intervention for this particular beginning phase is almost always at the group level unless the trainer is confronted by some particular individual. The type of intervention provides the group leader with one or more alternatives. Choosing the experiential type of response, the group leader may simply remain quiet, looking comfortably at the group, frustrating their expectations, and allowing the anxiety to build within the group. It is probable, however, that this will result in a group member finally asking, "Tell us a little bit about yourself, so we can get to know you." It may be seen from this example that the selection of a certain alternative (in this instance, remaining silent) leads to a "sequence of chained critical incidents" in which the future behavior of the group may be predicted by the nature of the response just made.

Another response intervention might involve the sharing of feelings. The group leader begins: "I'd like to share some of my thoughts and feelings with you about how I feel right now. I'm feeling pretty boxed in and a little uncertain as to how I should reply." (In this way he is sharing feelings and modeling behavior). "On the one hand, I hear you asking for some straight information and I'm certainly willing to give that, but I also seem to hear us trying to feel each other out, to locate our personal boundaries and limitations, to categorize and pigeon-hole. It seems to relieve the pressure and give us a direction." (This is a general but superficial interpretation of both content and underlying motivation). "I wonder if the rest of you feel that you really know each other that much better now?" (Here we have a movement from the experiential to the group conceptual level, encouraging sharing of ideas about the process just finished.)

The level of intensity is almost always very low during this particular interchange and at this stage of the group. On the structural level, the group leader, as a resource person, has the option at this point of introducing a structural sensitivity exercise—a sharing dyad (see below) is appropriate—an activity that encourages familiarity and cohesion among members. The trainer's decision to use this exercise will be determined by a knowledge of individual group members and their needs, the speed with which he would like to see the group consolidate its gains, and the importance he attaches to structural interventions. A typical and appropriate structural intervention exercise is described in its entirety at this point to illustrate the potentially increased effectiveness of combining a variety of trainer approaches.

The sharing dyad.   Although it may be utilized at any stage, the sharing dyad is most useful in the beginning stages of a group to build trust and break down resistances to intimacy. In the beginning, members usually find it easier to express themselves with one other person than with the whole group. Group members are first paired by any convenient method forming a dyad. These dyad meetings usually last from ten to fifteen minutes, depending upon the leader. Each member of the dyad is told to remain silent while one member speaks, and then to reverse the process. Both members of the dyad face the same direction, that is, one member of the pair always sits with his back to the other member who first speaks. The leader may state, "I want you both to get to know each other as fully as possible, to try to understand the other, to learn how to give and take from your partner, and how to produce creatively with him. Tell each other what you feel is most important and needs to be said both about yourself and your partner." The objective is to provide an opportunity for each participant to learn to express himself and to receive the expressions of another in such a way that a relationship can be built.

Following the dyad meeting, it has been found productive to bring two dyads together forming a group of four people, and to repeat the exercise, doubling the members in the groups until the entire group is formed again on a more trusting and freer interpersonal level.

CRITICAL INCIDENT II

A second and frequently occurring critical incident offers a prototype for recognizing and dealing with conflicts and differences between group members. These conflicts occur throughout the life of the group, even though this critical incident is primarily directed at the middle period of group life. While there are different types of conflicts involving different levels and issues, several fall into this general model. One example (Bradford, Gibb, and Benne 1964) is the following:

> Most T-Groups, within three or four sessions, face a sharp cleavage. . . . This cleavage grows slowly, usually comes to a crisis, and is resolved sufficiently for the group to move ahead—although it is never solved for all members (p. 143).

> Thus the cleavage between those who wanted assigned topics and those who were interested in exploring behavior deepened and widened. . . . It was at this point that the group session came to an indecisive and frustrating conclusion (p. 147).

I. Specify the context within which the event occurs.   It is becoming evident that there is a widening split between those group members who support task issues and involvements and those who endorse maintenance issues dealing directly with emotions. From the nature of the statements being given, there is a great deal of hostility and an inability to see the importance or relevance of the other's position. Following a particularly heated exchange, the group has fallen into a frustrating silence.

II. Specify the behavior and/or conversation that led up to and immediately preceded the choice point.

Group Member A: "I just can't understand why we should keep getting hung up all the time on personal or emotional issues when we need to work on establishing an agenda and reaching our goals."

Group Member B: "I don't think an agenda has anything to do with what I want from this group. I can't understand your attitude at all. The only thing that really matters ultimately is our personal feelings."

Various other group members give support to each of these positions and express confusion about opposing stands. The group now lapses into uneasy silence. What are the issues involved and the response alternatives available?

III. Specify the level, type, and intensity of the intervention.
First, it is obvious that the leader always has the option of remaining
silent, of not responding. This in itself is a type of intervention designed
to raise the general anxiety level of the group and sharpen the task-
maintenance conflict. However, if the leader judges that his continued
silence would not be productive, and that the group should first be
made aware of the value of integrating and utilizing the two concepts
of task and maintenance, he may intervene along the following lines:
"I'd like to offer you a few of my observations. For the past thirty
minutes, I've been sitting here feeling more and more frustrated,
maybe even feeling trapped or experiencing a sense of futility. I
wonder how many of you feel the same way?" (This is an experiential sharing and reflection of mood of the group at the group level, an
invitation to the group members to share what they all have in common—a sense of frustration.) "Some of the concerns we're expressing
here—working on tasks versus working on people—are the same concerns that man, and groups of men, have always struggled with to
create our own community, here and now." (This is a conceptual input
at the group level, identifying the issues and goals.) "I'd like to suggest
at this point an exercise which may help us to understand and manage
our mutual concerns better." (This introduces a structural sensitivity
exercise chosen both to emphasize the concerns of the group at this
point and to point to ways of coping better with the issues).

The structural intervention may help the leader guide the group to
an integrated approach to group functioning. The degree of intensity
is typically medium. The leader should, by the tone and nature of his
intervention, both reflect and express the cognitive and emotional
issues involved. A group leader who plays down the emotional issues
involved would deliver an intervention of very low intensity. Another
leader may prefer to underscore the emotionality of the split in the
group and consequently would choose a high-intensity intervention.)
The following structural intervention would be appropriate for the
critical incident.

Verbal and nonverbal communication dyad.   Often when people
try to express their feelings about each other verbally or to explain
themselves or some situation, they simply cannot "understand" each
other. This occurs when people are inarticulate, when they have strong
but hidden conflicts about their feelings, when they are actually not
aware of what their feelings are, or when they use words defensively to
obscure feelings. In these situations two approaches may be helpful.
The first involves verbal interaction and the second involves nonverbal

behavior. It is often most effective to use both, in the following order.

In the first method each participant is asked to stop talking about his own bias and try to state his adversary's position as clearly and sympathetically as possible. Usually the two will exchange seats to carry this out. Initial attempts are often caricatures; it is important to insist that the opposing argument be stated as if it were a reasonable position. This forces the antagonists to think of the merits of their opponents' arguments. The second method of clarifying an interaction is to ask the two participants to continue to communicate their own positions *without using words*. These two exercises should help members recognize the legitimate status of both positions—the importance of ideas and feelings, and the value of getting a task accomplished and enabling feelings to be expressed so that people are able to work together.

CRITICAL INCIDENT III

This final critical incident seems to occur most often during the middle to end phases of group life. It has been observed (Bradford, Gibb, and Benne 1964) in one or more of the following variations:

> In one T-Group, a number of events relating to feedback had occurred. . . . one anxious member had asked the group members to tell him anything they wished about himself. He was here to learn all he could. He could 'take' anything they said. His anxiety communicated clearly, however, and the group did not respond, except to show increased uneasiness. (p. 156)

> At the end, very simply, he asked them to respond in any way they pleased, but in ways they thought would give him more knowledge of himself . . . *not* to hold back their reactions to him. (p. 158)

The above references point to the emergence of issues dealing with members beginning to question their present behavior. This is usually concurrent with a request for an evaluation of on-going behavior from a group member, and a demand for more effective future behavior.

I. Specify the context within which the event occurs. The type of PTI delivered at the beginning of a training group meeting is usually designed to provide continuity between related sessions, and/or to establish a climate such as trust. This essentially involves an initial input that arouses or intensifies some productive emotional mood, perhaps a sharing of feeling that facilitates openness and trust.

In this example, the group leader has just finished a PTI involving the feedback process and productive risk-taking. One of the group members who is highly intellectual and cognitively oriented makes a statement directly to him. It is obvious from his appearance and tone of voice that he is highly anxious.

II. Specify the behavior and/or conversation that led up to and immediately preceded the choice point.

Group Member A: "I've been sitting here listening to you and I wonder—are you talking about me? Am I supposed to change? What am I supposed to do? I've always been relatively secure the way I am. Why should I change—or how?

In the moment of silence following this statement all eyes are on the trainer. What are the issues involved and the response alternatives available?

III. Specify the level, type, and intensity of the intervention response.   The level of intervention for this particular critical incident should take into consideration both the issues involved in the PTI and the benefits to both individual and group and should serve, if possible, to link them together. One alternative is simply to intervene at the group level in order to turn the individual's question back to the group. Thus, the response, "Perhaps this is a question with which each of us is struggling. What does the group think and feel about Bill's question?" While useful, this response may not take adequate advantage of the opportunity to integrate knowledge, values, and practical skills. We might contrast it with another alternative.

The group leader begins, "Bill, I had the feeling as I was watching and listening to you just now, that you were feeling pretty tense and uptight. The reason I mention it is that I feel that way, too, sometimes." (This is a direct intervention at the individual level, experientially reported. It serves the purpose of communicating both to the individual and the group that the trainer is aware of the feelings involved and wants to be supportive.) "I guess the questions you raised—can I find a place for myself in the group? Are people going to accept or reject me? How much should I risk revealing and how can I find out where I stand?—are questions we are all struggling with as a group." (This is a continuation of the intervention at the individual level, and directs attention to the larger, basic questions and issues to which the trainer wants to sensitize the group. Finally, the last few words identify the level as one of group concern.) "I wonder if the rest of you would share your feelings about this point?" (The intensity of intervention, in this instance, is judged to be high, and deals directly with very important, personal feelings in a straightforward manner.)

In the above instance, the model of leadership offered is one in which the leader uses his own feelings when they are genuine and when they are relevant to the productive growth of a group.

On the structural level the group leader has the option, as before, of supplementing his intervention with a sensitivity exercise. The following is offered as particularly appropriate.

Behavior prescription. This technique has its greatest potential during the end phase of the group. It requires that enough time has passed and yet that sufficient time remains for the individual to experience and apply the prescriptions given to him. The group member should be able to carry out such prescriptions in the remaining life of the group. It has been found to have limited value in the beginning stages, because of individual resistances and because appropriate norms have not yet been established.

The group is divided into small units of four or five persons, depending upon the size of the group. These small groups then move to individual rooms so that each group is separated from the others. The trainer has already told them: "In order to facilitate the resolution of some of the problems that we have been struggling with, I would like to suggest an exercise in which we can aid each other in both individual and group functions. It is very important, however, that we conduct this exercise in a supportive and nondestructive atmosphere. Here is how we proceed: In each subgroup one person will leave the room for ten minutes. During that time the remaining members will first diagnose this person's typical style of interacting with others, and secondly try to pinpoint definite, specific, helpful suggestions as to how he might be helped to engage in atypical but productive behavior both for himself and the group. I must stress the terms 'definite' and 'specific.' Don't make abstract generalizations like 'you're too much of an introvert, so try being an extrovert for a while.' Instead, give him definite and specific prescriptions to carry out that are generally atypical but productive. Thus, one person might be told to express anger toward the group more directly and verbally instead of remaining quiet. The process continues until everyone has been given a 'behavioral prescription.' We will all meet back here in 'X' minutes to see what sort of changes have occurred." The group leader may focus upon group functions as a general source of prescription, or he may choose to focus upon functions outside the group as in "back-home" problems. The choice of focus will depend upon the needs of the group and the amount of time allotted to carry out the behavioral prescriptions following the exercise. After the group has reassembled, there is usually little urging needed on the part of the trainer to begin a discussion of roles, functions, and effects that have appeared among the group members.

OVERVIEW OF CRITICAL INCIDENT APPROACH

The critical incident approach is an attempt to recognize and systematically arrange recurrent group phenomena to enable a group leader to effectively utilize a wide range of appropriate interventions. The recognition and collection of critical incidents with a number of appropriate alternative interventions and optional structural exercises should provide a valuable tool in teaching, training, and research. While we acknowledge that there is more than one set of responses to a given critical incident, we nevertheless assert that there are certain preferred alternatives which can be evaluated on the basis of empirical observations of their effects upon the group. In this manner, the beginning group leader may be able to develop an effective style of leadership based upon a knowledge of critical incidents and appropriate responses. The recognition and categorization of specific critical incidents as they arise will aid the group leader in his efforts to understand the phase or stage in which a group is functioning and the problems which are of greatest underlying concern. He will also be helped to intervene in ways that facilitate movement in a given direction. This approach in no way inhibits the spontaneous and human quality of the leader-group relationship, since the group leader is free to emphasize or reject intervention alternatives. The choice he ultimately makes will be a function of his experiences and his developing style of group leadership. Freedom for the group leader is increased, not decreased, by providing a wide range of possible intervention alternatives.

If the critical incident is to fulfill its function as a teaching, training, and research tool, it must possess the flexibility with which any on-going group may be described, since each theoretical approach—nondirective, psychoanalytic, gestalt, and others—has its own unique style of intervention. This should be reflected in the quantity of level, type, and intensity dimensions of the intervention cube. If the intervention cube is shaded with those areas that represent a specific intervention style, then a direct comparison may be made between theories, between areas that are over- or underemphasized, between experienced and beginning group leaders, and so on. By selecting representative examples from major theoretical approaches, by classifying the style of leader interventions, and by shading in the appropriate areas on the intervention cube, a specific identifiable intervention style emerges that instantly reflects the underlying theory.

The nature of an intervention is of paramount importance to both the understanding and control of group growth and development. If the fact is accepted that there is a large measure of regularity and consistency among groups over a period of time and if there are identifiable classes of responses available to the group leader, then an attempt to gather and systematize these incidents and apply appropriate modes of response would seem to be a necessity. The recognition and recording of various critical incidents as they occur during an interval of time would prove valuable in the determination of specific phases of group development, as Tuckman (1968) has postulated in his work. The ultimate benefits of our technological approach using a critical incident model, however, will be to the group that can effectively use knowledge, skills, and values in an integrated framework that will be broadly applicable to the real world.

REFERENCES

Bach, G. "The Marathon Group: Intensive Practice of Intimate Interaction." *Psychological Reports* 18, no. 9 (1965): 995-1002.

Benne, K. D. "From Polarization to Paradox." In *T-Group Theory and Laboratory Method: Innovation in Re-Education,* edited by L. P. Braford, J. R. Gibb, and K. D. Benne. New York: John Wiley & Sons, 1964.

Berzon, B. and Solomon, L. "The Self-Directed Therapeutic Group: Three Studies." *Journal of Counseling Psychology* 13, no. 4 (1966): 491-497.

Bonner, H. *Group Dynamics.* New York: Ronald Press, 1959.

Bradford, L. P. "Trainer-Intervention: Case Episodes." In *T-Group Theory and Laboratory Method: Innovation in Re-Education,* edited by L. P. Bradford, J. R. Gibb, and K. D. Benne. New York: John Wiley & Sons, 1964.

Bradford, L. J.; Gibb, J. R.; and Benne, K. D., eds. *T-Group Theory and Laboratory Method: Innovation in Re-Education.* New York: John Wiley & Sons, 1964.

Buchanan, P. C. "Evaluating the Effectiveness of Laboratory Training In Industry." *Explorations in Human Relations Training and Research,* no. 1. Washington, D. C.: NTL Institute for Applied Behavioral Science—National Education Association, 1965.

Campbell, J. P. and Dunnette, M. D. "Effectiveness of T-Group Experiences in Managerial Training and Development." *Psychological Bulletin 70,* no. 2 (1968): 73-104.

Fiebert, M. S. "Sensitivity Training: An Analysis of Trainer Intervention and Group Process." *Psychological Reports* 22, no. 8 (1968): 829-838.

French, D.; Sherwood, W.; and Bradford, D. "Changes in Self-Identity in a Management Training Conference." *Journal of Applied Behavioral Science* 2, no. 2 (1966): 210-218.

House, R. J. "T-Group Education and Leaderhip Effectiveness: A Review." *Personnel Psychology* 20, no. 1 (1967): 1-32.

Klaw, S. "Two Weeks in a T-Group." *Fortune* 64 (1961): 114-117.

Kuriloff, T. and Atkins, D. "T-Group for a Work Team." *Journal of Applied Behavioral Science* 2, no. 1 (1966): 63-94.

Miles, M. B. "Human Relations Training." *Journal of Counseling Psychology* 7, no. 3 (1960): 301-306.

Stock, D. "A Survey of Research on T-Groups." *T-Group Theory and Laboratory Method: Innovation in Re-Education,* edited by L. P. Bradford, J. R. Gibb, and K. D. Benne. New York: John Wiley & Sons, 1964.

Tuckman, B. W. "Developmental Sequence in Small Groups." *Psychological Bulletin* 63, no. 3 (1968): 387-399.

Weschler, D. and Reisel, W. *Inside a Sensitivity Training Group.* Los Angeles: University of California Institute of Human Relations, 1959.

Dilemmas
for the Trainer

SHERMAN KINGSBURY
NTL Institute for Applied Behavioral Science
Washington, D.C.

A central skill of a manager or of any leader is to be able to take effective action despite rationally unresolvable uncertainty about what constitutes a correct or best action. To choose to move or not to move in areas of neatly balanced forces is the constantly recurring challenge to the trainer in a training group.

Abraham Kaplan (1964) makes a clear distinction among puzzles, problems, and dilemmas. A puzzle is an uncertainty which can be resolved simply by finding out how to put one's thinking straight, by seeing the logical thing that was being overlooked. A problem is an uncertainty which can be brought to resolution by working on it in certain systematic ways, such as gathering appropriate information and making relevant analyses. Resolving the uncertainty of a problem takes time and work, but one can feel reasonably confident from the start that it can be done.

Dilemmas are a different matter. The uncertainty is persistent. No action makes complete sense, and inaction is unacceptable. The dilemma remains even after one has acted and evaluated the result. A particular action will not necessarily feel appropriate the next time the tension arises. A change in strategy may seem indicated just because the previous choice was made in a particular way.

The dilemmas I experience as a group trainer arise from my values about training and about myself and my relationship to others. In each situation one side of me says, "Do this." Another says, "Do that." And still another says, "Do nothing." To yet another part of me, doing nothing is unacceptable. Some may say that my problem is muddy thinking and that my values are not well worked out, but I do not think that is entirely the problem. Similarly, I do not believe that all a manager's dilemmas are to be resolved by straightening out his thinking. I do think that excitement, challenge, and reward of training (or of managing) come with taking action in the presence of real uncertainty, having courage to act not knowing if the action is rationally defensible, experiencing the consequences of the action, and regrouping and moving on.

HOW DEEP TO GO?

The contract between the trainer and the participant calls for learning about self and groups and their relationships; for self-improvement, self-initiated growth, experimentation, and emergence. It does not call for treatment, rescue, or deep regression. The existentially present reality of the group is the primary field of analysis and interpretation.

Most excursions into the there-and-then seem to be flights from reality. Occasionally, however, a group member will begin to explore and reexperience some past or deeply personal situation under very special circumstances in the group: several other members of the group seem to be in touch with him; testing is done to validate that he really wants to go in this direction; there is a shared feeling that the group will be severely blocked if it is not able to see this individual find his way past this area; people are tense, perhaps even fearful, but feel focused and helpful. Communication from the person may begin to show distortions in the form of transferences, misperceptions, slips of the tongue. The anxiety and emotionality of the situation intensify and are expressed through tears, rage, or depression. Clear testing of the situation still indicates that the individual and the group want to go on and feel it would be constructive to do so. Perhaps by now the trainer's clinical judgment tells him that the participant is moving toward exploration of some repressed conflict which is frightening and yet focal for him. Very rapidly this sort of thing can advance to the point that if the trainer diverts the exploration—no matter how —the participant may feel he was headed into something even more terrible and more unacceptable than he had feared.

This is a multi-faceted dilemma. Things are getting deeper, more intensely intra-personal, and less present-oriented than I really would like. I am committed, however, to the idea that the group is in charge of the agenda. I could try to resolve this by simply being quiet, by passively letting the group assume the entire responsibility for what is going on. But for me that is a "cop-out." I am there. I have responsibility for my inaction as much as for my action.

Given the intense character of this moment, the openness of the participant, and the support of the group, it is possible that this is one of those rare occasions when real and useful insight or experimentation can emerge in a brief time. But if it goes badly, the group can mire down in parlour psychiatry. I acknowledge and respect the time and skill generally required for psychotherapeutic progress with deep-lying issues. I also have respect for the huge steps individuals in groups can take when things are going well.

In this situation, it may be that I simply do not know where we are heading or what to do. Should I share this feeling with the group? I trust groups to move with real sensitivity if they are able to test out and move carefully through what they are doing. If I share my uncertainty, I risk diverting the group's attention from the participant's needs to mine. How often I must entertain the possibility that talk about the trainer's behavior is flight from more important, difficult issues facing the group!

I rarely choose to do nothing in such a situation. Sometimes I divert attention from the deepening personal exploration. Other times, if I feel there is a reasonable chance of a useful outcome, I move with the exploration, participate actively in it, and push it deeper. In some cases, the result of my action is strong movement by the group into new learning. There are times when the action on my part is completely ineffectual. Sometimes I choose to remain on the sidelines trying to communicate that I am paying close attention to what is going on, ready to become actively involved if I can figure out how to be helpful.

The situation tests my values and puts them into conflict. Whatever I do momentarily suppresses some of my values and underlies others. But I have not made a long-lasting choice of priorities among my values. The conflict remains with me after I have acted.

INDUCING DEPENDENCY VERSUS MODELING PASSIVITY

Any action the trainer takes may gratify to some degree the dependence needs of some members of the group. The more vigorous his action, the greater the dependence he is likely to induce. In equal measure, any action the trainer takes will serve as a model for the behavior of some members of the group. Inaction on the part of the trainer serves for some people as a model of passivity. The training group is a learning environment and I am deeply convinced of the truth of Raymond M. Hainer's opinion (1967) that if learning is the game, passivity is the enemy.

The dilemma (which arises most clearly in the early life of the group) is that if I act, I tend to induce dependence, which I wish to avoid; if I withhold action, I tend to model passivity, which I also wish to avoid.

Very often in a group I think I know just the expression, just the analogy, just the nonverbal exercise with which to bring real clarity into a muddled situation. Often the situation *is* clarified. But at what a price! I find myself increasingly pressed to produce *the* solution, to be an oracle or a guru. Some members of the group then turn to me like infant birds, beaks wide open, waiting for mother to drop in a choice worm. Others try frantically to say just the right things, to make analogies, or to propose nonverbal exercises—and these people seem to look for the applause of the crowd after each "turn." So, by being "helpful," I have induced group members to act out dependence needs or to compete with me (much the same thing, as the "competitors" depend on me as a model). While dependence is an appropriate issue for many members of our society to confront, I do not think it has to be forced into a group by the trainer's behavior. Groups have problems enough without trainers giving them problems just for exercise.

Is the only choice then to say nothing, to be passive? I thus avoid the risk of inducing dependence, but I also avoid the exposure of doing something risky, something that changes the subsequent judgment of the group. These consequences of passivity distress me.

The best definition of the trainer role I know is this: an effective member. This means that the trainer is concerned about his own learning in the group, his own gratification, and his standing with the other members. He values being open and trusting and confronting. He is aware of his own feelings and can make conscious choices about expressing or suppressing them. If he expresses them, he has several choices. His values are exemplified by his behavior. He values his own freedom and feels confined when another is dependent on him. He values his own learning and is suspicious of his own passivity in a tight situation.

But even if he is all this and more, he still faces the basic dilemma.

I do not see a clear resolution. I act or I suppress in a given situation. I have a hunch that I make better choices in this dilemma when I operate spontaneously without trying to set and follow a policy line.

For example, I am often quiet in the early sessions of a group. I have sometimes done this as a matter of policy, thinking it reinforced my ground rule that the group control its own agenda. A few groups, however, have confronted me with this policy, charging that I was protecting myself and not being helpful, and successfully demanded I change my behavior.

At other times, I have found myself inactive simply because I did not know what I could do and who I could be in that group. In that condition, I had nothing to say or do. In that state, I have sometimes been able to talk about my difficulty in knowing what I was able to do and have found the ensuing discussion helpful to me and constructive to the group.

If I can limit myself to talking about my own inner state, perhaps I can avoid the induction of dependence. But is that really being active? Is it really being all me? I am not able to settle the question.

FALSE DICHOTOMIES

In the past, I have been more strongly committed than I am now to the idea that it is important for a person to talk through his experiences in a group in order to develop cognitive clarity and a personal theory about the meaning of the experiences he has. Recently, however, I have found myself suspecting that some pretty good things were being talked to death, and that an experience which involved the whole person—mind and body, head and heart, reason and emotion—became so intellectualized that the feeling component of the insight was dulled or lost; the reality, intensity and, I have suspected, the transferability of the insight to other situations was drained away.

When I ask former laboratory participants what they recall about their groups, I get not intellecutual distillations but stories of specific events. When I ask what influenced them most and what they apply most often, I rarely get general formulations describing rationally what those events meant. My own answers to those questions center on critical events, usually emotion-laden ones, and to moments when my own behavior patterns took shape and when I connected group events with events from other times and places. The connections seem to occur in images rather than in words. Verbal formulations may follow the image connections, but the potency and existential validity of the insight lies in the images.

As my respect for the great communications mechanisms of sensory, motor, and image expression has grown, so has my concern that people frequently use words to suppress or repress communication, discovery, meaning, and learning in those other, more primitive modes of expression.

I do not want to sell short man's capacity for making rational constructs. I have worked with some people who seemed unable to begin to work or to believe that anything was happening unless they started with the rational. Often both participants and I feel that much more can be learned from an event if only we can understand it and its ramifications better. But I have little patience with myself or others when I hear the question, "Why do you feel like that?" I want to say, "That's an impossible question. Feeling is a direct, biologically-rooted response to an experience. Thinking about it afterwards is a critique, not an explanation why." Yet sometimes I have seen a person help himself by tackling that "impossible" question.

This dilemma is somewhat different from some of the others. There is no question where my values are. I want to be a fully feeling *and* thinking person. I hope that the training group will facilitate each participant's experience of his own feeling and thinking as fundamental, synergistic, and valuable human processes. I am deeply influenced by Abraham Maslow's view (1964, 1968) that the transcendence of such dichotomies as feeling/thinking or subjective/objective is an outcome of the process of self-actualization.

But are we "talking an event to death" or are we reaching a deeper, more general, more applicable level of meaning? I cannot always tell.

There is another way of expressing this dilemma: I am committed to the value of research and the building of theory under the discipline of reality-testing, but I am very troubled by some of the published research in behavioral science. In attempting to evaluate objectively the quality and effectiveness of training, the research is so essentially dull. Its results are elusive and seem to have been captured from a vital situation only in statistical nets of considerable delicacy. There is nothing elusive, delicate, or dull about the inner experience or behavioral shift of a person whose life has literally been changed by his experiences in a training group. For him, it is clear, intense, and exhilarating.

Perhaps all I am doing is criticizing the state of the science, but I think something more than that is going on—something that has to do with the denial of the reality of feeling on the irrational ground that it is not rational. A lot of "objective" research published in the field of applied behavioral science has the quality of talking valid experience to death.

The notion that reason and emotion are mutually exclusive pervades our society. I want reason and emotion unified in my own behavior and experience, and I want to do something better than I know how to do now with these issues in the groups I lead.

INDIVIDUAL AND ORGANIZATION

The context of the training group and the value orientation of most trainers create a social system which values openness, genuineness, authenticity, congruence, interdependence, personal development, self-actualization, emotionality, warmth, confrontation, activity, creativity, experimentation, reality testing, and so on. While most trainers do not want to impose their values on others, they do want to create conditions in which people become aware of their values and are free to make choices about them. The training-group values, however, once they are perceived in action in a strong group, are very attractive to many people, and numerous participants shift their values in the directions indicated above during and after their group experience.

While all this is going on, we trainers are also trying to convince the management of organizations that group training is leadership training and will facilitate productive organizational life. Much research has been done to establish scientifically that such improvement is indeed observable. Many of us have attempted to show that the values found in the training group are the same as those which belong (either by "law of nature" or in the interest of productivity) in large organizations.

Perhaps time will show that to be the case. Nevertheless, I am uncomfortable because the values in many organizations (observable in their behavior, not necessarily in their policy statements) are not consistent with training-group values. Instead, suppression of feeling is valued, confrontation is hazardous, experimentation is ritualized to avoid innovation. We encourage such organizations to send people to laboratories. Some, embracing the new group values, return to the parent organization less functionally adapted than before—determined, even, to find new jobs. Surely it is no accident that right now many trainers are leaving organizations, trying to establish themselves as part-time consultants or academicians because, they say, they require greater freedom and autonomy. The emergence of the field of organizational development from the training-group culture is probably directly related to the conscious or unconscious recognition of this value difference.

The dilemma is this. I am strongly in favor of the individual's autonomous growth toward self-actualization. I am committed to the training-group values. Am I acting consistently with those values if I manipulate organizations by helping individuals discover and confront their own alienation from the values of the organization that is paying for their expenses at the laboratory and their salaries while at it?

I have tried to confront this issue in many organizations. Usually I am told that a value shift is a risk the organization is willing to run, but I cannot help wondering whether that is not just brave talk.

This dilemma occurred in a slightly different form in one of my groups. A member, the only black man in the group, held a responsible-sounding, middle management position in the public health department of a medium-sized southern city. At first, he seemed elderly, passive, conceptually impoverished, and limited in vocabulary. At times he fawned like a real Uncle Tom. He came to trust the group late in the laboratory, and only after much testing, and a remarkable change took place. He seemed younger, stronger, more active, and vigorous. His voice deepened, his sentences were more complex and penetrating, his southern accent fell away. He told us we were the only whites he had ever trusted enough to let his mask slip. He was able to behave in this second way only with a limited number of trusted black associates and friends, for he was convinced that to show his second self would be to lose his job and destroy his chance to exercise even the limited influence he had.

Shortly before the laboratory, I had read John LeCarre's *The Spy Who Came in from the Cold,* a story dealing with a man's agony in maintaining a false identity in a hostile environment in which he dared not let his mask slip for a moment. To know people in the enemy camp he could trust enough to let the mask down did not help; it only increased his chance of making a fatal slip.

To be allowed to know this black man in his second persona was a significant learning experience for all the whites in the group. But did we help him? Did we strengthen his ability to live behind the mask he felt he must assume, or did we vitiate his ability to be a spy out in the cold? I would like to think that for him to have been able to trust some whites for even a brief time would help in the long run, but did we make it harder for him to survive *until* the long run? I still do not know.

The issue is the same with some businessmen. Training may be an education for freedom; I think it is, but I am not always sure what is responsible behavior with individuals who cannot allow themselves to be free, or with organizations that do not actually value what I mean by freedom for their people.

CONCLUSION

I do not have satisfactory resolutions of any of these dilemmas. Much of the satisfaction I receive from the work comes when I am able to act despite them. Sometimes hindsight will support my action and I feel gratification; sometimes hindsight says I was wrong and hopefully I can learn from analysis of that situation.

There are, happily, two ways of looking at a dilemma. Whatever I do to resolve a dilemma is to some extent wrong, but it is equally true that whatever I do is also to some extent right.

The greatest mistake a trainer makes is to be unwilling or unable to analyze with the group the basis of any action he takes and the outcome of it. Assuming that learning is the game, there are few mistakes if the trainer is willing to work with the group in bringing his own behavior into analysis and to demonstrate that he is committed to the struggle to learn from it.

REFERENCES

Hainer, R. M.; Kingsbury, S.; and Alriches, D. B., eds. *Uncertainty in Research, Management, and New Product Development.* New York: Reinhold Book Corporation, 1967.

Kaplan, A. *The Conduct of Inquiry.* San Francisco: Chandler Publishing Co., 1964.

Maslow, A. H. *Religions, Values, and Real Experiences.* Columbus: Ohio State University Press, 1964.

———. *Toward a Psychology of Being,* 2d. ed. New York: Van Nostrand Reinhold Co., 1968.

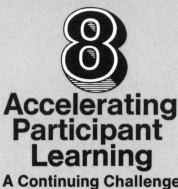

Accelerating Participant Learning

A Continuing Challenge in Trainer Intervention*

SAMUEL A. CULBERT
University of California
Los Angeles, California

MUCH of my professional time since the mid-1960s has been devoted to training group trainers. This work has increased my awareness of differences in trainer styles, values, and theories of learning. Moreover, it has alerted me to the things I do as a trainer, to my thoughts about training and about others who are coming into this profession, and in particular, to the characteristics that distinguish my style from that of others. In this chapter, I articulate some of my unique characteristics with openness and candor in the hope that my comments will stimulate others to dialogue.

In a recent paper about trainer intervention (Culbert 1970), I provided a model for accelerating group learning which is broad enough so that any trainer can superimpose on it his theories about how people learn and his techniques for helping them do so. This model contains five assumptions.

1. Trainers *can* through their participation accelerate the natural learning processes of training groups.

* Special thanks to David R. Peters for his helpful comments on an earlier draft of this chapter.

2. The ultimate goals of a training group are not immediately attainable.

3. Experienced trainers can predict the paths for reaching these ultimate goals in spite of revisions which must be made as group events unfold.

4. Trainer predictions (whether explicit or implicit) usually have a directive impact on the group's process.

5. Guidelines for the trainer's participation derive from attention to those issues which a particular phase of the group's development is contributing to the accomplishment of the group's ultimate objectives.

In the paper mentioned above, the discussion of this model emphasized what the trainer may systematically do to guide his group toward the personal growth objectives established by the group's existence. The present chapter contains some of the specific methodologies which I use when working with the model, the rationales for my behavior, and my thoughts about the moment-to-moment participation issues a trainer faces. These issues are grouped into three categories: (1) the unique responsibilities of the trainer role; (2) the singular opportunities of a trainer for influencing others; (3) and the human demands of participation as a trainer in a group.

ISSUES FACING GROUP TRAINERS
RESPONSIBILITIES OF THE TRAINER ROLE

By responsibilities, I refer to the obligations for performance attached to the trainer role as the result of the expectations of others, of expert knowledge, or of self-expectation.

Responsibilities resulting from the expectations of others.   Issue: Can the trainer role be diminished to that of model group member?

An assumption I would like to erase is that the trainer is just another participant. Many contend that a trainer is simply a more experienced group member or the best group participant. In reality, while he is both of these, he also has some unique responsibilities.

Certainly the trainer is a model, whether by his own intent or because others who are in the process of trying to discover guidelines for their participation in the group will see him that way. Participants will expect him to be someone who has successfully dealt with many of the struggles currently confronting them in the group. And in all likelihood, the trainer will also see himself this way. Moreover, participants will quickly observe that when the "votes" are tabulated, the trainer has voted more than once, he is a power figure and others will seek to gain similar power by supporting his views.

I believe, however, that it is the trainer's struggles, not his successes, and the ways he deals with intrapersonal and interpersonal dilemmas, not his solutions to them, that give him what singular value he has as a model. For example, a while ago I had the experience of listening to a participant tell of a struggle that was causing him considerable pain. Since I felt deeply with him, I decided that I would share something parallel that I had struggled with a few years earlier. His reaction was indeed a lesson for me: "Hot dog for you, Sam. You got over yours. What does that do for me?"

Modeling is an unfortunate term because it can imply that something about the trainer's behavior is a performance for others to replicate. I use the term to mean that a trainer can use his real and natural interactions, with their existential outcomes, to illustrate the potentialities of certain kinds of behaviors and relationships.

Responsibilities resulting from the trainer's expert knowledge. There are a number of responsibilities which should be assumed by the trainer when no one else in the group has thought—or has expertise —to pursue them. Sketched below are ten which the trainer might be uniquely qualified to handle.

A trainer is responsible for keeping participants aware of what is happening. The trainer should provide a road map, relating here-and-now activities to group goals in order to assist participants when they get lost. For practical purposes, people are nonparticipants when they are confused or when their thoughts are drifting to something else. Before a group begins, I ask participants to let the rest of us know if they become lost, mentioning that in this way we all have a chance to reexamine group focus and its usefulness to our learning. At the trainer level, I thus have an opportunity to admit I am also lost or to highlight group process and to communicate a broader understanding of its potential than new participants can recognize by themselves.

A trainer is responsible for developing group norms consistent with his learning theories. The norms of trust, exposure of differences, and exchanging of perceptions are among those which lead participants to see blind spots and to experiment with new behavior.

A norm I try to support is that participants share their personal needs when they ask someone else to change. For example, let us suppose that group members confront a silent person about his nonparticipation. If formulated in terms of a "should"—every responsible member should voice his views—the whole group is in danger of missing a very important learning: "Why do the confronting members need the quiet one to speak?" The group can simply decide that the quiet one is trying to manipulate the group, demanding visibility and support by means of his silence. However, this conclusion limits the learning for everyone. Confronting members often do not really face the anxieties the silence creates. They may fear it masks criticism. They may be motivated by their own needs for inclusion and acceptance to form a group norm that everyone must participate. They may be volunteering someone for attention to keep the focus off themselves. For his part, the silent person never really gets beyond the interpersonal patterns that have characterized his everyday relationships. He does not discover the extent of the control he exercises, the power he can have without silence, or the rich opportunities for interpersonal connections that systematically fall beyond his reach. All these learnings become possibilities when a group norm obligates participants to share their own needs in asking someone else to change.

A trainer is responsible for providing accurate perspective for the feedback received by participants. The trainer should balance hostility with warmth and support with confrontation. For instance, when someone is receiving a great deal of critical feedback from three or four vocal group members, he often loses perspective about just how widespread the criticism is. When I think this is happening, I point out to the group that this person is acting as if everyone were critical of him; I thus give others who may feel differently a chance to voice their feelings. Even when a group is unanimous in criticism, I try to introduce multiple perspectives by asking participants to express that self-information which reflects the unique problem posed for *them* by this "objectionable" characteristic. Failure to provide an accurate perspective can lead to eventual resentment of the group by the criticized participant as he gathers more accurate information from his relationships with others outside the group.

There is a special variation of this responsibility that trainers must keep in mind when sharing their own feelings. Most participants think of their expression of feelings as revealing very intense matters. Trainers are more used to expressing feelings, even subtle ones. They frequently overstate or speculate about feelings to teach a participant something. A trainer should be careful to point out when his purpose is didactic, and he should qualify overstated feelings by such remarks as, "I'm only 20 percent annoyed." Because the trainer is a power figure, failure to qualify the degree of his emotional expression can be intimidating.

A trainer is responsible for keeping the tension level of the group at an optimum level for learning. Research has clearly demonstrated that tension bears a curvalinear relationship to learning and, I would add, to relationship-building. Too little tension leaves participants uninvolved and disengaged; too much polarizes them and cuts off communication among them. A technique that I frequently use for raising or lowering group tension levels is to spend time helping participants sharpen their statements to one another. For instance, after silence someone might say, "For the first time I felt good about one of our silences." When I want to raise tension levels, I ask the participant to say more about why this silence differs from previous ones. This can help make him aware of the sources of his tension. When I want to reduce the tension, I ask him to say more about what is contributing to his comfort.

A trainer is responsible for lending his vitality to a group. Experience-based learning is a very demanding process which requires more momentum than is usually needed in order to overcome the barriers to personal learning. If this were not so, this type of learning would occur much more frequently than it does in our daily routines. The trainer's aptitude for spotting learning opportunities and his experience in generating excitement over the possible results of these opportunities provide him with a bank of vitality which he can lend to the group. Of course, there are key moments when group members need to experience their lack of energy in order to develop their *own* momentum; the best contribution the trainer can offer at these times is his silence.

A trainer is responsible for acting as referee from time to time. Frequently a trainer sees members going back-and-forth with statements such as, "You did this. . . ." "No, I didn't. You merely see it that way because. . . ." At some point the trainer can save the group a lot of time and frustration by asking for data and helping to produce it and by setting up rules for talking, such as the common, "I think you could hear one another better if you used 'I' instead of 'we.' " He can also provide perspective with a statement of the following type: "You're so wound up with one another that I don't think either of you is going to get through. Why doesn't each of you pick someone else who knows what you're trying to say and ask them communicate for you?"

A trainer is responsible for providing opportunities for group members to work on the centrally important theme of relations with authority or power. Everyone comes to a group with problems about authority, power, receptiveness to influence, and the like. Authority and power struggles are born early in a person's life and take a long time to resolve. They usually have numerous daily consequences. An important, omnipresent dimension of a training group is that it gives participants a chance to do further work on these issues. It presents a powerful format for attacking them, and the trainer is the key to this process. In contrast to daily encounters with authority where open expression of conflicts usually knocks a participant out of dialogue with the person in authority, the trainer remains in dialogue with each participant over a period of time. Participants, then, can use their relationships with the trainer either for diagnosis or for experimentation with new behavior. Most often this requires interacting with the trainer's masculine side: the part of him which is intellectual, challenging, directive, personally assertive, or willing to fight openly. Unfortunately, despite the preponderance of male trainers, only a minority seem to train with their masculine sides salient. Most interpret the trainer role as predominantly feminine—even maternal—interacting by giving support, nurture, responsiveness, guidance, or reasonableness.

A trainer is responsible for identifying and helping break up group games which interfere with learning. This is a very difficult challenge for a new trainer since these games are often organized around one of his weak sides. Groups can subconsciously sense a trainer's idiosyncrasies and play on them to get control of a situation. A group game to which new trainers are especially vulnerable is the unconscious collusion to protect the image of the leader as strong and knowledgeable. Casting the trainer in this role supposedly provides security to group members. Of course, there are many collusions which group members enter into to protect their own weak sides, but these are usually easier for the trainer to spot and interrupt.

Following are two examples of group collusion which I encountered when observing new trainers.

1. The group talked as though they had established a very warm atmosphere, but there was no apparent reason for it. My first thought was that whatever produced the warmth the members were alluding to had taken place at an earlier session that I had not observed. Then, however, the conversation veered away from an opportunity for two participants to appropriately recognize their appreciation for one another. No one objected when the subject was shifted suddenly to another subject which produced a seemingly warm interchange among the participants. Later the trainer and I discussed his own personal problems with intimacy and after some time we concluded that his group was mirroring these problems. They were giving the illusion of

intimacy and depth as a defense against their anxiety in displaying the caring and vulnerability required for achieving real
intimacy.

2. The trainer was very aware of my presence as a consultant,
   despite our having discussed the possibility of this awareness
   before the group. He was very concerned with impressing me,
   and my own needs unconsciously reinforced this concern. The
   training session produced no beneficial results. Participants were
   slow and quiet and refused to build upon one another's comments. The trainer reacted to this by becoming increasingly
   active; he singlehandedly was trying to be the group. The session
   ended in frustration for everyone; for the trainer because of his
   performance, and for the participants because of their inability
   to capitalize on the leadership "offered" them. In my subsequent
   discussion with the trainer, we posited another strategy. He
   could have helped generate another kind of process and smoked
   out live issues by saying to the group, "There doesn't seem to
   be much happening tonight. Are there any reasons why we just
   don't knock off?"

In asserting the trainer's responsibility for breaking up group games,
I am not advocating that he enter and save the group whenever things
are not proceeding well. Part of participant's learning is in learning to
shape the group process around themselves. In my thinking, however,
the trainer has responsibility for contributing his assessment of interaction patterns—even when letting the group members "do it themselves." The group may or may not be able to use these contributions,
but it is helpful if members see the trainer as pitching in rather than
as sitting back passively. For example, in moments of group malaise,
the trainer should be searching his silence for ways to help, even if
this means telling the group that he has been thinking for the last
fifteen minutes about what to do but has not been able to come up
with anything.

*A trainer is responsible for helping participants separate diagnosis
from a mandate for change.* Realizing the existence of a problem does
not necessarily reveal its solution. Group members often react angrily
when the trainer points out something they know to be true but which
they do not like about themselves, although the trainer's motivation
for telling them may have been constructive. In such cases, it is likely
that members project upon the statements a stronger criticism than
was probably intended. Any criticism may actually be about their in-
effectiveness in getting what they want for themselves or about the

problems their behavior creates in a relationship with them. The members, however, feeling inadequate because they cannot immediately change, are self-critical and thus defensive.

The trainer can perform a beneficial service to group members merely by finding support for them against their own self-criticism. Participants need to discover that there are good reasons for the difficulties they have in changing. The trainer can help with this by asking a participant to repeat his description of the criticized characteristic so that the other participants can see it clearly. Typically this reveals problems in the accuracy with which the participant sees himself and underscores any gaps in his understanding of his motivations.

Since it is usually the narrowness of the insight that has blocked previous attempts to change, separating diagnosis from change usually makes available behavior alternatives. In such situations, the trainer is dealing with a real-self/ideal-self discrepancy. The participant is frustrated because his behavior is not more like his ideal of how it "should" be. A more accurate real-self picture usually reveals "good" reasons why the participant behaves the way he does and, in the process, confronts unrealistic aspects of the ideal-self image. The anxiety aroused by too large a gap between real- and ideal-self images is reduced. Thus, providing an accurate real-self picture often leads participants to greater self-acceptance and frees them to change, or not to change, their behavior.

A trainer is responsible for helping a participant separate the positive, goal-congruent aspects of his behavior from those aspects which are viewed negatively by others and which cause him to want to change. Group members frequently experience the feeling that they are being asked to change a favorite quality, even though they cannot quite articulate what they like about it. When dealing with so-called normals, the trainer must remember that there are adaptive aspects of all behavior and that these aspects must be considered lest the person being asked to change feel a sense of personal loss. Separating the adaptive from the maladaptive, however, is not a task that the trainer can count on other group members (with dynamic and complex links with one another) to perform.

For instance, a participant's aggressive behavior when angry can block the expression of others. Given a choice, the aggressive participant probably does not want to do this. On the other hand, the angry behavior also has useful aspects for him, such as allowing him to release tension and freeing him to be a more interesting companion for others. The message, "Stop being so aggressive," needs to be received with greater precision; the message is not just "Stop being aggressive," but also "Stop violating my boundaries with your aggressiveness." The challenge to the trainer is to manage, when possible, the following process: (1) Make the consequences for the person objecting to the aggressive behavior more apparent to the aggressive person; (2) Get the aggressive person to state his values about these consequences (the reactions of the objector) without losing his sense of the adaptive aspects of the aggression; and (3) Get both to collaborate in modifying the troublesome aspects of the aggressive person's behavior. When accomplished, this kind of collaboration can lead to deep expressions of warmth as each person in the conflict experiences from the other respect for and support in the dilemma. The objector gains the understanding and respect of the aggressive person for the problems he is experiencing with him, and the aggressor gains support in his ability to change his behavior without giving up some aspects which are valuable to him.

Responsibilities resulting from a trainer's self-expectation. Issue: Must the trainer require participants to accept as a matter of faith his assumptions about the kinds of behavior that produce learning?
My response to this issue is a resounding "no"—of course tempered in practice by my limitations in articulating training-group processes and by my own behavior as a critical part of those learning processes. I strongly believe that the most central value of the training-group process is that participants learn how they have learned. In fact, my ultimate objective as a trainer is to teach participants how to produce similar learnings in their daily activities. (I will go into this more fully in a later section of this paper.) This objective is hard to gain when the trainer takes the nondisclosing role of guru. To the extent that the trainer is either not articulate or is unwilling to discuss his assumptions, he is subtly building up his own charisma at the expense of participant learning. On the other hand, some trainers believe that immediate solutions to problems, transcendental experiences, and exploration of the depths of interpersonal connections in the group are the most important outcomes of a training group; these trainers can make good use of the role of guru-trainer to produce such outcomes.
Early in a group, participants frequently require more informational support than the trainer can usefully impart. For one thing, participant needs for information are usually based on emotions which they do not want to admit. Thus, these feelings are not easily engaged. At such points, the trainer may seek to engender confidence in his own abilities in lieu of information. I believe, however, that even under these circumstances it is better for the trainer to build confidence in

himself by means of an in-the-group track record than by relying on prestige or status brought from out-of-the-group activities.

For the trainer to discuss his assumptions about learning-producing behavior gives each participant more responsibility for group process as well as for his own behavior. It challenges each person to be the architect of his own learning and to involve others as they are relevant to this process. Not being encumbered by the expectation that he will manage each participant's learning frees the trainer for data-producing and integrating roles which only he can fill.

Participant responsibility is not possible when the trainer makes a statement that interprets behavior without revealing his data, when he picks at words rather than reciprocally engages participants, or when he supports and feeds transference rather than clarifies group perceptions of himself as a person. In addressing this issue, I make a point of sharing my data with a group by replacing "Somehow I get the feeling that . . . ," with "Let me share . . ." interventions and statements of the reasons for a particular sharing.

There are some other obvious benefits that accrue personally to trainers who attempt to make their assumptions public. These trainers get immediate feedback about the accuracy of their theories and the usefulness of their interventions, with implicit suggestions for modifications. They also learn by being asked questions to which they do not yet know the answers. By making assumptions public, trainers also can learn while demonstrating the experience-based methodologies of data collection and analysis, while experimenting with new behavior, and while generalizing from new learnings to modify related theories.

Issue: To what extent must participant learnings be made explicit?
Learning must be made explicit to a considerable extent. An important trainer responsibility is to arrange impromptu examinations of what the learning participants indicate (often without words) they experience. In dealing with personal learning, people can hedge on their intentions to change unless they publicly put their learnings into words. Verbalization and public acknowledgment seem to serve three major purposes: (1) They press the learner to address gaps in conceptualization which cause him to be tentative about that which he already knows; (2) They produce a concrete expression of the learner's commitment to act to which he can later refer as a bench mark for evaluating his behavior; (3) They elicit support from others in unlocking the learner from old patterns which are discrepant with his new desires for participation.

Explicit statements of participant learning are also valuable to the trainer. I am often surprised to find that the meaning of a group experience for a participant is not what I had assumed. As a trainer, I feel an obligation not to brainwash people to see things differently than they do. Explicit expression allows both participants and me to be aware of our differences and to recognize subsequent opportunities for data collection which are relevant to dialogue and mutual understanding.

Certainly there are rich implicit learnings that defy description and that in some cases would be diminished by discussion. Such learnings center around expressions of intimacy. I call such experiences "existentially pure." With the passage of time, however, people become less vulnerable when talking about these experiences, so that we can learn from them without violating their memory. I jokingly tell participants my main commitment is to a "learn-in," not a "love-in."

OPPORTUNITIES OF A TRAINER FOR INFLUENCING OTHERS

I have already mentioned that the trainer gets more than one "vote" in the democratic processes of the training group.* Even if the trainer leaves the room, some participants in the group are guessing how he would "vote" if he were present. This is a fact no matter how much a specific trainer might protest.

Issue: Should the trainer strongly influence a training group's climate in terms of his own preferred style for group interaction? The trainer should decidedly influence a group's climate, as long as his preferred style provides enough latitude so that participants can learn using variations suited to the ways they learn best.

Group training is still an art. For practical purposes this means that different trainers can achieve similar results by doing things in their own individual ways. Each trainer has his own theories of how people learn and how he can best contribute to these learnings. While all of us have a tendency to state our theories as if they were equally valid for others, we privately acknowledge that, in part, our theories are formal justification for our doing the thing we uniquely do best. It is in the participants' best interests for the trainer, when necessary, to structure the group so that he can employ his best style. Without detracting from the validity of this assumption, I have also learned

* I learned this most vividly from Leland Bradford, former head of the NTL Institute for Applied Behavioral Science. How it delighted me to hear him say during an NTL Central Office Staff meeting, "I cast one very strong vote for. . . ."

from my work with interns and my research (Culbert 1968) that most trainers have a far greater range of participation styles than they typically express. Accordingly, I both encourage new trainers to do what they feel they do best and also to experiment with new ways of accomplishing their training-group objectives.

As an example, I would like to mention one of the things which I do well in a training group. I use my own personal involvement in the group process as a key means of illustrating data which are critical to diagnosis and problem identification. Typically I am after data that are not quite at the level of group consciousness so that they could not easily be brought to the surface by others. I begin by engaging the participants (or the group if my hunch is at the level of group process) on the dilemmas with which their behavior faces me or the feelings they stir up in me. The purpose is to get myself involved in an interaction in which I experience the behavior I want to comment about. In the process, I am a rather open participant and am very responsive to discussing "my piece of the action." It has been commented that there are real "handles" on me if someone wants to get back at me as a way of discharging his defensiveness.

When the critical data have been made visible in my interaction and my feelings as well as those of the person or persons I was addressing are at a point of at least temporary resolution, I invite the others in the group into the conversation. With the data more evident, they are able to be more articulate about similar issues they have been experiencing with the person with whom I was involved or with others in the group. I conclude my participation by conceptualizing the data I observed both in my interaction and in the subsequent comments of others and then try to complete the bridges to others who could have been involved but have not yet participated. Although I intend this kind of participation for diagnostic purposes, it frequently stimulates a learning process by producing a disequilibrium between the behavior the participant wants to change and the anxiety which was previously kept under wraps by this behavior.

Intentionally structuring a training group to support the trainer's unique style is a process which requires constant introspection if the trainer is to remain effective. There is always a risk that the focus will be more on the trainer's needs than on those of the participants. The opportunities to attain professional effectiveness while fulfilling personal needs makes the trainer role an unusually attractive one. Those who fill it have a context for centrality, self-disclosure, influencing and helping others, having their sensitivities appreciated, demonstrating effectiveness as a person, being seen as sexually attractive, and so on.

While many such expressions can be satisfied simultaneously with participant growth and learning, some block the participants. I have never yet observed a trainer whose needs did not occasionally get in the way of other people's learning. The challenge here is for the trainer himself to be an open system with means for monitoring his actions, for assessing their consequences for others, and for changing his training behavior when appropriate. Flexibility—the ability to change within the group—is more often than not contingent upon the trainer's ability to find ways of fulfilling the same needs outside the group. All trainers confront this problem to some extent.

Just as individual trainers have their own styles (albeit some less effective than others) for facilitating group learning, participants too have styles which characterize the conditions under which they learn best. For example, given alternatives, some people prefer aggressive interaction and others require a group climate of considerable support. While some day we may know enough about learnings and training styles to form optimum matches, today we have to content ourselves with finding trainers whose styles, regardless of specific characteristics, provide enough freedom so that participants can learn in the individual ways which are best suited to them.

The key characteristics in providing participants with this kind of freedom are breadth of trainer repertoire and personal willingness to try different alternatives. This does not mean that the trainer need be all things to all people—only that he exercise flexibility and a willingness to try different types of interventions and to work within climates that are codetermined by participant needs. For example, I recently tried a variety of interventions in an attempt to help a participant get beyond his cynicism. I first dropped the seed of a confrontation between the participant and another group member who was trying to get closer to him. I personally empathized that the reason for his cynicism was probably not that he did not care, but that he cared too much. I encouraged others to talk with him about his isolated position in the group. None of these interventions helped him. He finally was able to make considerable progress when I engineered a role play in which he confronted himself as if he were another group member trying to get through his cynicism to say something that was personally important.

Issue: Does directive action on the trainer's part interfere with the democratic learning processes of his training group? The democratic processes of a training group confront participants with how much of their potential for change is self-determined. Moreover, the processes produce data about each person's unique style of learning, exerting leadership, and reacting to the influence of others. In subscribing to the usefulness of these processes, most trainers used to feel it was necessary for the leader role to be filled with nondirective behavior. The democratic group processes were initiated by confronting participants with an unstructured and ambiguous situation and then the trainer implicitly challenged them to make something out of it. In coping with this trainer-structured dilemma, participants produced data representative of their coping styles. The group could analyze and relate to these data once they found out what they were supposed to do. Marrow (1964) presents an excellent example of this type of training. The trainer's role, in the simplest sense, was not to tell the group what to do but periodically to ask members to analyze the group's process or to share their own reflections about the salient dynamics and learning conflicts facing the group or individual members. Colleagues who trained this way tell me, however, that they were not responding to a table of random numbers when they chose a particular time to ask the group to reflect. There is no doubt that their directiveness was subtle.

It is rare to find such a group today. For one thing, participants seldom come to groups without first speaking with a number of others who have had training-group experiences. They not only know what kind of group processes to expect but sometimes know about some of their trainer's salient personal characteristics. Trainers are no longer content with group learning rates produced without a substantial amount of trainer participation. They want to experiment with their intuitions and their theories for accelerating participant learning. Trainers also acknowledge that their own participation is an important buffer against their own frustration and the boredom that is produced by a nondirective style. Thus, in acknowledging the directive aspects of the trainer role, the issue has become, "How can the trainer give his directive participation to the group so that he does not interfere with the democratic learning process necessary for certain kinds of participant learning?"

The key to this issue is that the trainer must provide sufficient information for participants to evaluate his direction against their own objectives for participation. This entails the trainer's being explicit about his objectives, clearly explaining why he thinks the process he is suggesting will accomplish the goals he has suggested. It also involves the trainer's explaining whether he is acting on a hunch or whether he has no idea at all about what the group might do. Such information leads participants to a different type of dependency than

TABLE 1. Phase Progression in Weekend Human Relations Group

Time	Specified Phases of Progression	Dynamics Which Evolved in the Group	Group Task Implicit in the Dynamics Evolved	Specific Within-Phase Trainer Behavior Emphasized
Friday evening	1. Developing a climate of trust	Group story telling: members attempting to make comments consistent with what had preceded.	To determine whether there is enough member similarity to begin risking disclosure of individual differences.	Sharpen and clarify participant statements in order to facilitate interparticipant dialog. Call group members' attention to the trust elements of what is being discussed.
Friday evening & Saturday morning	2. Exposure of individual differences	Members present encapsulated self-statements revealing differences.	To test, simultaneously, reactions of others to differences and willingness of others to respect (self) defenses.	Establish norms of openness and respect for differences; support those members who wish to remain "closed" but assist them to articulate their reasons for taking this position.
Saturday morning	3. Exchanging perceptions of others	Members interact spontaneously with one another and build potentially growthful relationships.	To discover whether others could really be resources for personal learning.	Support feedback through encouraging participant interaction and involvement with others. Personally model here-and-now, self-disclosing participation, gradually curtailing activity with time.

Saturday afternoon	4. Individual problem-solving	Use of relationships in the group and here-and-now processes as vehicles for helping others look at their own contribution to "back-home" problems.	To capitalize on the full potential of the group resources developed.	Point out similarities between within-group relationships and out-of-group problems being discussed. Identify here-and-now group processes and their possible connections to the relationships under discussion.
Saturday evening	*5. Group problem-solving	Participants relate spontaneously shared problem without being controlled by the attitudinal differences of others or seeking to influence others to be more like themselves.	To work on issues having relevance for all group members without compromising the quality of the individual resolutions resulting from individual differences.	Remain quiet and unneeded.
Sunday morning	6. Reconnaissance and evaluation of personal learning	Free-wheeling participation with individuals experiencing periods of reflection, conceptualization, feedback, and the gambit of self and other confrontations and emotionalities.	To conceptualize the weekend's learning on an individual basis and to test these self-formulations with others.	Help members gain clarification, feedback, and back-home conceptualizations by identifying appropriate sources (persons) of information including oneself. Summarize group processes and challenges for further individual growth.

* This phase was spontaneously designed by the group members.
SOURCE: S. A. Culbert, "Accelerating Laboratory Learning through a Phase Progression Model for Trainer Intervention," *Journal of Applied Behavioral Science* 6, no. 1 (1970): p. 45.

that created when they are asked to do something by the trainer without much more explanation than is implicit in it as coming from someone who is usually right. It is my desire, when being directive, to focus my directiveness at producing data for better democratic decision-making by participants. My directive behavior is usually focused on developing group processes and seldom at influencing specific decisions such as whether the group should accept an observer or discuss Bill's feelings before hearing from Pete. While I am usually willing to share the consequences I believe will follow from specific actions contemplated by the group, I try not to control the extent to which participants experiment with behavior for which I predict less than optimal consequences.

A very difficult situation for me is seeing a participant make a decision on the basis of adequate data but with an inaccurate interpretation of it. This is often seen in the person who explains to a group that openness only results in hurt for him. When asked if he is sure this is so, he produces a string of examples to prove the validity of his assertion. Continuing to contest his position would appear to be arguing with him over conflicting values. Remaining silent is to go along and give the impression of supporting the conclusion drawn by the participant. In such situations I tend to be a risk-taker, feeling that I do have a responsibility to provide each participant with a *choice* and feeling that at present this person does not have one. Usually I make him aware of my disagreement with the conclusion he has drawn from his data. I try to engage him in further data analysis, using data collected more currently from in-group events. For instance, with someone who is defending the desirability of not opening up, I call his attention to both the consequences others are experiencing for their openness and to the consequences he is experiencing for his lack of it.

Issue: Are there guidelines for knowing when to comment at the individual, interpersonal, group, or organizational levels?

Issue: When should the trainer react to content discussion and when should his comments be addressed to the process or dynamics of the discussion?

Issue: How does the trainer decide to intervene in the first person to initiate a personal interaction, in the second person to respond to someone, or in the third person to help others get into dialogue?

Each of these issues confronts the trainer with the potential usefulness of a theoretical or practical frame of reference which could present him explicit guidelines for making his interventions. Not many trainers give much thought to a theory or set of practical objectives when they make their interventions. Usually trainers base interventions on their intuitive feeling for the requirements of the immediate situation or in terms of an overall project such as that of getting group members to be learning resources for one another.

I have recently described (1970) how, before a training group's beginning, I attempt to build a cohesive frame of reference for my participation. First I interact with participants to reach joint agreement about the overall objectives of the group. I next try to predict the phases of development through which the group will have to progress toward its overall objectives. These predictions are open to modifications as the group actually unfolds, but the specified phases provide me with a frame of reference for understanding group events and provide insurance for participants that they will cover the necessary ground for achieving their objectives.

To illustrate, table 1 summarizes a weekend group whose overall objective was "to increase self-awareness through looking at the ways participants dealt with individual differences (Culbert 1970, p. 45)." The first, second, and last columns of this table are self-explanatory. The third column describes the salient dynamics evolving in the group as the members worked at each phase of the group's development. The fourth column describes my understanding of the task which was implicit in the group's dynamics at each phase. Not included in this table is a description of the systematic steps I took to facilitate the group's progression from one phase to the next.

Issue: Do better trainers really make fewer mistakes?   The trainer's role permits a great deal of latitude. All trainers can and do make many mistakes without seriously impairing the learning processes of training groups. We err in reading group emotionality, in being sensitive to the feelings behind a participant's statement, in indulging our needs, and in projecting our conflicts onto participants. While I probably make substantially fewer and probably less serious errors now that I have been training awhile, there is little doubt that I am always making a sufficient number to demonstrate my contention that participants learn in spite of trainer mistakes. Certainly it is also true that some trainers make many more errors than others. However, the number and quality of errors are not the main differences between effective and ineffective trainers. Effectiveness is determined by the trainers' ability to hear and to learn from the comments, or feedback, evoked when he makes an error.

Some constellation of cues always is present when a participant feels misunderstood. Less effective trainers are those who miss these cues, respond to them defensively, or do not know how to react to them. More effective trainers are those who see these cues and respond to them with openness, although they may not, even in retrospect, know how to react "appropriately." Trainer openness to feedback not only has immediate consequences for participant learning but also helps to establish a group climate where others can make mistakes without undue criticism.

A distinction can also be made between *merely* effective and *very* effective trainers. Participants who have merely effective trainers experience quality learning and considerable growth in their training groups. They receive feedback, have important insights, and experience emotionality bearing on struggles which are central to their current life goals. They even experience breakthroughs having major impacts on their life styles. When the group is over, these participants frequently return to their daily routines with real feelings of personal renewal.

Participants with very effective trainers also experience considerable growth in their training groups. When they learn something or experience growth, however, they also learn about the process of how they just learned. The rewards are considerable. Not only do they improve their situations with regard to current struggles, but they also learn how to cope better with the problems they will encounter after the group. They learn a technology for generating the personal and interpersonal data required in analyzing the periodic growth crises that characterize all of life. When faced with key life struggles, they not only will know about the resources available in a training group, but they will also have some ideas for creating similar resources among their current acquaintances.

HUMAN DEMANDS OF TRAINER PARTICIPATION

Training-group participants usually define themselves as normals developing their human potential and seldom as neurotics working to shore up deficiencies. Implicit in this self-definition is the expectation that they will be treated authentically and not clinically. Even though the distinction between normal and neurotic is frequently blurred, the role of trainer does entail using one's authentic self as an instrument of learning for others. This means taking risks and exposing parts of one's self that are not yet fully developed and with which the trainer is struggling. Such involvement, coupled with the intense, emotional encounters which take place in training groups, put numerous human demands on the trainer.

Issue: During a deeply moving encounter, can a trainer give rein to his own feelings when he has responsibility for others? When a participant overextends the limits of his emotional expression, trainers have a responsibility for protecting the participant and for making sure that structures are raised or missing perspectives brought out. This is a particularly challenging responsibility since at times of heightened emotionality it is likely that the trainer will also be experiencing poignant feelings and thus be less able to keep an eye out for others. Certainly this is the case when the trainer is personally involved in an interaction or is relating to an emotional experience of his own.

Three ways come to mind for handling this dilemma. The first is for the trainer to maintain some minimum amount of surveillance of others while becoming personally involved. This means hedging his involvements somewhat by staying in touch with his diagnostic understanding of the participants in his group. The trainer thus becomes involved to the extent that he can be responsive to cues signaling him to switch tracks, relying on his understanding to provide him quickly with perspective on whatever problems come up. For some trainers this means an availability for almost complete absorption in the moment, and for others it means somewhat less personal involvement. Who was it who said his highest human goal was to remain lucid in his ecstasy?

The second way of handling this issue is for the trainer to withhold his full involvement until he knows participants well enough to feel that the group has sufficient resources to cope with small crises. Participants must be responsive enough to provide one another with support as needed. Knowing that at least minor crises will get adequate coverage reduces the trainer's need for vigilance. If something major comes up, there will be resources available until the trainer can cap his feelings and regain his perspective.

A third way of dealing with this issue is to play the odds that no crisis will be so severe that it cannot be retrieved and adequately put in order at some later time. I find this assumption made most often by trainers who are not clinicians, and I do not believe it to be valid. I tell interns that the only trainers who have not faced a crisis of a magnitude that demands their immediate and total availability are trainers who either are not facilitating important learning or who have not trained very much. Moreover, being alert has implications for participant growth. James Clark,* contends that an even bigger challenge in being alert to

---

* In a personal communication.

emotional peaks is for the trainer to be able to distinguish when the peak contains possibilities for accelerated growth and then to use his training and experience to give direction to the participant rather than try to ground emotionality. I find this a very difficult, but important, thing to do.

Issue: Is it essential for a trainer to be "honest" and "open" at all times? Authenticity, honesty, genuineness, openness, and congruence are words which are frequently used synonymously but which actually communicate a range of concepts. Of these words, congruence is the concept which has primary utility for me.

Congruence means that a person's thoughts or feelings and the words he uses or the actions he takes are consistent. Rogers (1959) in the context of two-person helping relationships adds to this definition the idea that the consistency of thought and action must be perceived by those with whom an individual is relating. Inasmuch as the perceptions of others are determined, in part, by their own needs and motivations, a person's actions will be congruent with his own thoughts and feelings more often than they are experienced as congruent by others.

As a person, in my everyday activities, I am always on the alert for situations in which I can appropriately be congruent and for people with whom I can risk congruence. As a trainer, I am committed to being congruent to the extent that I am able. I make explicit use of my congruence and of my incongruence—as perceived both by myself and by others—in addressing the learning goals of others. Table 2 summarizes some examples and consequences of trainer congruence. Although somewhat oversimplified, it illustrates how each of the four cells indicated can be split in half (dashes) to show the consequences of trainer participation which facilitate and which block participant learning.

In trying to be congruent, I always intend to be honest, to represent accurately the things I choose to say. I do *not,* however, always intend to be open, to express that which I know and which is relevant to a group member or group situation. I think of myself as manipulative at those times when I am honest and selectively open without also being congruent. In furthering participant learning, I may think it quite congruent not to take action or not to reveal my thoughts and feelings. There are a number of reasons why I might remain silent: I might be having difficulty translating my clinical insights into words which would accurately communicate; my expression might rob someone else of the chance to share similar feelings; my expression might be too early in terms of an individual's emerging capacity to use it; or my nonparticipation would serve as a challenge providing others an opportunity to move beyond their passivity and to experiment with their own styles of leadership.

Issue: Should the trainer make his own problems part of the group process? There are actually two questions in this issue. How much of his struggles should the trainer share when he has alternatives for expression? How should the trainer deal with his own struggles when, as inevitably happens, they are interjected into the group's process as salient characteristics of his relationships with others?

I have found that there is a point in each group's life when group members are especially thirsty for the personal and "human" participation of their trainer. Prior to this time they may be solicitous of him, but probably for reasons other than his humanness. Disguised in the members' apparent concern for the trainer may be issues such as his role in individual authority struggles and opportunities for flight. As long as group members focus on the trainer, they can avoid their problems in relating to one another.

At the critical time when most group members become genuinely interested in the trainer as a person, they also are probably using their interest to symbolize their growing independence. Most likely they will begin to support the trainer as he reduces the number and character of his differences in participation and begins to resemble a regular group member. At this point, others usually pitch in to fill the maintenance functions the trainer had been performing.

Looking at the situation from the trainer's viewpoint, it may be that he has a need for participation which does not coincide with the group's natural timing for including him as a participant. To the extent that the trainer is able to find alternative outlets for these struggles (perhaps in other colleagues), he ought to refrain from interrupting or personally determining the group process. At such points, the trainer can rely more on technique and less on the use of his own person as an instrument for the learning of others.

The preceding comments speak normatively about "the time" for a trainer's inclusion as a group participant with personal struggles. Certainly there are many situations, almost from the group's beginning, in which the particular sub-project being addressed by the group may provide an appropriate context for problem disclosure by the trainer. The trainer may even believe that, rather than offset the curtailment of any learning objectives, his immediate participation will free him for further contributions. Of course, all this is quite academic when the trainer does not have a choice about whether he will disclose his

TABLE 2. Trainer Congruence: Examples and Consequences for Facilitating and Blocking Participant Learning

	Participants View Trainer's Behavior As Congruent	Participants View Trainer's Behavior As Incongruent
Facilitating learning	Trainer feels good about himself and his relations with others. He feels creative and useful. Participants trust the trainer and his motives. They are more apt to listen carefully and to lower their defenses.	Trainer's commitment to himself provides momentum for him to support others in their confrontations of him. He utilizes discrepancies in viewing his congruence as a means for understanding the resistances of others. Participants see the importance of self-commitment in the face of group consensus. They learn more about "inquiry" as an alternative to personal defensiveness.
Blocking learning	Trainer gets carried away with his own importance. He fails to provide others an opportunity to express their feelings and insights. Participants defer too much. They behave as if their own self thoughts are less important than the ideas of the trainer.	Trainer defensiveness is aroused by the frustration and vulnerability generated in being "misunderstood." Participants become unaccepting of minority dissent. They use this condition as a means of justifying their defensiveness to trainer inputs.

Trainer Views His Behavior As Incongruent

	Trainer Views His Behavior As Congruent	
Facilitating learning	Trainer finds support for his own lack of personal clarity. He may even disclose his dilemma to the group and explicitly solicit consultation. Participants view the trainer's personal commitment to training-group values of openness, honesty, and personal growth.	Trainer is confronted by participants over the problems created for them by his lack of congruence. He reacts sympathetically to confrontation rather than refusing to change. Participants find that their abilities to confront can yield positive results. They also find that the trainer has an "in-process" self-image rather than one of perfection.
Blocking learning	Trainer is overindulgent to his own needs for too long a time. The absence of group opposition deprives him of one kind of vehicle for getting back in touch with himself. Participants work on trainer-focused projects while thinking that the trainer is responding to their needs.	Trainer fights and tries to defend an untenable personal position. Participants feel alienated from the trainer. They may even conclude that they have been punished for their confronting this discrepancy in trainer behavior.

struggle or when he lacks a frame of reference for differentially evaluating the utility of his interventions. I have spent many moments in groups without having either a choice or a frame of reference.

A particular trainer problem or struggle may be crucially relevant in releasing a group for a period of heightened learning. This is likely when the trainer is himself the center of a group conflict, or when, through exposing his own struggles, he can act as a catalyst for others with similar struggles. At such times, the trainer has a unique contribution to make if he is willing to share his thoughts openly. He makes a far greater contribution if he can discuss his personal struggles in relation to specific group participants than if he discusses them in longitudinal terms. At first glance, this strategy appears to expose less personal vulnerability than talking about problems in the context of one's back-home situation. An equal amount of personal risk is experienced, however, if the trainer focuses his disclosure on how his own struggles contribute to problems others are experiencing in the group. Moreover, if the trainer is not clear about his contributions, or does not stay with the discussion long enough for his role to become clear, he may stigmatize participants with an attribute which will confuse their relationships with others in the group.

Not only does the trainer's sharing of personal struggles serve as a model for participant learning and growth, but it begins to clarify the issues other participants bring to their struggles with the trainer. When the trainer acknowledges his actions, and thereby subtracts his input, what is left can be more clearly analysed and acknowledged by others.

Trainers want participants to leave their groups thinking highly of them. But far more important is that participants leave with a many-sided picture of the trainer. This is a key contribution which trainers can make to participant growth. Many trainers are personally attractive, sexually desirable, and very empathic; some are conceptual giants or powerful confronters. But very few, in my experience, manifest these qualities in their everyday activities to the extent that participants will see these qualities in their training groups. A statement I heard Chris Argyris make to a company president comes to my mind with respect to this issue. He said, "You know, Pete, the longer people work for you the more they come to like . . . [the company] and the less highly they seem to regard themselves." I believe an idealized image of the trainer has a similar impact on participants. Their real-self picture suffers in comparison with the trainer's competence and attractiveness. And the real-self/ideal-self gap for most people is wide enough without the trainer's widening it further with a one-sided self-presentation. I believe self-acceptance to be every bit as important a learning project for training-group participants as self-improvement.

Issue: What personal characteristics are most essential in predicting excellence as a trainer?   Recently I supervised the selection of interns and others who were being trained by the NTL Institute as group trainers. In this capacity I received letters of recommendation written by almost every professional who had an active interest in the field of training. They recommended what seemed to me to be a very diverse group of people with very diverse personal characteristics. Few writers mentioned the same characteristics; for that matter, it was rare to find two recommendations for the same applicant emphasizing the value of the same personal characteristics.

Notwithstanding this diversity, I have my own pet theories about which characteristics best predict excellence. The two characteristics on which I consistently seem to rely are social competence and an aptitude for accurate viewing of one's own contributions to interpersonal dilemmas.

I realize that *social competence* must sound like a strange attribute to list as most important; for that matter, I am not even sure that I can be very articulate in stating exactly what I have in mind in using this term. During my training as a clinical psychologist, I noted that many excellent clinicians were failures in relating to people at the social level. They had difficulty discussing topics on which they were not particularly authoritative or in which they were not particularly interested. An example comes to mind of a therapist whom I observed during my internship. He was a masterful therapist and I learned a great deal from watching him. Also, his patients seemed to make excellent progress. This same man, however, would literally walk sideways down the narrow corridors of our clinic so that he would be saved the embarrassment which apparently came from not knowing the cordial exchanges that follow, "How are you today?"

The therapist in this example may not have had more severe personal conflicts than many who are excellent group trainers. My point is that, for whatever reasons, his problems were of a nature that impeded the *range* with which he could engage other people. Experience has led me to conclude that the range in authentic engagement of others outside of the structured training group seems to predict the range of availability and competence within it.

Extended discussion concerning *accurate viewing of contributions to interpersonal dilemmas* does not seem necessary since numerous references to this attribute are embedded throughout this paper. This is not a characteristic that most trainers develop naturally, although most have a natural aptitude for it. In many instances, a person's primary motivation for becoming a trainer is that he sees training as a means of developing this aptitude. Most who have acquired accuracy of self-perception seem committed to it as a central life value. It is essential to note, however, that no one who has acquired it is accurate in viewing himself in relation to others more than part of the time. Thus, for purposes of predicting trainer excellence, this characteristic also includes accuracy in picking up cues which indicate that one is inaccurate in viewing his contributions to interpersonal dilemmas.

Meta-values   Two meta-values permeate most of what I do as a trainer. The first is interpersonal bias and the second is a strong commitment to assist participants in learning how to make out-of-group applications of their learning.

By interpersonal bias I mean that no group event or trainer intervention can be considered by itself for full understanding. There are several reasons for this assertion, perhaps the most obvious being the added learning available when group events are viewed from multiple perspectives. The previously mentioned example of group members' response to a silent member illustrated this point.

Examining motives functionally in terms of the interpersonal projects they are intended to service enables people to view themselves descriptively rather than moralistically. Evaluation becomes, to a greater extent than is typical, a matter of seeing whether a participant's behavior brings him closer to his interpersonal projects. This has considerably greater utility for personal growth than reflecting behavior against the "shoulds" of one's ideal-self or those which a participant introjects from the expectations of others. In everyday activities, these "shoulds" sacrifice self-acceptance for self-improvement. Discovering that no fundamental behavior change is necessary is a valuable and often overlooked contribution that training groups make to participants.

Perhaps the most important characteristic of emphasizing the interpersonal lies in the applicability of this learning strategy to participant worlds outside the group. Interpersonal correlates exist in the group for each step of the experimental and introspective methodologies (for example, Schutz, 1967) emphasizing insights and substantive learning.

These correlates are diagrammed in figure 1. Care has been taken to insure that each element in the column on the right (interpersonal) gets coverage equal to that of the elements on the left.

At a minimum, I believe the interpersonal encounters of the training group have value merely because they demonstrate that participants can push the boundaries of experience and interpersonal relationships beyond the limits within which they typically live. The potential is much greater. The enlarging of boundaries presents disequilibriums to typical living patterns and this, with the proper support, can stimulate

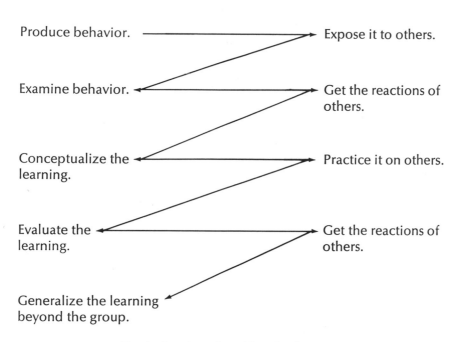

Fig. 1 Experience-based Learning Processes.

change toward expansive new boundaries in nonlaboratory activities. Too often, however, training-group learning does not transfer easily to nonlaboratory situations (Campbell and Dunnette 1968). In fact, trainers themselves have difficulty in doing this, as witnessed by the number of times trainers commiserate at the end of a lab that all they have to look forward to are the wife and kids.

Training groups can be structured to provide handles for helping participants bridge their learning to nonlaboratory worlds. I believe this structuring is most important, and I expend a considerable amount of energy on it. Accordingly, there are several types of interventions which I make to help participants cross the bridge from laboratory to nonlaboratory situations.

At the conclusion of learning episodes, I call attention to the contributions made by each person's style of participation. For example, I ask the group members to think about what just took place and ask them to summarize the conditions they saw contributing to these events. I also am likely to turn to those involved and inquire whether their responses were the ones they typically make in similar situations or whether there was something unique about their present reactions. Not only does my questioning encourage people to develop their understanding of what they individually bring to interpersonal transactions, but it also produces an awareness of the factors contributing to the learning processes which they have just observed.

In summarizing, I encourage participants to collect the impressions and reactions of the others present and to answer questions they might have about what has just taken place. Since I too participate, we all have a chance to expose the attributions we have made about what we just observed. Moreover, by this process we add dimensions to our developing relationships. Argyris (1968) believes that making attributions is an undesirable type of trainer intervention. In some ways I agree, and I tried to express this in my comments about defeating the propensity of people for letting "shoulds" influence their behavior. But I naturally make many attributions and participants usually make even a greater number. Therefore, I try to emphasize the importance of collecting information regarding attributions and of learning from the parts of one's self which are exposed in the process. New data about self are revealed when a person attributes one set of motives to data that equally well could support another. In the process, the entire group has the highly important and generalizable experience of collecting data which might have clarified some touchy issue if only they had asked themselves whether there was a chance they could have misunderstood the other person.

Another bridging intervention that I use is that of encouraging group members to bring critical back-home struggles to the group's attention. I do this after some valid basis for trust has been established and the problem-solving potential of relationships has been demonstrated by addressing the here-and-now problems in the group. My expectation is not that the group will be able to solve all, or any, critical back-home problems. Not only is it probable that these problems have persisted for some time, but also most are of an interpersonal nature and could only be solved by having the relevant parties present. I believe, however, that the ultimate validity of the training-group experience comes in focusing group resources on problems that really count. I encourage participants to discuss similarities between the problem-revealer's role in his problem and characteristics of his relationships with others in the group. This almost always leads to personal insights which are directly applicable to a participant's life outside the group.

If the group process is not developed to the point mentioned above,

I do not encourage—and often block—revealing critical back-home problems. While I usually will tell a participant that I do not think the group has yet made the most of its capacity for dealing with his problems, I often have another fear in mind. During the relationship-building phase that precedes collaborative problem-solving, everything a person says can be used against him. It is not that anyone is particularly malicious, but issues of power, love, and ambivalence often entail interpersonal acrobatics. Participants are usually quite vulnerable when addressing back-home conflicts, and I neither want to see anyone deeply hurt nor do I want other members to become afraid of discussing their own critical problems and thereby to forfeit a valuable opportunity for learning.

I will, however, often encourage disclosure by a participant who has given out cues that indicate he is deeply troubled about some out-of-the-group situation. I feel remiss in my responsibilities as a trainer if I do not give everyone a chance to participate. What constitutes a "chance" for a given person is always an individual decision. Usually I will call a participant's attention to the unique qualities of the training group which might justify his disclosure; I will also mention anything I know which might indicate that disclosure is a poor strategy—the presence of someone who might misuse this information in another context, for example. But most important, I ask the participant to state the conditions under which disclosure would be a good strategy and I encourage him to collect data bearing on these conditions. This gives others a chance to contribute their personal support.

CONCLUSION

This chapter is a personal consolidation; it gives me a new bench mark for my own growth and discovery, something like composing a journal at the end of analysis. Learning to become an effective trainer and learning to conceptualize seem very much tied to what I have learned by facing my own personal struggles. Then too, I have noted that trainers who try to circumvent their struggles when leading training groups often tend to be bland or inappropriate. The challenge which I continually confront is to find ways of facing my struggles without blocking or confusing others. When I succeed, I am often able to find ways to make my struggles useful to others.

I have wanted in this chapter to stimulate you to think about what you do and why. I realize that many of the positions I have taken are controversial and that many readers will have differences with me. My wish is that we both will learn from our differences. I hope my positions will stimulate you to new clarity and that I will hear of your views and have a chance to extract the learning that our differences can generate.

REFERENCES

Argyris, C. "Conditions for Competence Acquisition and Therapy." *Journal of Applied Behavioral Science* 4, no. 2 (1968): 144-177.

Campbell, J. P. and Dunnette, M. D. "Effectiveness of T-Group Experiences in Managerial Training and Development." *Psychological Bulletin* 70, no. 2 (1968): 73-104.

Culbert, S. A. "Accelerating Laboratory Learning through a Phase Progression Model for Trainer Intervention." *Journal of Applied Behavioral Science* 6, no. 1 (1970): 63-78.

Culbert, S. A. "Trainer Self-Disclosure and Member Growth in Two T Groups." *Journal of Applied Behavioral Science* 4, no. 1 (1968): 47-73.

Marrow, A. J. *Behind the Executive Mask.* New York: American Management Association, 1964.

Rogers, C. "Theory of Therapy, Personality, and Interpersonal Relationships, As Developed in the Client-Centered Framework." In *Psychology: A Study of Science,* vol. 3, edited by S. Koch. New York: Wiley & Sons, 1959.

Schutz, W. C. *Joy.* New York: Grove Press, 1967.

Design Developments in Group Training

Transactional Analysis As a Training Intervention

The late MICHAEL G. BLANSFIELD
President, Blansfield, Smith & Co.
Carmel, California

IN the 1960s, interest in the format and content of advanced sensitivity-training laboratories increased. Many people working in
applied behavioral science felt that an intensified sensitivity training
session was the appropriate way to deal with this interest. Others felt
that laboratories billed as advanced should concentrate their activities
on specific focuses, and laboratories such as "Personal Growth," *
"Conflict Management," and "Consultation Skills" resulted. One of
my solutions to the problem of making a sensitivity-training laboratory
truly advanced is to use transactional analysis as an initial training
intervention.

Transactional analysis, described by Dr. Eric Berne (1961, 1964), provides an optimistic and relatively jargon-free description of personality
and of the dynamics of intrapersonal and interpersonal relationships.
Its major premise is that each of us has three ego states, that is, sets of
attitudes and emotions linked to sets of behaviors. The three are called

---

* This laboratory focuses on creativity, body awareness, and contact and is drawn
primarily from the work of Dr. and Mrs. John Wier of Los Angeles, California.

Parent, Adult, and Child (capitalized to distinguish them from the actual parent, adult, or child). At any point, one of these ego states may be "running our show." It is possible to shift very rapidly from one to another, and our doing so depends usually upon the situation, or the person or persons we are with. For example, a friend who is being his Child (perhaps having fun or, alternatively, sulking) may engage our Child (who wants to have fun too) or our Parent (who responds to the Child with a lecture on sulking).

In most people the ego states have areas of overlap or "contamination"; the Parent or the Child or both usually contaminate the Adult. The overlap of the Parent over the Adult results in such irrational judgments as prejudice. The overlap of the Child over the Adult can cause phobias, manias, compulsions, or other neurotic behavior.

The state of being our Child is characteristically fixated in terms of age. That is, in the physically mature person the Child is of a consistent general age level and has a fairly predictable set of characteristics. The fixation occurs at some point between birth and maturation and is the result of a traumatic event, the memory of which is often repressed. Events and relationships in early life can also lead to a phenomenon called **decommissioning,** the "putting to sleep" of some part of one or more of the ego states. For example, a boy with a passive father and an aggressive mother may deal with the resulting role-model conflict by repressing or decommissioning the part of his Parent which he integrated from his father's behavior.

It often becomes apparent that one of the ego states operates more often than the others. This gives us some clues to the location of the "executive," the part that tends to control the actions. Ideally the executive should be in the Adult, where it can summon the Parent or the Child rationally and appropriately. However, the executive can be and often is located in the Parent, the Child, or in the areas of contamination.

BEGINNING PHASE

In beginning a program using transactional analysis, I usually explain that I am proposing a more structured beginning methodology than group members may have anticipated. I say that, with their concurrence, I will teach them something about a rather new psychiatric theory and ask them to use this lesson for self-analysis and reporting, and that we will then pursue whatever course the group wishes. At this point I always ask for expressions of feeling about the proposals. It

seems very important to uncover feelings of resistance to the intervention and to explore them until the whole group selects another
beginning methodology or the resistance is overcome. The possibility
that one or more members of the group will withdraw has not occurred
in my experience to date. (By the beginning of 1969 I had used this
methodology with at least twenty-five groups over a four-year period.
Groups of mixed sex and professional background, averaging twelve
per group, met usually for a week.) The groups to which I have proposed this approach have generally been enthusiastic about trying
something new. Our verbal contract has always contained the clear
understanding that during the process group members may ask questions or express resistance. Perhaps four persons of some three hundred
have actually done so. Questions arise almost exclusively about Berne's
theory, not its use in the group.

I next informally poll the group to confirm that we agree about our
immediate methodology. If we do, we proceed to a simplified presentation of the theory, a lecture-dialogue that usually lasts about three
hours. I try to cover the formation and characteristics of the three ego
states, their functioning, and the concepts of age fixation in the Child,
executive power, contamination, and decommissioning. Berne's theory
of transactions is not referred to at this point; it is dealt with later if
appropriate. In this initial phase, I try to convey only enough about
transactional analysis to enable each participant to describe himself in
terms of his understanding of the theory. Nor do I deal extensively at
this point with psychopathology or pathogenesis, for the populations
I work with are relatively stable and self-selecting and want increased
insight and understanding, not psychotherapy. An early emphasis on
neurosis or psychosis might cause them to conceal data they viewed as
excessively deviant from group norms.

APPLICATION OF THEORY

After an open-end question period I tell the group that I have
explained only part of the theory and that in a very simplistic manner.
I assure participants of my availability to assist them with their inevitable work and its interpretations, shades of meaning, and definitions.
I frequently illustrate the three ego states musically by playing selec-
tions from the light opera, Man of La Mancha. The song, "I'm Only
Thinking of Him," sung by Don Quixote's niece and housekeeper,
illustrates the Parent; "Aldonza," sung by a serving girl as she tries to
force Don Quixote to see her as she sees herself, is an illustration of

the Adult; Don Quixote's "The Impossible Dream" is an example of the Child in each of us. On the basis of an intuitive sense of differences, I then pair participants in "consulting pairs." For example, I try to pair a fairly silent, reserved person with one who is voluble and open. This pairing is one in which each can serve as a resource for the other at points of resistance to or difficulty in their next task. I stress, however, that it is not a dual effort.

Each person is to develop at least ten (and preferably more) words or phrases that describe his behavior in each of the three ego states. He is to estimate the age of his fixated Child, the approximate location of his executive, and the size and locations of his areas of contamination. The data is recorded on large sheets of newsprint. Each person then makes an informal record of the events that seem to him to have shaped his personality constellation and prepares to report on them. This task takes most group members at least four hours. Misunderstanding of self and/or theory cause much initial confusion.

After the newsprint sheets are finished, each group member reports pertinent autobiographical information and discusses his personality constellation. He is questioned by members of the group and is usually given additional data about the ways he has been perceived by the group. As each person reports on his schema of learning and insights (the initiation and subsequent rotation of reporting is a group decision), which are group wishes, the balance of the week is used to deal more extensively with the accumulated data.

During the preceding process my role varies. When group members are engaged in self-analysis, I usually help primarily by answering questions about procedures or by further interpretation and clarification of the theory Once the reporting commences, I tend to serve to clarify obvious misunderstanding of the theory and to underline significant personal content or highlight data relationships to provide a base for richer and deeper understandings. After the data reporting and discussions, I encourage the group to proceed in whatever way it wishes.

ACTION OUTCOMES

The members usually proceed to intensified grouping with frequent references to the material evolved about each person. A fairly consistent outcome of the process is a greatly enchanced understanding of the complexity and consistency of the self. For example, the description of the Parent helps a participant understand how he may act as a manager at work and/or at home and why he tends to act that way and indicates, through group feedback, some of the consequences of his Parental behavior. Group members are frequently surprised to find that only a portion of the Adult is available to them. With the help of the group they then begin to work on methods of enhancing and freeing the Adult. By discovering and trying to change previously unanalyzed, nonfunctional behavior, group members also become consciously aware, often for the first time, of the repressive role of the Parent on the Child and the consequent reduction in fun and play in their lives.

Another frequent outcome is the liberation of repressed feeling about "forgotten" episodes. As the week goes on I frequently hear, "I haven't thought of that for years." "I've never told anyone that before." "You [the group] know more about me than my husband [or wife or best friend]." In the right circumstances, the approach can also rather quickly liberate repressed feelings of some magnitude. Working in a group recently, a thirty-seven-year-old vice president of a major corporation presented a personality constellation that puzzled me. His description of his Parent was that of a brutal and cruel person, yet his Adult and Child were logical and loving. I felt this was a paradox that should be explored. I pointed out the discrepancy I saw and the participant got up, went to his newsprint chart (we had hung them on the wall but had not yet begun the reporting process) and wrote under his Child the word "cry." I asked him, "When did you cry, Jim? After looking at the floor for a few minutes he said, "When I was ten I awoke one night and heard a commotion in my parents' bedroom. I crept down the hall. Their door was ajar, and I saw my father beating and then raping my mother (the child's perception of the reality of the moment). I crawled down to the bathroom and lay on the floor in the dark crying for about an hour, and then had my first autosexual experience. Since then I have hated my father and have had at best unsatisfying sexual relations with women. I have never told anyone else about this before."

Feelings and behaviors of this nature and depth may lead to requests for extended help of a nature that a sensitivity-training laboratory cannot supply. Such reporting is important partly because it occurs in the first place and partly because it occurs in a context that permits appropriate therapeutic referral if the participant requests it. In this instance and numerous other of like nature, this has been the end result of reporting. This is not to say that group discussion and exploration of such a problem would be prohibited. However, in the limited time available, it is very unlikely that I would encourage pursuit of this problem for the balance, or even a major portion, of the group life at the expense of the remainder of the group.

CONCLUSION

The transactional analysis intervention is an action-oriented approach. It is concerned with organized self-understanding and, where appropriate and possible, with the alleviation of nonfunctional behavior. The trainer must be willing to take an action-oriented role rather than an interpretive and relatively passive one. He must also have a sound intellectual understanding of the Berne theory and an emotional acceptance of and commitment to it.

It is most helpful, if not essential, that participants have completed at least one prior laboratory experience and that they know in advance that the experience may be quite different from their previous laboratory experiences in entailing extensive and guided self-revelation. In addition, it is helpful if they are referred to books on the subject before the program begins.

To me one of the great values of the intervention is that it provides in systematic framework a great deal of personal information that the usual sensitivity-training laboratory brings out haphazardly or not at all. The helping relationships which I see as the most important tools of the sensitivity-training lab are developed by data that is systematically gathered.

Group members gain new insights and increased understanding of their own needs and drives. They understand each other in more integrated, meaningful ways and develop feelings of empathy and identification with each other more rapidly than in the usual sensitivity-training laboratory. They also tend to be more empathic and supportive in their feedback.

REFERENCES

Berne, Eric. *Games People Play: The Psychology of Human Relationships*. New York: Grove Press, 1964.
————. *Transactional Analysis in Psychotherapy*. New York: Grove Press, 1961.

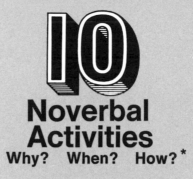

Noverbal Activities
Why? When? How?*

GOODWIN WATSON
Antioch College
Yellow Springs, Ohio

A^T the opening session of the American Association for Humanistic Psychology in San Francisco in September 1968, a trainer directed the nonverbal activities of some eight hundred adults in a large ballroom. For a time, participants milled about with closed eyes, encountered and touched others, tried briefly to envision the unseen person, and moved on.

At a resort in Minnesota in December 1968, forty business executives crawled around on the floor with closed eyes, exploring by touch and feel the others they encountered. Later these same executives gathered in quartets around card tables, cooperating without speaking in an effort to create satisfactory group finger paintings.

RAPID INCREASE

Illustrations like these could easily be multiplied—a California research institute has compiled an inventory of some three hundred

* The author wishes to acknowledge the assistance of Miss Joyce Goodrich for her help in preparing the materials in this chapter.

nonverbal group activities. The increase of nonverbal activities in training groups, sensitivity training, and encounter groups has been astonishing. No other innovation has so significantly altered the original training-group design in which members simply sat around a table and talked (or remained silent). The nonverbal activities at such places as the Esalen Institute have been described in newspapers and popular magazines reaching millions. Laboratory experiences incorporating nonverbal techniques have been conducted under the auspices of colleges, churches, school systems, and business corporations. Have participants gained anything but a personally exciting set of parlor games to try out on their friends?

NEED FOR THEORY

Participants usually describe their reactions to nonverbal techniques in general terms like interesting, unusual, stimulating, or unforgettable. Those who hear about such experiences secondhand often use a different set of terms: gimmicks, silly, acting out, bawdy, frivolous, shameless, or undignified. (The last two descriptions accord with the purposes of some of the methods—to reduce shame and cut through the separateness of dignity.)

But these are hardly precise terms. Why and when and under what conditions is nonverbal expression better than verbal? What are defensible criteria for the use of these new techniques? In no aspect of training-group leadership today is there more need for sound theory.

We shall begin our analysis by discussing ten areas in which non-verbal procedures may be useful.* Later we shall examine the activities in the light of several systems of theory. We can then summarize some recommendations to trainers. (We prefer Carl Rogers' term *facilitator* to the more conventional word *trainer*.)

Getting started. The milling around described in the first paragraph is one opening gambit, in this case an ice-breaking technique. The purpose of the crawling exercise in the second paragraph is to overcome barriers of dignity and prestige and in childlike behavior become more open to early feelings. This "regression in service of the ego" can be important in freeing creativity.

Another procedure is to form pairs of people who mirror each other's movements, often to music. In a second dyadic exercise, two

---

* A number of these headings were contributed by Mrs. Neila Horn of Boston, who has been developing a comprehensive set of categories.

people look closely at one another, studying facial expression, structure, shape. Then, with closed eyes, they try to reconstruct the image of the partner's face from memory and, finally, by sensitive touching.

All of these activities obviate the unproductive discussion which is likely to arise when people introduce themselves by describing their back-home roles and affiliations. Attention is directed to the here-and-now rather than to the there-and-then, and to specific feelings rather than to arguments and concepts. Sometimes activities of the kind listed here are used, along with brief periods of discussion, in an opening micro lab.

Building trust.   All theories of laboratory training recognize that development of trust is essential. In a common trust-building activity, one members stands in the center of a tight circle of his peers, closes his eyes, and lets himself fall backward. The others catch him; they may roll him around the group. The analogy between reliance on the group for physical support, however, and a real faith in their trustworthiness as confidantes is not perfect. One man who had said very little that was personal in his training group went through the falling-catching exercise. He said later that he had no fear of not being caught, but was still unwilling to expose his private life to the others.

Another activity used to build trust in many groups today is a kind of gentle lifting and rocking. One young woman who was carefully lifted and rocked by her group experienced sensations reminiscent of those she had felt toward people who had given her comfort when she was in labor. In a workshop for executives, a man who described his difficulties in trusting people was raised and lowered, then rocked gently, and again lowered by his group. He was in tears as he reported the flood of trusting feelings he had experienced. A year later he wrote of the experience as one of the most influential of his life. In contrast, the person who was passed by two rows of hands around a double circle experienced it as only a pleasant back massage and an enjoyable sense of movement without any noteworthy personal meaning.

Still another exercise which lends itself to trust-building is the blind walk. Participants operate in pairs. One member of each pair closes his eyes. For four to five minutes his partner leads him carefully through the room, into corridors, and perhaps out-of-doors. (Sensitivity to one's surroundings as well as trustingness may be increased if the guide provides opportunities for the blind partner to feel objects of differing textures and to sense changes in temperature and weather.) Participants then switch roles. In such a clearly defined situation, issues of dependence and independence are very susceptible of evaluation.

Increasing awareness.   A group may begin a session lying on the floor with closed eyes while a quiet, gentle voice leads a guided meditation, calling attention to a score of sensations often present but usually ignored. Charlotte Selver (1966) has pioneered this kind of training in the United States. Her aim is to help create an integrated person whose potential is released because he has become more fully aware of feelings and sensations and is freer to respond to them— a person who has regained many of the open sensitivities to self, to others, and to surroundings which were present in infancy and childhood. Miss Selver has developed restorative experiences done while lying, sitting, standing, or walking slowly. She feels that two persons who concentrate with open sensitivity on one another, not trying to do anything except to be responsive to their interaction, can become very truly in touch without actually touching. She says, that most people want to do something for their partner instead of simply being there. Once this capacity for responsiveness is felt, however, interactive experiences (in which something may or may not be done) become more valuable, and their quality seems deeper and more subtle.

In one of the exercises, one of the dyad lies quietly on his back on the floor while the other sits behind the head of his prone partner. When given a signal by the latter, the sitting partner puts his hands on the recumbant person's head, face, or hair. He keeps his hands lightly in each place long enough for the other to savor the sensation. The quality of the touch tells the partner a great deal. It is a form of communication sensed by both. This experience may also include firmly yet gently lifting the head and slowly moving it up, down, and to the side before returning it slowly and gently to its resting place. If the reclining partner is able to trust the one lifting his head, he will "give it up"—not use his neck muscles to control its movement. The aftermath has sometimes found the participants describing one another in terms like "You look absolutely beatific," or "You seem so at peace."

Another technique for increasing awareness is to tap or slap oneself "alive." The intensity of touch depends on what feels right for each part of the body. The procedure is to slap or tap face, arms, chest, legs, hips, or back, and at the same time, without trying to control or alter breathing, to be aware of changes in it. The goal is not a floppy, droopy relaxation, but a healthy aliveness, a sense of being in harmony with one's own inner needs and with the environment.

Facilitating disclosure and diagnosis.   A wise and experienced facilitator learns a great deal about individuals from the way in which they sit, stand, speak, gesture, or walk. Even very simple movements can be revealing to the trained eye of the leader, and what he can see he can help his group members to see.

In one exercise, couples lie on their backs on the floor, their bodies touching only at the shoulders, and their feet extended in opposite directions. Each raises the hand closest to his partner and, listening to music with varied moods and tempos, "dances" with his partner's hand. Initiative or dependence, cooperation or competition, hostility or affection, insensitivity or empathy, stereotyped movement or creativity—these and other personality dimensions may be revealed.

In one laboratory of school administrators, a strong bamboo pole about six-feet long happened to be standing in the corner of the room. Spurred by a sudden inspiration, the trainer suggested that four group members, two on a side, hole the rod with both hands. Then the trainer said, "Don't talk, but but do anything you like with the pole." The participants might have created a dance. Instead they immediately launched a violent struggle for control. One man in particular tried to dominate the other three; their resistance grew. Later the participants and observers commented on their surprise at the competitive attitudes which emerged so clearly and strongly.

Confronting.   An exercise often used with strangers in an early session asks them to form lines against two opposite walls, with each participant facing a partner across the room. If men and women are about equal in numbers, opposite sex pairs are sometimes formed. At a signal, and perhaps with music, each person moves very slowly toward his partner. Each attempts to adapt his own pace to that of his partner. They watch each other closely for clues about how close to approach, trying to sense where invisible "life-space-shelters" encounter each other. The aim is to come as close as the shelters permit without violating the comfort range of the partner. The exercise is then discussed. If the activity is repeated with other partners, the repetition seems to decrease the distance between participants' shelters.

Another exercise introduces the dimension of dominance and submission. Partner A places his hands on the shoulders of Partner B and tries to push B to his knees or even to force his forehead to the floor. Then A lifts B up and the roles are reversed. Feelings during this confrontation are also discussed. The issue of male dominance is particularly likely to arise in mixed pairs.

One of the most common kinds of confrontation is when one member volunteers (or is selected as a volunteer) to go around the group, pausing in front of each member, to express nonverbally some kind of genuine feeling. This works best if it is limited to one or two rounds in any single session, as it becomes forced and time-consuming if all members participate.

Confrontation issues can be joined when members are asked to reach nonverbal consensus. For instance, in one group quartets were asked to determine which member of the four was most tense. This initially produced disagreement. When it was decided, however, members were able to agree on ministering actions—flexing limbs, stroking, holding, and patting. This is an entirely nonverbal supportive encounter. Some in the quartets ministered *to* the subject, but some truly communicated *with* him in their nonverbal interaction. Similar exercises can be used to confront members with feelings such as apathy.

An important kind of feedback can be developed nonverbally by arranging in a row as many chairs as there are group members. One dimension of group interaction is selected, at first by the facilitator but later by other members. If the dimension is "influence within the group," the chair at one end of the row is designated "most influence" and the chair at the other end "least influence." All group members are asked to go without speaking to their proper places in the line. The confrontation develops when each member looks at those above and below him in the influence hierarchy. Some see others as out of place. Each tries by gentle gesture to move these persons up or down in rank position. When disagreements develop, other members are appealed to (still nonverbally) as arbiters. Sometimes the pressure to move a member up or down in the scale becomes more vigorous than gentle. Real struggles occasionally arise. The same device can be used to rank members on warmth, hostility, competiveness, empathy, or any other trait observable in the group. Each member is confronted by different perceptions of where he truly belongs and by differences between his self-images and the impressions prevailing in his group.

Including and excluding.   From the secret clubs of childhood to the adult community, a major distinction is that between the "ins" and the "outs." One useful device for making this factor more apparent is a sociometric diagram. Each member is given a sheet of paper with a circle in the center to represent himself. He then draws circles to symbolize the positions of other members of the group. Those to whom the member feels closest are drawn close to his own circle. Those toward the outside of the sheet are the ones who seem distant and remote. Members seen as belonging to informal cliques are included within a dotted-line circle. The exercise is sometimes modified to include other dimensions. Persons are drawn in colors which seem appropriate to the artist. The size of the circle may vary also from large for the more influential members to small for those who have minimal impact on the group. Drawings are passed around and discussed.

Another kind of exercise sometimes used near the beginning of the laboratory requires that participants form trios which then split— deciding on whatever basis feels right—to become a pair and an excluded singleton. The pairs then work together or form quartets. The singletons form new trios and repeat the separating and pairing process. This can be painful, even traumatic, for individuals who are several times excluded. On the other hand, individuals who do not easily exclude others may benefit by the opportunity to practice rejection when it is really felt. One reason for doing this exercise early in the laboratory is that some can comfort themselves with the thought that they do not yet really know others and are not yet known by them except superficially.

A physical expression of the desire to belong is the "break in." A college girl whose whining had led others to exclude her tried to break through the closed ranks of the group circle. She spent nearly half an hour bucking the tight wall, but eventually slipped inside. This did not wholly restore her self-esteem, for she asked, "Why were others accepted without a struggle; why did I have to battle my way in?" At the same time, she knew she had won against odds, and she was more fully accepted by other members than she had been before. The physical contacts also contributed to a sense of intimacy and solidarity. (The "break out," the simple reverse of this exercise, can lead to feelings of greater freedom and openness.)

Releasing anger.   Most people have been taught to repress angry feelings. The resentment which is held in may find expression in chronic tensions of the body, distortive thinking, and in generally hostile attitudes which poison interpersonal relations.

A calmly spoken statement, "I am now feeling angry at you," does not go far enough to trigger real emotional release. Hence, members of sensitivity-training groups are sometimes encouraged to make threatening gestures, to stamp and scream, and to pound a pillow or couch with both hands locked together. A punching bag might well be routine equipment; perhaps better would be one of the inflated, big-as-life objects which can be socked again and again in a reenactment of anger.

Rivalry and competition are present at times in most groups, and a widely known technique for bringing out these feelings is some form of wrestling. Thumb wrestling, arm wrestling, Indian leg wrestling, or just plain grappling in an attempt to down the opponent can be tried. These "fights" seem to serve as a catharsis for the participants and, to a lesser extent, for the observers. Usually both the winner and the loser feel better after the struggle. Who comes out on top has become less important; each respects the other more and they are drawn toward comradeship. A contest with the facilitator often helps to free feelings bound up in attitudes toward authority figures.

Sometimes the need for a good fight is not clearly related to rivalry with any single individual. In one group a charming, able girl grew increasingly tense and preoccupied. Suddenly she said, "I want to fight one of the men! Any one!" It did not matter who, as long as he would really put his full strength into the battle. After a tussle which ranged into all corners of the room, she was definitely held down. She arose able to cry and to laugh more freely. It is hard for trainers who themselves have been brought up to avoid honest conflict to appreciate, until they have experienced it, that the aftermath of physical struggle is likely to be increased closeness, spontaneity, warmth, and good humor. This is similar to the reaction after "breaking in."

Sometimes a more playful, symbolic fight is sufficient. In one group where tension was felt, the perceptive facilitator asked one of the male members what he felt like doing. That man responded by asking all the other men to stand and gather in a group. Then he began bumping his shoulders against theirs, and they bumped one another and him. In this case, possibly because he needed affectionate but somewhat competitive contact with other men to ease his rather rigid ways of relating, he had chosen a man-style encounter which was structured to include those values but to avoid a win-lose situation. The mood was an affectionate expression of strength, and it felt right for everyone.

Another kind of symbolic fight can be done with loosely rolled newspapers which make quite satisfying noises and do no real damage. A good donnybrook can be very refreshing when a group is bogged down.

Fantasy.   Fantasy exercises are not strictly nonverbal, but they differ from rational disclosure in much the same way as do the various action techniques. The variety of fantasies which groups can generate is inexhaustible. One form imagines the group together on some adventure—on a ship or climbing a mountain or exploring new territory. Another asks that members see one another in fancy dress for a masquerade, as fictional or historical characters, or as animals. More inward-moving processes are evoked by imagining oneself as very small, then entering and going on a trip within one's own body. There is also the group fantasy of a strange cave in which, after overcoming obstacles and terrors, one finds something especially meaningful.

The mini-dream is another productive technique. Participants are relaxed and quiet; eyes closed, they drift toward sleep. They are told that at a signal they will probably begin a dream. They are asked not to use effort to imagine something, but rather to relax and let images and happenings develop as on a television screen. After a few minutes the dream is terminated and shared. Sometimes a group can fantasy cooperatively, each adding a phrase or sentence which carries forward what others have contributed. Group discussion follows. If someone introduces a discordant image, the incident can also be explored.

Finger painting or working with colored crayons can provide nonverbal expressions of fantasy. A procedure we have found especially rewarding is to ask members to let an abstract design emerge unplanned. Participants select a color at random and make a line or form. As colors are added and the picture takes form, the participant asks, "What is the significance of this? What, in my life, or in this group, could it represent? What does this begin to feel like?" From this point on, the artist can consciously develop the image to bring out the meaning or to elaborate some key items. Group members then describe their reactions to the drawings. If the pictures are hung in a meeting room and left for several days, their meaning often becomes clearer.

These fantasy techniques are related to some of the experiences for developing awareness. They might also have been discussed under the heading of *Facilitating disclosure and diagnosis.* They provide many clues to inner conflicts, frustrations, and aspirations. Moreover, the expression alone can be good for the participant even if it is not brought into a framework of interpretation and diagnosis. The life of the mind and body is playful as well as purposeful.

Enjoying.   Many nonverbal activities are fun, and this in itself can be a justification for their use in some groups at some times. Much depends on the purposes of the individual and the group session. Groups in which members are paying for personal therapy or for increased skill in leadership and problem-solving have a right to expect procedures which carry more significant opportunities for learning than fun alone provides. In such groups, nonverbal techniques are inadequate if they are merely titillating and amusing.

A good case in point is the "greeting card factory" exercise which was often used in NTL Institute laboratories about ten years ago. It was lively, competitive fun, and some memorable verses emerged. Gradually, however, it was abandoned because the resultant learnings about the organization and management of a productive enterprise were too meager.

The simple parlor game must be related to the deeper purposes of the group and its dynamic state. A group achieves its purposes using both work and play, humor and seriousness, but too much of either may mean that the group is avoiding here-and-now issues, that defenses are not being touched and opened, or that involvement and trust have not been achieved within a democratic atmosphere.

Ending.   The end of a group that has become a living social unit may call for some kind of appropriate ritual. One which we have found productive is the exchange of gifts from a magic store. Each member tells what he has bought there to give to each other member. It is a fantasy exercise which produces meaningful feedback.

Perhaps the most frequent nonverbal termination is formation of a tight circle in which each member is warmly held by those beside him. The group stands quietly through the surge of feelings until "fullness" is felt. Spontaneous humming or singing may help to achieve this feeling of completion.

A variant of this arose spontaneously in one college laboratory when the student body president sought out his political rival and they linked arms; others quickly joined the moving chain. They circled the room and then moved into a spiral which brought everyone into a close-pressed coil. After a period of silent communion, the members went their separate ways.

THEORETICAL CONCEPTS

Too many groups and facilitators pick nonverbal techniques without considering whether the "gimmick" is really the most appropriate procedure for the persons involved, for the group, or for the present stage of personal development and group life. Critical evaluation must have foundation in theory. There are a number of systems within which nonverbal activities can be understood and evaluated. The systems can only be mentioned here, not fully presented.

Training-group theory.   Since most readers are familiar with this approach, and various aspects are elaborated in other chapters of this book, it will be sufficient to simply recall such terms and concepts as these: initial leadership vacuum, rivalry for power, growth of trust, movement from dependence or counter-dependence toward independence, a stage of pseudo-harmony when negative attitudes are repressed, risk-taking, experimental trial of new behaviors, feedback, decision-making, and true consensus.

Nonverbal procedures are likely to be especially facilitative in expressing competition for control, testing trust, getting beyond pseudo-harmony, building readiness to try new behavior, supplying data for feedback, and sharpening awareness of unspoken attitudes and feelings.

One important clash between traditional training-group theory and the newer exercises occurs in the realm of dependence. If a micro lab of brief encounters is conducted by the facilitator as an opening session, some behaviors such as self-disclosure and direct confrontation may be speeded up, but the facilitator is likely to be seen as a director. After suggesting nonverbal activities several times, we often find that the group expects us to continue to bring out new tricks. If we then return to the traditional nondirective trainer role, the group seems to have even more difficulty accepting responsibility for its own procedures than if this relationship had been established in the first sessions. This conflict can be relieved somewhat if the group works together long enough for members to develop the ability to propose appropriate nonverbal activities. A similar result has been noted in groups whose members have been through several laboratories in which a variety of nonverbal procedures have been experienced. The members are quite willing to suggest and to direct these, and the facilitator can easily remain in the role of interpreter.

In most groups of inexperienced participants, the facilitator will have to choose between the values of the learning which comes to members when they are quite freely self-directing and the values which come from conducted activities. In the short weekend groups which have become very frequent, the traditional pattern of the training group seldom has time to evolve, and facilitators tend to take a more directive role.

The apparent conflict between a need to help the group be self-reliant and a desire to suggest appropriate nonverbal activities can be minimized if the facilitator clearly respects democratic values and sees himself as only a member with some special resources. He then offers his suggestions in such a way that they can be amended or rejected. He encourages other members to devise ways of helping the group. He calls attention to any tendency, even the unspoken one, to rely too much on him.

Learning theory. Most learning theory postulates a situation in which learner complacency is disturbed. The learner initiates behavior which he has previously used with apparent success. If this fails, he reexamines the situation and tries something else. If it succeeds, the behavior is reinforced and is likely to be used in other situations perceived as similar.

Nonverbal exercises bring out this sequence with unusual clarity. The challenge of the situation evokes trial of unaccustomed responses which may prove effective or ineffective or be felt as personal triumph or failure. Successful nonverbal experiential learning leads to intense and deep responses at a feeling level. The affective element in this kind of learning, followed by description and discussion, tends to touch more deeply and to be more readily recalled than purely cognitive, verbal learning.

If the purpose of the training group is improved behavior in an organizational setting back home, obvious differences in the situation may limit the transfer of what has been learned from verbal or nonverbal encounters. Studies of transfer of training have shown that if new learning is really internalized, the probability is increased that it will be applied in other situations. The implication is that group members should be encouraged to do more than respond actively to specific directions. If as they consider their experiences in the group, they can form new attitudes, insights, or concepts, they can carry away more that will be useful in other settings.

Too few participants see their back-home situation as very similar to their laboratory experiences. This sad fact produces the expected result: participants report that they have had a satisfying experience, but they do not attempt transfer. Rather, they look for another chance to enter a group and reenact what they found satisfying. We get what Bugental has called "groupies"—those who only dimly exist between the workshops in which they can really come alive.

Psychoanalytic theory. Group therapy which is psychoanalytically oriented centers mainly upon the analysis of transference, resistance, and the strengthening of the ego. Nonverbal activities afford excellent opportunities for experiencing and observing transference. The facilitator may be experienced as a good or a bad parent. Other members' responses may be directed initially at siblings, mother or father figures, or love objects. The quality of each relationship shows more clearly during incidents of conflict, physical contact, joint movement, or psychodrama, than in verbal reports. Most training groups do not encourage the association of memories to present behavior, and so fall short of reaching full potential of the experience for therapeutic growth. The dimension of depth is missing. Behavior in the here-and-now is reflected in feedback but is not consciously related to its origins. To add the "historic" factor does not mean that the facilitator has to set forth his own interpretations. He will be much wiser, if he wants to move in this direction, to encourage soliloquy about earlier versions of the present dynamic relationships. It may be expected that if more time is kept free for individuals to ruminate on connections between their present experiences and their earlier memories, more participants will come away with insights they can transfer to new situations.

Intensive work in the area of sensory awareness can produce a marked transference. At the end of a Selver course, one participant wrote, "Out of my experience with the work, I developed a feeling of great, warm, easy, trusting love. It was as if I had turned her into the good mother and was again experiencing what a tiny child must feel in a healthy symbiotic state. It was not controlling—it was allowing and cleansing."

Analysis of resistance can easily be, but rarely has been, associated with trying new nonverbal activities. Gestalt therapy often encourages a patient to dramatize an encounter between two imagined persons, one a spokesman for a new venture, the other against it. To enliven the dialogue, two chairs may be set up; the patient moves from one to the other as he changes roles. Again the historic dimension plays a large part in the understanding.

The fact that most educated persons implement their defenses with words is a strong argument for more nonverbal approaches. The evasion and parrying which can persist in talk sessions breaks down rather quickly in more physical encounters. Feelings may be gotten to more readily and more intensely.

As for ego building, the wider variety of activities is a great help. People who are not easily articulate are given new channels for influence and experience and for demonstrating competence. The highly verbal may find even minor success in nonverbal performance especially rewarding. Beneath their loquacity often lingers a suspicion that they are fooling the world with words. A successful nonverbal experience may do more to enhance their self-image than winning another score of debates.

Semantics.   Alfred Korzybski (1933, p. 19) and his followers have called attention to the disorders which spring from regarding words as truly equivalent to their referents: "The map is not the territory."

One formulation of experience along the time dimension begins with an event. It next recognizes the sensory perception, the emotional reactions, and the behavioral and movement responses which this produces. The symbolic linguistic expressions come last. As long as we remain in the realm of words, we risk making no, or only a very slight, connection with the more primitive layers of behavior response, feeling, and sensory awareness. The nonverbal movement is really coming to grips with phenomena more fundamental than signs and symbols. Words should follow, not take the place of, real encounters.

Sociological theory.   A sociological approach to laboratory training groups looks at the norms. The process of growing up in families, schools, churches, and other community institutions has instilled a set of usually unconscious norms. One "should" or "should not" say, feel, or do. The "shoulds" overlie experience until real feelings are no longer recognized.

What the training group, encounter group, or psychotherapy group does is to provide a new set of norms. Since the norms prevailing in the larger society are, in part, restrictive and crippling, the countervailing norms of the laboratory groups are felt to be liberating. Real anger can be expressed without polite cover-ups. Warm feelings or sexual feelings can be openly recognized instead of evaded. Obligation to the true self replaces pressure to achieve. The discovery of real, many-faceted persons supplants the view of self and others in a role. The result is a new and more authentic experience of self and of relations with genuine others.

A concept from anthropology, that of culture shock, is helpful in understanding the difficulties in transition from the back-home norms to those of the laboratory. Some resistance, bewilderment, and belittling of the new norms are to be expected. They are suspected of being contrived and pretentious. It takes time to learn to appreciate and use the countervailing culture. That the new culture is experienced only tentatively and provisionally may be a major argument against the weekend group; pretended conformity to the new norms may be more frequent than real assimilation and understanding.

The transition from the utopian cultural island to the established community may be even more difficult. Some who have not been deeply and vitally affected by the laboratory experience find it rather simple. In Rome, they do as the Romans do. Back in the old rat race they run their usual treadmill. Others react by planning to return to other groups as soon and as often as possible. Still another adjustment is to develop a satisfying inner life and to participate only peripherally in the workaday world. A better adaptation is made by those who become, within the limits of their influence, change agents. Thus we find that more businessmen have been able to make significant changes in their family life than in corporate procedures and attitudes. A few who have been deeply involved in the laboratory experiences, both verbal and non-verbal, and who have changed their whole concept of what it means really to live, may become alienated from all that pertains to the Establishment. They may "turn on and drop out." The student protest movement is giving some young people social support in an effort to achieve values rather like those achieved in successful verbal and nonverbal encounters.

Life against death. Norman Brown (1959) has carried psychoanalytic theory to a new level and one of special relation to the non-verbal procedures. In contrast to Freud, he assumes that an unrepressed life is actually possible. He contrasts the death-directed efforts of repression, separation, individualism, conformity, renunciation, and guilt with such life-enhancing values as freedom, spontaneity, play, living in the present, acceptance of the whole self, interdependence, and joy in living.

An honest look at many laboratories organized around managerial training and powered basically by achievement motives reveals very little challenge to the corporate culture, with its controls, correctness, schedules, and limited goal-seeking. Most nonverbal activities tend to emphasize release from the pressure of obligations, awareness of and respect for the body, creative quest for richer experience with others, and playful enjoyment. They come much closer to the life side of the life-death dichotomy. Sooner or later the whole laboratory enterprise may face a divisive conflict between the two styles of training. Organizational effectiveness and self-actualization may be incompatible goals.

Other theories. This section is by no means exhaustive. We might have explored the connection of nonverbal experiences with Adler's "Gemeinschaftsgefühl"; with Horney's categories of moving toward, against, or away from others; with our need to correct what Sullivan called "parataxic distortion"; or with the balance Jung sought among the four functions of sensing, feeling, knowing, and intuition. We might, if we were better acquainted with Asian psychology, have viewed nonverbal experiences in the light of Yoga or Zen. There is a place also for openness toward things in heaven and earth that are not dreamed of in most of our philosophies.

SOME RECOMMENDATIONS

- Nonverbal activities can make an important contribution but they should not be adopted wholesale or used indiscriminately.
- A good facilitator will offer the possibility of nonverbal activities when they seem appropriate and in such a way as to preserve democratic control by the group over its own program.
- A good facilitator will, before suggesting or approving a nonverbal exercise, ask himself why it is appropriate and if there are other or better ways of achieving what the group, or certain persons in it, presently need.
- A good facilitator will sense empathically the readiness of group members for new forms of activity and will move with them, encouraging each to advance at his own rate, and allowing for a range of individual differences.
- A good facilitator is guided by insight into what is happening within the group and within each individual; he may act on this insight but should not try to explain all his diagnoses. He also submits his insights to an ongoing process of checking whether the responses he expected actually occur.
- A good facilitator can relate what is happening in the group and in each individual to a body of concepts and theory which he has found experientially and intellectually satisfying. He acts on these ideas but does not try to "teach" them to the group. Neither should he refuse to provide a helpful explanation if the members request it.
- On the basis of his systematic thought and his empathic insights, a good facilitator will be constantly evolving new activities, both nonverbal and verbal. If a trainer finds himself repeatedly relying on a limited set of devices, verbal and nonverbal, he may be following a course of least resistance rather than reflecting truly involved, creative, yet solidly grounded thought and behavior.
- A good facilitator will use activities in a developmental sequence, starting with the relatively simple, and moving gradually, as his group grows in competence, toward deeper involvement and more complex performance.
- A good facilitator will provide ample opportunity for group members to review, appraise, think about, associate to, understand, and apply what they have been experiencing. A series of unexamined experiences brings little learning.
- A good facilitator may begin with conscious attention to such guidelines as these and to the relevant theory. Eventually, as his own experience matures, he will find himself able to do the right thing at

the right time on the basis of what he feels and observes. A new trainer may be tempted to neglect the disciplined critical thought which underlies good learning in a group and to try immediately to do intuitively whatever feels right. This is perilous. Intuition without a foundation of disciplined thought, sound theory, and extensive experience is not sufficiently trustworthy. Leading a training group, or any other group, in either verbal or nonverbal procedures looks deceptively easy when it is well done by an experienced facilitator. We are about to suffer the painful consequences of amateur leadership of groups in the performance of activities which have been picked up as gimmicks and inappropriately used.

There are too few publications which supply theoretical foundations for insight into the consequences of various forms of nonverbal activity. The bibliography which follows offers some points of view which may prove helpful in developing more adequate theory.

BIBLIOGRAPHY

Brenner, C. *Elementary Textbook of Psychoanalysis.* New York: Doubleday & Co., 1957.

Buber, M. *I and Thou.* New York: Charles Scribner's Sons, 1958.

Bugental, J. F. T., ed. *Challenges of Humanistic Psychology.* New York: McGraw-Hill, 1967.

Burton, A., ed. *Encounter.* San Francisco: Jossey-Bass, 1969.

Groddeck, G. *The Book of the It.* New York: Random House, 1961.

Grossman, C. and Grossman, S. *The Wild Analyst; The Life and Work of Georg Groddeck.* New York: Dell Publishing Co., 1965.

Gustaitis, A. *Turning On.* New York: Macmillan Co., 1969.

Hall, E. *The Silent Language.* New York: Doubleday & Co., 1959.

Howard, J. *Please Touch; A Guided Tour of the Human Potential Movement.* New York: McGraw-Hill, 1970.

Isherwood, C.; Heard, G.; Huxley, A.; and Vivekananda, S., eds. *Vedanta for the Western World.* New York: Viking Press, 1960.

Jourard, S. *The Transparent Self; Self-Disclosure and Well-Being.* New York: Van Nostrand Reinhold Co., 1964.

Kapleau, P., ed. *The Three Pillars of Zen; Teaching, Practice, and Enlightenment.* Boston: Beacon Press, 1965.

Lowen, A. *Physical Dynamics of Character Structure.* New York: Grune & Stratton, 1958.

Malamud, D. I. and Machover, S. *Toward Self-Understanding, Group Techniques in Self-Confrontation.* Springfield, Ill.: Charles C. Thomas, Publishers, 1965.

Maslow, A. *Toward a Psychology of Being,* 2nd ed. New York: Van Nostrand Reinhold Co., 1968.
Murphy, G. and Lois B. *Asian Psychology.* New York: Basic Books, 1968.
Perls, F.; Hefferline, R.; Goodman, P. *Gestalt Therapy.* New York: Dell Publishing Co., 1951.
Reich, W. *Character Analysis.* New York: Farrar, Straus, and Co., 1949.
Rogers, C. *Freedom to Learn.* Columbus, Ohio: Charles E. Merrill Publishing Co., 1969.
Schilder, P. *The Image and Appearance of the Human Body.* New York: International Universities Press, 1950.
Schutz, W. C. *Joy.* New York: Grove Press, 1967.
Shattuck, E. H. *An Experiment in Mindfulness.* New York: E. P. Dutton & Co., 1960.
Shepard, M. and Lee, M. *Marathon, 16.* New York: G. P. Putnam's Sons, 1970.
Whyte, L. L. *The Next Development in Man.* New York: New American Library, Mentor Books, 1950.

REFERENCES

Brown, N. O. *Life against Death.* New York: Random House, 1959.
Korzybski, A. *Science and Sanity.* Lakeville, Conn.: International Non-Aristotelian Library Publishing Co., 1933.
Selver, C. "Report on Work in Sensory Awareness and Total Functioning." In *Explorations in Human Potentialities,* edited by Herbert Otto. Springfield, Ill.: Charles C. Thomas, Publishers, 1966.

Group
Methods and
Organization
Development

Some Differences between Laboratory and Nonlaboratory Organizations

Implications for Group Trainers Who Desire to Be Organization Development Consultants

JERRY B. HARVEY
The George Washington University
Washington, D.C.

SHELDON A. DAVIS
TRW Systems
Redondo Beach, California

GROUP trainers are frequently asked to apply their skills to improving the functioning of organizations. Such requests reflect both the trainers' success in the laboratory setting and the real potential of the impact of laboratory method on the culture, its organizations, and institutions.

However, the group trainer who has tremendous influence in the laboratory organization frequently finds that his effect on "real life" organizations is limited or even nonexistent. For the trainer who is used to the euphoric closing of the laboratory and the concurrent adulation of its participants, the experience of being impotent, irrelevant, or unsuccessful is, at best, jarring and, at worst, devastating. We think the latter experience is unnecessary.

Understanding the differences between laboratories and other organizations is important if a sensitivity trainer is to become skillful as an organization development consultant. One reason trainers are frequently ineffective in nonlaboratory environments is that they are unaware of some of these differences. As a consequence, they enter such organizations with assumptions and skills which may be irrelevant or dysfunctional. In addition, they may lack certain skills which are required in order to be effective. The trainer may be faced with the need both to develop new skills and assumptions, and to divest himself of others he has used in the context of the training laboratory.

We would like to articulate some of the similarities and differences between laboratory and nonlaboratory organizations and discuss their implications for sensitivity trainers who aspire to be organization development consultants. In addition, we suggest ways in which the trainer may better prepare himself to work effectively in organizations.

First, it is important to provide definitions of organization development and laboratory training and to distinguish between laboratory training in general and sensitivity training in particular.

When we speak of organization development (also referred to as OD), we mean change interventions which are based on the theoretical work of, among others, McGregor (1960), Lewin (1951), Likert (1961), Blake and Mouton (1964), Maslow (1965), Argyris (1962) and Schein, Bennis, and Beckhard (1969). These theories provide impetus for more effective problem-solving, better decision-making, more reliable communication, decreased demotivation, increased collaboration, the integration of human values with technology, and greater consequent organizational productivity within all kinds of organizations. Specific applications of the theories take place with respect to matters such as the organization of production processes, the manner by which control is exercised, the reward systems within the organization, and the structure and character of relationships existing among individuals and units within the organization. In its most general sense, organization development concerns the ways and means by which behavioral science knowledge is applied to the integration of human and technological systems to fulfill the requirements of organizations for productive functioning.

Laboratory training, on the other hand, is a form of experience-based educational technology which is designed to teach individuals about interpersonal, small-group, and organization behavior. It generally involves sensitivity training (training groups) (Bradford, Gibb, and Benne 1964) as a central part of its training design, although there are other experience-based educational strategies—for example, those involving instrumentation (Blake and Mouton 1962, pp. 61-76)—which are encompassed by laboratory method. Thus, sensitivity or group training is one form of laboratory method which, in turn, is only one type of behavioral science intervention that might be applied to organization development efforts.

In this chapter we will restrict ourselves to behavioral science interventions based on laboratory method and will not deal with any of the other change technologies such as systems analysis, cost effectiveness, and survey research, any of which might be employed in organization development work.*

A second set of definitions important to our discussion concerns the distinction between laboratory and nonlaboratory organizations.

When we talk about a laboratory organization, we are referring to a sensitivity-training laboratory. Structurally, a laboratory organization generally includes a training staff and a group of participants who are strangers † to one another. The learning design usually involves some combination of training groups, general sessions, and exercises. The overall purpose of the organization is to produce learning about individual, group, intergroup, and organization phenomena through the medium of experience-based educational technology.

In contrast, a nonlaboratory organization is one such as General Motors, the Baptist Church, the Boy Scouts, or the University of Texas. Although the purposes of these organizations vary, they are not in general predominantly those of learning about self and others, and the basic process underlying the organizations' operation is not experience-based learning.

Finally, in discussing the sensitivity trainer, we refer to the person whose role is that of a staff member in a training laboratory organization. On the other hand, the organization development consultant is the trainer who leaves the training laboratory and takes a role in the life stream of nonlaboratory organizations. The roles are quite different.

SIMILARITIES BETWEEN LABORATORY AND NONLABORATORY ORGANIZATIONS

As a point of departure, it is important to recognize that the training laboratory is an organization. For the trainer who revels in the idea of

---

* Another paper could certainly be written about the means by which laboratory method and other approaches to organization development might be creatively combined so that the employment of the various methods does not lead to destructive win-lose competition among them.

† We specifically use "stranger" laboratories as the prototype laboratory organization because they are the most opposite in character from nonlaboratory organizations. As stranger laboratories become "cousins," "diagonal," "family," and "interface" laboratories, the difference between the laboratory and the nonlaboratory organization diminishes.

non-structure and expresses dismay at the prospect of working within a structured organization, this may be quite disturbing. Nevertheless, the trainer's acceptance of this fact is important, for it is because a training laboratory is an organization with structures and dynamics similar to those of nonlaboratory organizations that the transfer of laboratory learning experiences to nonlaboratory organizations is possible.

In the language of "formal" organizations (Argyris 1957), a training laboratory has a number of characteristics in common with any other organization.

A hierarchy or chain of command.   In its most complex form, the laboratory has a dean (top management), a training staff (middle management), and a group of participants (labor or workers).

Although power and exercise of power may be different in the hierarchy of a laboratory organization from that in other organizations, the laboratory still has a formal, identifiable hierarchy through which formal power and influence are exercised.

A span of control.   According to Argyris (ibid., p. 64), "The principle of span of controls states that administrative efficiency is increased by limiting the span of control of a leader to no more than five or six subordinates whose work interlocks." For the laboratory organization, the same principle is in operation. Learning efficiency is increased by limiting the span of control of the trainer to no more than twelve subordinates whose learning needs are similar. The names of the learning groups may vary (T Groups, clusters, instrumented groups, or development groups), but the important point is that the concept of span of control does exist in the laboratory setting.

Task specialization.   This principle states that organizational effectiveness is increased by assigning specialized tasks to the organization's members. In the industrial organization, such specialization may take the form of a limited mechanical task such as "left rear wheel assemblyman." In the laboratory organization, this specialization may take the form of "Smith is a good group trainer, but don't let him design exercises." Or "Let Jones do the lectures for all of us so we can concentrate on other elements of the design." Or "The role of a participant is to learn, not to run training groups or give lectures to the total laboratory population." The content of the specialization is not as important as the fact that task specialization takes place in the laboratory organization as well as in the nonlaboratory organization.

Output.   A characteristic of all organizations is the output of some product. In General Motors, it is automobiles. In the Boy Scouts, it is character. In the training laboratory, it is learning about self, inter-personal relations, small-group behavior, relationships between groups, and organization dynamics. Thus, the output of the training laboratory is identifiable and measurable in the same sense that production is measurable in other organizations.

Implicit norms and mores.   All organizations have implicit norms and mores governing behavior. These norms are seldom found on the formal organization chart or in a statement of organizational rules and regulations. For example, an executive of The Bank knows it is in-appropriate for him to show up in a turtleneck sweater, Bermuda shorts, and sneakers, and a laboratory trainer knows it is inappropriate for him to appear for work wearing a Brooks Brothers suit and a felt hat.

There are probably many other similarities, but to elucidate them is unimportant. The basic point is that laboratory and nonlaboratory organizations have structural elements in common and that these elements provide the potential for transfer of laboratory learning to nonlaboratory organizations.

DIFFERENCES BETWEEN LABORATORY AND NONLABORATORY ORGANIZATIONS

Laboratory and nonlaboratory organizations also differ dramatically in a number of ways which are important to the trainer in conceptualiz-ing his role in a program of organization development. These differ-ences occur in the following dimensions.

Population.   People who volunteer for laboratory training differ from those who do not. To be sure, persons who come to stranger laboratories come from a variety of organizations, professional groups, and levels within their organizations. In addition, they have widely varying religious, ethnic, and socioeconomic backgrounds. However, they are homogeneous in one important sense. They volunteer for human relations training and are, therefore, different in personality structure from the modal person in the back-home organization who does not volunteer or who may actively reject an opportunity to par-ticipate in such training. Stated simply, the person who attends Human Relations III in Bethel, Maine, or the Ojai Lab, or the Boston University sensitivity-training course is not the modal person who works for

Procter & Gamble, or joins the priesthood, or enlists in the U.S. Marines.

One of the authors did a brief study of all 67 participants who appeared for a volunteer Human Relations Laboratory at Bethel in 1963. He gave the Dogmatism Scale (Rokeach 1960) to determine whether low dogmatics (defined as persons who are capable of evaluating, interpreting, and acting on information according to its intrinsic, structural merits) or high dogmatics (persons who respond to irrelevant elements in evaluating information such as outside authority, anxiety, or social pressure) change the most as a function of a laboratory education experience. To the author's surprise, the mean dogmatism score for the 67 participants was 130.9 (S.D. 21.3), a score which falls in the low-dogmatic range when compared to various populations reported by Rokeach. Most of the participants fell into low- and medium-dogmatic categories. Of the 67 participants, 29 had scores below 130, a score considered as low dogmatic. Only 3 had scores in the high dogmatic range of 180 and above, and those 3 ranged only from 183 to 187, which placed them in the lower end of the high-dogmatic range (Harvey 1963).

Since one of the frequently stated goals of laboratory education is to make people more data-oriented, as opposed to authority-oriented, the implications of such population homogeneity are exceedingly important. That is, voluntary sensitivity-training laboratories draw those persons as participants who have the least to gain from the learning and whose values and skills coincide most with the values and educational technology underlying laboratory training. Thus, the trainer's values and technology for working within the laboratory setting are congruent at the outset with those of the participants. As a consequence, he is faced with a nearly automatic success experience. As one trainer put it, "The participants are fish and the laboratory is pure water." When he leaves the laboratory, however, and enters an organization where the population's values may be quite different from or at least less similar to his own, he frequently runs into difficulty. The "magic" of the training group and the acceptance and effectiveness of laboratory-based change strategies may not be inherent in the personalities of the nonlaboratory population. Different change technologies and skills may therefore be required.

Life span.   In the terminology of Bennis and Slater (1968), the training laboratory is a temporary system. It has a life span ranging from a few days to a few weeks. Participants and staff gather for short periods to pursue limited goals and then disband. Most other organizations are not temporary in nature; they have continuity. (The consultant is frequently brought in to help insure that continuity be maintained by inculcating a capacity for self-renewal in the organization's structure.) Implicit in the temporary nature of the training laboratory are several characteristics, the most important of which is that the participant lives much more in the here and now. He does not have to pay homage to his past or plan for his future in the same sense as the person whose performance-appraisal files are in the personnel office, or the person who is vested in two more years. This freedom from being time-bound in the laboratory and the freedom to exist apart from the coincident strictures of having a past and a future in his back-home organization make both the individual and the total laboratory organization much more amenable to change. Consequently, very different change strategies on the part of the organization development consultant are required when he enters an organization whose time boundaries extend both into the past and the future.

Building versus changing.   Closely related to the concept of time is the fact that in the laboratory the problem is to build an organization. In other organizations the problem is to change existing structures or create new ones.

At the beginning of a training group, there are no shared agendas, no shared goals, no agreed-upon leadership structures, and no common norms governing members' behavior. In effect, a vacuum is created, and into this vacuum participants and staff project their assumptions about interpersonal, group, intergroup, and organization behavior. As these individual assumptions are articulated, projected, clarified, and shared, the laboratory organization builds and takes shape. To be sure, the individual brings personal norms, values, and behavior patterns which may undergo change, but shared norms and goals, values, and formal structures and hierarchies are not present at the start of a training-laboratory experience.

Nonlaboratory organizations, on the other hand, have intricate sets of informal norms, mores, and relationships, some of which are informal and some of which are formally articulated in organization charts. In addition, they have formal administrative structures (such as salary administration procedures and budgetary processes) and technologies (production processes) which frequently act in opposition to needs of human beings for healthy human functioning (Argyris 1957, Blake and Mouton 1964, McGregor 1960). These structures and technologies are also a potential source of tremendous organizational inertia. Therefore, one major task facing the organization development consultant is to break down dysfunctional norms, attitudes, work patterns, and organization structures, and to replace them with models more congruent with the needs for healthy human functioning. As opposed to working primarily to change individual behaviors (the task which most trainers see as central in the laboratory setting), the task of the OD consultant in a nonlaboratory organization is to create conditions in which existing dysfunctional organizational structures and dynamics are altered, modified, or replaced.

The nature of the system.   Most nonlaboratory organizations are sociotechnical systems (Marrow, Bowers, and Seashore 1967). Thus, they have human systems such as values, mores, attitudes, and communication patterns, but they also have technological systems with which the human system interacts. In its most apparent sense, the technological system is a production process, involving a variety of hardware, machinery, and equipment. In addition, most nonlaboratory organizations have administrative/bureaucratic procedures such as performance appraisal, salary administration, control systems and accounting technologies to support their production operations. Generally, the technological system is directly related to the organization's output, be it automobiles, clothes, or religious conversions. But frequently the tail wags the dog: the technology for producing that output frequently shapes the human system in the organization. As Argyris (1957) and Blake and Mouton (1964) have pointed out, the technological and human elements of organizations are frequently in opposition and conflict.

Laboratory organizations, on the other hand, are essentially social systems. They have no technology in the form of machinery, and few supporting administrative processes opposed by human needs. In the most general sense, the product of a laboratory is learning about human behavior. Thus, the human system and the product of the organization are basically in agreement. Consequently, in the laboratory, nearly any behavior—even cases of near psychotic behavior (Haigh 1968)—is acceptable, supported, and certainly not in opposition with the aims of the laboratory. While there are individual predilections and assumptions to overcome and new human systems to build, few bureaucratic or technological systems must be modified or integrated. (It is possible, of course, to consider the largely unapparent system of hierarchical organization including training groups, staff management practices, and the value system of the staff, as systems that need modification, but those are human systems, not technological or bureaucratic ones.)

As a specific example, it is one thing for a participant to learn that participation and involvement enhance the production of the training laboratory, and another to translate the concept of participation to development of a budgetary system or a production process. Herein is the challenge which the organization consultant does not have to face in the environment of the training laboratory.

Individual versus organizational orientation. Laboratories are oriented toward individuals and small groups. Organizations are oriented toward organizations. (This is a pragmatic observation, not a value judgment.) For direct evidence concerning the individual orientation of laboratory organizations, one only has to turn to reviews of research such as Campbell and Dunnette (1968), Durham and Gibb (1967, pp. 27-41) or Knowles (1967, pp. 42-71). Most of the research has been concerned with the effect of laboratory educations on individual behavior: What did Joe Jones learn? How did he apply it? Did he enjoy it? Is he more effective because of the experience? Does he still beat his wife or does he still let his wife beat him? Do his subordinates see him as being more trustworthy, loyal, helpful, friendly, cheerful?

There is less research concerning the effect of laboratory education on groups as groups: Do groups improve in their effectiveness in making decisions as a result of their experience in the training group together? Virtually no research has been done on the effectiveness of a laboratory as a total functioning unit other than the gross judgments made by participants and staff who say that "it was a great lab" or that "the lab of '65 was greater than the one in '54."

The way decisions are made concerning the conduct of laboratories themselves is a case in point. In general, most trainers (managers) make decisions in the laboratory by asking, first, what is good for Bill; second, what is good for the training group; and third, what is good for the laboratory as a whole. Following is a hypothetical example.

> Sonja is in the midst of a personal crisis and her training group is giving her feedback. It is also time for the all-laboratory, tower-building exercise. The staff meets before the start of the exercise and Sonja's trainer speaks. "We are really going in our group. Sonja is in the midst of a crisis. The group is very involved; I don't think we had better take part in the exercise.

Those who have been in the situation know the outcome: the exercise is canceled, or the rule of "trainer option" invoked so that Sonja's individual learning (or, at most, the group's learning) may proceed. The point is not that such a decision is inappropriate; since a laboratory is generally conceptualized as a personal and small-group learning experience, it may be most appropriate. The point is that such a decision is generally made by the individual trainer based upon what is best for the individual or the group, not what is best for the total laboratory, and that the value system underlying that decision-making process is different from the value system underlying the decision-making process in most nonlaboratory organizations.

The individually oriented decision may make sense in terms of laboratory output, but not in terms of the output of a nonlaboratory organization. Look at the Sonja situation in an industrial organization.

> The foreman comes to the plant manager and says, "Sonja is in the midst of a personal crisis and would like her production group to help her out. Of course, that will mean we won't complete the gizzitts in time to combine them with the gizzitts the other divisions are producing in order to make the rockets fly. But I think if we deal with her crisis, we will learn a lot, even if it does mean we will have to put the launch off for a couple of weeks."

The staff meets, and as you might guess, the nonlaboratory decision is made quite differently from the laboratory one. There may be some accommodation to Sonja's misery, but the prediction is that the needs of the total organization to be coordinated and to make the launch on time will take precedence. Decisions are made on the basis of what is good for the organization in its broad sense, not on what is good for Sonja.

The relationship of trainers to the organization.   Another important difference between laboratory and nonlaboratory organizations is not so much in the characters of the organizations themselves as in the relationship of the trainer to them. The laboratory trainer is a line manager. He has formal power and authority in the laboratory organization, in contrast with the organization development consultant who is a staff person.

In traditional managerial terms, the laboratory trainer plans (designs the laboratory). He controls: the most basic, unassailable control being that he insures laboratory method as opposed to other learning technologies to provide the focal educational process for the participants. He coordinates: along with other staff members, he decides when training groups should come together for a total community experience. He directs: "No, you cannot use physical violence in settling your differences in the training group. If you do, you will have to leave the lab. A little arm wrestling is okay, but fistfighting is out." He meets with other staff members in executive session (staff meetings) to set policies, solve problems, and make decisions. To be sure, his style of influence, his willingness to accept influence from subordinates, his capacity to collaborate, and his overall style of management may be drastically different from the style of traditional managers in non-laboratory organizations. Nevertheless, he has formal power and influence in addition to expertise which is greater than that of the participants.

When the trainer moves from the laboratory into the OD consultant role, his sources of power change. Little or no power springs from the authority of his position, as it does in the laboratory. The degree to which he has impact depends upon his technical competence and his influence (consulting) skills. In traditional managerial terms, he is a staff person. He can diagnose, advise, sell, formulate alternatives, and suggest. He cannot, however, "order" a team development lab or an interface problem-solving session between sales and marketing. He can try to convince someone from the organization to set up such a meeting, but that process of influence is quite different from making a decision to have a theory session on Wednesday afternoon in the laboratory setting. The skills involved in the persuasion process are quite different.

The reward system.   In the laboratory setting, the reward system is different from that in most nonlaboratory organizations. Although the laboratory staff generally is paid, the rewards for both staff and participants are essentially intrinsic in character (Harrison 1969).* That is, the rewards come from the exhilaration of learning something new about oneself, from learning in general, from colleagueship, from acceptance, from encounter, and from engagement in an existential experience for its own sake.

In the nonlaboratory setting, the basic reward system is extrinsic in character. The most apparent example is the system of monetary rewards. In fact, as Argyris (1957) has pointed out, monetary rewards within the organization may provide the means by which organization members may buy the freedom to engage in outside activities which bring them intrinsic rewards: "I'll settle for a job at Amalgamated Incorporated in order to really live during my time away from work." This certainly does not mean that nonlaboratory organizations do not have, or cannot have, intrinsic reward systems. It does mean that for the most part they do not; and therefore the change agent must take into account different motivational systems when he plans his change strategy.

* Harrison, R. 1969: personal communication to authors.

Availability of data. In the laboratory organization, data are readily available to the trainer. Most of his time is spent in a single training group and virtually all of his time is spent within the laboratory organization itself. He sees much of the data generated. Indeed, he is an integral part of the generation process. Seldom does anything happen in his training group that he does not have an opportunity to see or know about. To be sure, he may not (in fact, he most assuredly does not) see everything, and when he does see the events available to him, he may misinterpret, distort, or fail to understand their significance. But the data are there, readily available for analysis, examination, and interpretation.

In the nonlaboratory organization, data are not as available for a variety of reasons. To begin with, the trainer is not part of the organization in the same way he is part of a training group. As an outsider he may in a variety of ways be blocked from the data essential to understanding the organization's operation. To be sure, over a period of time he may develop the trust relationship with organization members which is necessary to be privy to behavior and other forms of data he needs. But developing that trust relationship takes far more time and energy than in the training group.

Secondly, the trainer does not generally "live in" with an organization. He is not there all of the time so data available to regular organization members, by nature of their permanance, are not so available to him. He may be there only a few days a month, and much can and does happen between visits.

Third, if the consultant conceptualizes, as he must, the total organization as being his client, he can never have access to the detailed data that are available if he limits his work to some small, circumscribed organizational subpart. In one sense, his dilemma is similar to that voiced during a laboratory by many group trainers who say, "I don't know what's going on in the other groups. I feel isolated. Tell me about yours." The consequences are different, however. In the laboratory, lack of total organizational knowledge does not generally hamper the trainer's performance since his focal client group is the training group. In the nonlaboratory organization, lack of connections with other organizational subparts can be disastrous since organizations consist of interdependent units, and what happens in one part has important consequences for other parts.

Finally, in the laboratory organization, the trainer must grapple primarily with data involving human behavior. In nonlaboratory organizations, he must not only deal with human behavior, he must also be prepared to deal with data of a technological and administrative nature if he is to be maximally effective.

Feedback on performance. In the laboratory organization, the trainer gets immediate feedback about his performance and self-worth. In fact the laboratory, with its emphasis on feedback, provides a constant feedback flow, and a trainer can easily and constantly monitor his impact. Since the laboratory is a temporary system, his total impact can be judged at the end of a relatively short time. Generally the feedback he receives is positive and unequivocal: "I think this has been the most exciting experience of my life and you are the most responsible for it." Even if the feedback is negative and equally unequivocal, the system disbands, and the trainer can try his luck (or skill) in a new temporary system.

The consultant in the ongoing organization does not generally have access to such immediate feedback, and in general the feedback tends to be more equivocal: "That was an experience we had in the team-building lab, but I am withholding any judgment about it until I see if we turn a greater profit at the end of the year." Or "I got a lot out of it personally, but I don't know if your work really has much relevance to the organization." Thus the trainer who works in the "real life" organization may find it hard either to evaluate the effectiveness of his performance or to get a clear picture of his own self-worth. As we shall later discuss, this fact has both technological and emotional consequences for the trainer.

Summary of differences. To recapitulate, there are a number of differences between laboratory and nonlaboratory organizations which have implications for trainers. The differences are summarized as follows.

1. Participants in laboratories are similar in personality structure. Their value systems are essentially congruent with the values of laboratory training and laboratory trainers. Persons from non-laboratory organizations tend to have much more diverse, or at least different, personality structures.

2. Laboratories are temporary systems. Nonlaboratory organizations tend to have continuity and long-term existence.

3. In the laboratory, the problem is to build an organization. In other organizations, the problem is to change existing organizational systems.

4. Laboratories are social systems. Nonlaboratory organizations are sociotechnical systems.

5. Laboratories are oriented toward the individual and small groups.

Nonlaboratory organizations are oriented toward the organization.

6. Laboratory trainers are line managers. Organization consultants are staff persons.

7. Laboratory organizations provide rewards which are essentially intrinsic in character. Nonlaboratory organizations tend to provide rewards which are extrinsic.

8. Data are more readily available in laboratory organizations than in nonlaboratory organizations.

9. Feedback is more readily available and less equivocal in laboratory than in nonlaboratory organizations.

IMPLICATIONS FOR SENSITIVITY TRAINERS

Assuming that the above differences exist, what are their implications for the sensitivity trainer who is asked to ply his trade in the real world?

The trainer must be prepared to employ a broad range of intervention technologies. Assuming that a nonlaboratory organization is a sociotechnical system, and that the human system itself is intricately interrelated, it is clear that change interventions must take place in a variety of ways in both the social and the technological/administrative structure. For the trainer whose professional life has been spent in laboratory organizations and whose basic life system is social, the operational definition of the concept of "multiple interventions" is simple, although for many, quite threatening. It tells him that training groups are not enough; sensitivity training is not organization development.

Perhaps an example would highlight this point. Recently, one of the authors was approached with the following, only slightly exaggerated, story from a manager of a large industrial organization.

Recently, production dropped off on the number 9 machine, morale was low, people were at one another's throats all the time. We called in a consultant and he suggested that we get together in a training group. We all took off a few days, went to a motel and aired out feelings. We went back to work with no apparent results. Production was still lousy and people were still mad at one another. Finally, we called in an engineer who suggested that we repair the crankshaft, and both production and

morale went up immediately. I'm a little puzzled about the first consultant's approach.

Without doubt, sensitivity training has a place, an important place,
in organization development technology. It is very useful as a basic
training experience which can allow persons to develop and test new
values and behaviors (or rediscover old ones), and to gain a beginning
understanding of the implications which those values and behaviors
might have for work-related activities. However, as the basic technology of organization change, the training group is both limited and
restricted in application. To be sure, some of the basic values inherent
in group training such as diagnosis, openness, trust, and the legitimacy
of analysis of behavior may be intrinsically valuable. But these values
have enormous potential which can be achieved only as they are put
into practice and become a part of one's everyday behavior in his
organization. That is really what organization development is all about
—to integrate the deepest needs of human beings with the needs of
the organization for productive functioning. Therefore, the values of
the training group are only useful if they are applied in a variety of
ways, at a variety of levels, to a variety of organizational processes such
as decision-making, the conduct of meetings, systems of accounting
and fiscal control, layoffs, hiring, firing, transfers, demotions, promotions, cost reduction, production process, and so forth.

If a sensitivity trainer is to become an effective organization development consultant, he must be prepared to enter the human system of
an organization with a variety of interventions, in addition to training
groups, such as one-to-one coaching, team-building (Kuriloff and
Atkins 1966), confrontation meetings (Beckhard 1967), a third party in
conflict resolution (Walton 1968), and interface management sessions
(Davis 1967). In addition, he must be able to translate what he knows
about human behavior into terms relative to the technological system
of the organization.

**The trainer must put proportionally more energy in the transfer
of knowledge of human behavior into organizational systems.** Since
the laboratory organization is essentially a social system, transfer of
learning about human behavior is not a basic problem for either staff
or participants. For the most part, neither participants nor staff has to
worry about such things as budgets, machinery, production processes,
profit and loss statements, absenteeism, or labor turnover. The culture
is self-contained and relatively open to influence. If a person learns
that openness is rewarding in the laboratory, he can transfer that learning immediately to his experience in the laboratory. How he applied

the concept of openness to performance appraisal, salary administration, the conduct of meetings, or the budgetary process is an entirely different matter. For example, should salaries be set in open discussion by all members of a work group and be known to everyone?

Since these variables generally exist throughout the organization, a consultant can exert tremendous influence on the total organization if he can translate his knowledge of human behavior into terms like these. For example, if the consultant can apply his knowledge of the human need for freedom, openness, and participation in the operation of a budget, he can integrate what are frequently competitive systems. Needless to say, facilitating such transfer of knowledge is difficult and in an organization development program it requires proportionately more energy on the part of the trainer than he generally expends within the framework of the laboratory organization. But it is when the human system and the technological/bureaucratic system are meaningfully integrated that real organization development takes place.

The trainer must learn to work with the total organization. In the laboratory organization, the trainer generally sees his basic job as conducting a successful training group, and his educational or change strategy is focused toward that end. Since individual learning and group learning are generally the criteria of successful training output, such a circumscribed change target is wholly appropriate.

However, in organization development, the organization is the unit of change. Since organizations are a series of interrelated units, what happens in one part affects the other. The literature of planned change is full of examples in which productive change in one part of the organization disrupts another (Harrison 1962, Buchanan 1965). As the cited authors have shown, the trainer who conducts a change program for one part of the organization without planning for its impact on other parts is doomed to misery, if not failure.

Dealing with the organization in its totality instead of in disparate parts also has implications for the theory employed by the consultant. In the training laboratory, individual or small-group theory is appropriate since the emphasis is on the individual or small-group learning. It is possible, for example, for a sensitivity trainer to conduct a successful training group using individually oriented theoretical formulations —psychoanalytic, for example. But to operate within the framework of an organization, a more comprehensive theoretical model is required. At the least, the trainer should be prepared to think in terms of the theories of Blake and Mouton (1964), McGregor (1960), Argyris (1962), and Likert (1961). All have developed reasonable coherent theories of organization, and more importantly, theories which allow the change agent to deal with the organization in its totality as well as its component parts.

One other point must be made. It is possible for a group trainer to operate by intuition, as opposed to theory (although we do not recommend it). It is less possible for a consultant to deal with organization change with "seat of the pants" technology. In other words, the organization change specialist needs a theory which allows him to conceptualize and carry out a change program for the total organization. Such a theory is useful as a cognitive map, as a tool for diagnosis and analysis, as a guideline for developing a comprehensive change strategy, and as a means of explicating the sought-for human/technological value system. Adequate theory provides the means for developing a coherent approach to organization development. In addition, theory allows both client and change agent to develop measures for assessing results. In summary, the trainer who employs an individually oriented theory or no theory at all limits his probability of success. He needs a theory of organization if he is to do an adequate job.

The consultant must be prepared to deal with persons who are different from himself.   Since laboratory populations tend to be homogeneous and share the trainer's values, the trainer may be lulled into the false assumption that all persons will respond equally well to laboratory method. Consequently, he may automatically assume that change interventions which work in the laboratory will be appropriate in a nonlaboratory organization. For example, most trainers automatically assume that a training-group intervention in the laboratory organization is appropriate. It actually is, because its lack of structure, its free-floating character, its value systems of openness, trust, inquiry into behavior, and the legitimacy of expression of feelings are not dramatically incongruent with the values of those who volunteer for the laboratory-training experience. But nonlaboratory populations are generally quite different. Consequently, to impose a training group as an organization change intervention in an organization whose members possess values and personality structures unlike those of volunteers for traditional sensitivity training is a certain way for the consultant to ensure the rejection of his efforts. In Festinger's terms (1957), the dissonance is too great. For example, in situations involving structured, rigid, dogmatic, authoritarian persons, it is theoretically probable that an instrumented approach (Blake and Mouton 1964) is a more appropriate way to introduce change into the human system; the structure of an instrumented approach introduces less dissonance into the system than an unstructured one and, therefore, offers the possibility of change instead of rejection.

Again, the point is that it is not automatically valid to assume that technologies and approaches will be appropriate in the nonlaboratory organization because they are effective in the laboratory organization. The organization consultant must be prepared, both theoretically and technologically, to introduce change in a variety of ways—such as coaching, counseling, instrumentation, or structural design—that are not generally used as central interventions in the laboratory setting.

The trainer must make long-term commitments.   Realizing that organization development involves the total organization and that complex human, technological, and administrative systems—each having its own inertia—must be changed, it is simple to see the implication for the consultant. He must be prepared to make a long-term commitment to the organization because the process of organization development is long-term. In fact, it may even be considered perpetual. To overcome cultural inertia, to inculcate new human values into the organization, and to integrate those values with the organization's technology and bureaucracy requires a continuing process of diagnosis, intervention, and change. Indeed, in spite of their built-in resistance to change, organizations are systems in transition. In a Darwinian sense, if they do not change, they die; and since cultural values and technology constantly change, the integration of these two elements is a never-ending process. Ultimately, of course, the goal of the organization development consultant is to assist the organization in developing a commitment to the norm of change so it can adapt to varying technological and human requirements. But to develop that norm is a long-term process and requires a more extended time commitment than the trainer is required to make in the training laboratory.

The requirements of long-term commitments may be particularly vexing to the trainer. For many persons, the attraction of working in a sensitivity-training laboratory organization is the short-term nature of the commitment, and the limited responsibility. It should be apparent, however, that such short-term commitments are not technologically feasible if organization development is to be achieved.

The trainer must actively seek data.   Since data are less available to the organization development consultant than to the sensitivity trainer, the consultant must, like a detective (Steele 1969), actively seek it. The emphasis is on active seeking as opposed to passive waiting.

Seeking data can take a variety of forms: systematic interviews, action research, or designing specific sessions or programs such as confrontation meetings (Beckhard 1967) where data collection, dissemination, and discussion are legitimized. It may also take the form of research projects wherein data are systematically collected and analyzed with publication in mind. Whatever the form, the process must be active. The trainer who waits for clues to come to him will find himself working on inconsequential cases.

The trainer must deal with his own loneliness.   To most trainers, one of the basic attractions of working in the laboratory organization has been the attraction of collaborating with a group of stimulating and accepting peers. It has been one of the few organizations in which professionals could collaborate with one another rather than compete. The format of the laboratory organization, its temporary character, its opportunity for intense, continuous interaction over a short period of time, and its built-in system of providing immediate feedback have combined to make the trainer's life emotionally satisfying. Words like accepted, connected, and involved crop up frequently when laboratory trainers try to describe the character of their relationships with peers.

It is not unusual, on the other hand, to hear statements such as "Labs are fun, OD is work." Or, "Working with X organization sure doesn't give you the 'charge' that you get in a lab."

Since loneliness can be dysfunctional, a trainer must be willing not only to accept his loneliness but actively to plan to deal with it. Attempts to overcome feelings of isolation and lack of support include pairing with another trainer, or joining an OD team periodically for both technological planning and emotional support, or building in projects such as periodic participation in laboratories for "rest and recreation." In the same way the trainer must take an active stance in seeking data, he must take an active stance in planning for his own emotional support. He cannot assume that it will be automatically forthcoming.

The trainer must develop new skills.   Underlying this whole discussion is the notion that the laboratory trainer must develop new skills if he is to be effective in a nonlaboratory organization. The question may be asked, "How can he develop skills appropriate for nonlaboratory organizations when most of his professional life is spent in training laboratories?"

First, it is possible to develop a great many skills by participating in laboratory organizations which are relevant to nonlaboratory organizations. One way in which this can be achieved is consciously to treat the laboratory itself as an organization. For example, if laboratory staff members conceptualize themselves as managers and make decisions on the basis of what is good for the organization rather than what is good for the individual or the training group, the interdependence and interrelatedness of staff, participants, laboratory administration, and community will be brought into sharp focus. The interdependence of subparts is one of the focal dynamics of nonlaboratory organizations.

To give a specific example, if a staff conceptualizes a laboratory as an organization where the parts are interdependent, the decision-making process of "trainer option" would never occur. In short, the process of grappling, as a staff, with issues which confront non-laboratory organizations will better prepare staff members to work in such organizations. For such grappling to occur, however, the laboratory itself must be conceptualized as a total organization, not a collection of subparts which run in semi-independent or parallel fashion.

Second, thinking through the implications of organization theory for organization process can provide worthwhile preparation. For example, how can the concepts of openness, owning up, and leveling (Argyris 1962) be applied to salary administration? What would be a 9/9 way (Blake and Mouton 1964) of organizing a production process? ("Production process" is consciously used instead of "production line" since production lines cannot be 9/9.) How can performance appraisal be carried out according to Theory X or Theory Y? (McGregor 1960). Dealing with theory in a speculative abstract sense provides a way to approach a variety of problems involving the integration of human behavior with technology and bureaucracy. Such problems of integration are not generally available in laboratory organizations.

A third way to gain necessary experience is to "hire out" as an apprentice to work with a more experienced organization consultant. As one person put it, "Working with someone who has had a wide range of experience keeps me from having to reinvent the wheel." For professionals who are used to being full staff members in the laboratory organization, an apprentice role may be trying, but our experience is that it is probably the most productive way to gain organization development skills.

CONCLUSION

We have identified a number of similarities and differences between sensitivity-training laboratories and nonlaboratory organizations. The similarities provide the potential that laboratory method has for being relevant to "real life" organizations and institutions. The differences, if they are not recognized, prevent the laboratory trainer from being maximally effective as an organization development consultant.

REFERENCES

Argyris, C., ed. *Interpersonal Competence and Organizational Effectiveness.* Irwin-Dorsey Series in Behavioral Science in Business. Homewood, Ill.: Dorsey Press, 1962.

Argyris, C. *Personality and Organization.* New York: Harper & Brothers, 1957.

Beckhard, R. "The Confrontation Meeting." *Harvard Business Review* 45, no. 2 (1967): 149-155.

Bennis, W. G., and Slater, P. *The Temporary Society.* New York: Harper & Row, Publishers, 1968.

Blake, R. R., and Mouton, J. S. "The Instrumented Training Laboratory." In *Selected Readings Series V: Issues in Training.* Washington, D.C.: NTL Institute for Applied Behavioral Science, 1962.

————. *The Managerial Grid.* Houston: Gulf Publishing Co., 1964.

Bradford, L. P.; Gibb, J. R.; and Benne, K. D., eds. *T-Group Theory and Laboratory Method: Innovation in Re-Education.* New York: John Wiley & Sons, 1964.

Buchanan, P. C. "Evaluating the Effectiveness of Laboratory Training in Industry." *Explorations in Human Relations Training and Research,* no. 1. Washington, D.C.: NTL Institute for Applied Behavioral Science, 1965.

Campbell, J. P., and Dunnette, M. D. "Effectiveness of T-Group Experiences in Managerial Training and Development." *Psychological Bulletin* 70, no. 2 (1968): 73-104.

Davis, S. A. "An Organic Problem-Solving Method of Organizational Change." *Journal of Applied Behavior Science* 3, no. 1 (1967): 3-21.

Durham, L. E., and Gibb, J. R. "An Annotated Bibliography of Research: 1947-1960." *Explorations in Applied Behavioral Science,* no. 2. Washington, D.C.: NTL Institute for Applied Behavioral Science, 1967.

Festinger, L. *A Theory of Cognitive Dissonance.* Stanford, Calif.: Stanford University Press, 1957.

Haigh, G. "A Personal Growth Crisis in Laboratory Training." *Journal of Applied Behavioral Science* 4, no. 4 (1968): 437-452.

Harrison, R. "Impact of the Laboratory on Perceptions of Others by the Experimental Group." In *Interpersonal Competence and Organizational Effectiveness,* edited by C. Argyris. Irwin-Dorsey Series in Behavioral Science in Business. Homewood, Ill.: Dorsey Press, 1962.

Harvey, J. B. "Type of Influence, Magnitude of Discrepancy, and Degree of Dogmatism as Determinants of Conformity Behavior." Unpublished Ph.D. dissertation, University of Texas, 1963.

Knowles, E. S. "A Bibliography of Research on Human Relations Training." *Explorations in Applied Behavioral Science*, no. 2. Washington, D.C.: NTL Institute for Applied Behavioral Science, 1967.

Kurilopf, A. H., and Atkins, S. "T Group for a Work Team." *Journal of Applied Behavioral Science* 2, no. 1 (1966): 63-94.

Lewin, K. *Field Theory in Social Sciences*. New York: Harper & Row, Publishers, 1951.

Likert, R. *New Patterns of Management*. New York: McGraw-Hill, 1961.

Marrow, A. J.; Bowers, D. G.; and Seashore, S. E. *Management by Participation*. New York: Harper & Row Publishers, 1967.

Maslow, A. *Eupsychian Management*. Homewood, Ill.: Richard D. Irwin, 1965.

McGregor, D. *The Human Side of Enterprise*. New York: McGraw-Hill, 1960.

Rokeach, M. *The Open and Closed Mind*. New York: Basic Books, 1960.

Schein, E.; Bennis. W., and Beckhard, R., eds. *Organization Development Series*. Reading, Mass.: Addison-Wesley Publishing Co., 1969.

Steele, F. I. "Consultants and Detectives." *Journal of Applied Behavioral Science* 5, no. 2 (1969): 187-202.

Walton, R. E. "Interpersonal Confrontation and Basic Third-Party Functions." *Journal of Applied Behavioral Science* 4, no. 3 (1968): 327-344.

12

Is the Training-Group Consultant Approach a Method of Organization Development?

ROBERT R. BLAKE

JANE SRYGLEY MOUTON
Scientific Methods, Inc.
Austin, Texas

AN excellent organization is one permitting fullest effectiveness, flexibility, and potential for long-term growth. Theory, logic, facts, and data are given priority over precedents and past practices in decision-making. There is a capacity to anticipate the future as well as to learn from present and past performance. In the corporate context, an ultimate measure is the capacity to achieve these aims while earning a high return on investment over an extended time. Comparable indicators are possible for nonprofit organizations.

Organizations develop "naturally"; they also decay "naturally." Like nations they rise and fall. The inevitability of change is axiomatic. The problem is to understand the dynamics of change and to gear strategies to those dynamics so that organization development can be brought about in deliberate and systematic ways.

We have three basic purposes in this chapter. One is to make explicit some assumptions about change which are exerting strong influences in corporations. These assumptions determine which actions for bringing about change are selected and which are rejected. Our second purpose is to provide an interpretation of what appear to be the sounder assumptions regarding the induction of change. We will present a series of propositions as foundations for a science of organization development. Our third purpose is to link a variety of assumptions to the training group as a change strategy to show how actions follow from assumptions. It is possible to ferret out the assumptions underlying a variety of other approaches to change—classroom instruction, management consulting, general semantics, survey research methodology, and psychiatry. We will concentrate, however, on the training group as a method of change, supplemented by consultation used in organizations. The question that will be examined is: "In the light of modern knowledge of organization development, how sound is the training-group consultant approach?"

We have learned much from this approach, in which we invested something in the neighborhood of twenty man years by 1960. We find ourselves particularly indebted to it for its focusing on the fundamental problems of change. That we find it limited in its comprehension of organization change dynamics and as a method of bringing about organization development does not reduce the depth of this indebtedness.

FUNCTIONS OF ASSUMPTIONS IN HUMAN AFFAIRS

The scientific enterprise might be regarded as a self-correcting way of determining which set of assumptions best fits reality. Testing and verification convert assumptions to principles which then come to have an absolute quality, even though later scientific work often demonstrates that what was a principle at one level contained unjustified assumptions.

One way of revealing assumptions is by identifying dilemmas of development. Every executive is in a position to resolve the dilemmas in one way or another as he seeks to enhance his organization's capacity for success. Behavioral scientists face them when dealing with change from the point of view either of research or of application.

A dilemma arises when a choice must be made between two or more sets of assumptions and the basis of choice is unclear. If the assumptions are congruent with the actualities, the results may be predictable. Invalid assumptions, however, may lead to strategies and tactics which yield no improvement or which reduce performance and promote unmanageable resistance. Thus, identification and appreciation of the dilemmas involved in a situation is of greater significance than knowledge of tactics.

Assumptions made in real life are unlikely to be as definitive as we suggest. But these are the kinds of assumptions, either spoken or unspoken, that guide decisions about change. There are also other relevant assumptions and the dilemmas themselves are interrelated in complex ways.

The test of one set of assumptions by comparison with another is merely an experimental verification of operational results, and designing conclusive experiments and conducting field applications has been difficult. To formulate foundations of a science of organization development, therefore, it is necessary to rely upon less rigorous field studies and case histories.

THREE KINDS OF DEVELOPMENT

Change is thought of in various ways. For some, the process of change may be limited to evolutionary modifications or revolutionary turnings, while for others, it may be engineered according to specifications of systematic development. If one subscribes to the first view, his strategy and tactics of change are quite different from those he would choose as a believer in systematic development.

Evolution.   Evolutionary adjustments occur when change is small and takes place within broad status quo expectations. An underlying assumption of the fact that evolutionary accommodation rarely violates traditions and precedents is that progress is possible if each problem is dealt with as it arises. Thus, changes are likely to be eclectic and piecemeal and to occur one by one on a pragmatic basis. Because they are adjustments within the status quo, they seldom promote great enthusiasm, arouse deep resistance, or have dramatic results. Solutions that prove sound are repeated and reinforced; those that are unsound disappear. The outcome is based on the belief that, beyond survival, growth and development are most probable for the business enterprise which finds solutions to each concrete problem on a situation-by-situation basis.

"Kicking a man upstairs" to make way for new blood is one example of evolutionary modification. Another is to live with a manpower surplus until attrition ends it. A third is to constrict an operation to avoid loss while living with inflexibilities in a union contract.

Acceptance of evolutionary concepts is widespread among managers and behavioral scientists alike for several reasons. The changes often represent progress and rarely constitute significant departures from past practices. They are reasonably easy to understand and accept and are therefore unlikely to provoke resistance. There are limits, however, to expecting significant evolutionary development. Only those problems that force themselves into focus are likely to be dealt with, and they are not necessarily the most important. Furthermore, an evolutionary approach takes the status quo of the system as a given factor even though the status quo itself may present the real barriers to progress. Prevailing values often prevent awareness of deep problems, and if some brief awareness occurs, organizational norms make these problems harder to tackle. Also, evolutionary processes are likely to be so slow that even though change occurs, its rate and tempo are such that the organization may in fact be falling farther behind. The processes may be little more than accommodations, adjustments, and compromises involving style and technique rather than form or character. Still, despite its limitations, the evolutionary approach is highly characteristic of American corporate life.

Revolution.   Processes of change can be regarded as revolutionary when the shift results in overturning the status quo. Revolutionary change causes violation, rejection, or suppression of old expectations and compels acceptance of new ones. It is often susceptible to interpretation within the framework of the Hegelian dialectic.

Changes of the revolutionary type are likely to be affected through the exercise of power and authority. Moving a textile plant from New England to the South to break a union is one example. A "sweep clean" edict that results in summarily firing a plant manager and replacing him is a revolutionary method for the one discharged and may have revolutionary consequences for those who remain. A similar example is forcing a budget cut across-the-board as a desperation move for reducing losses, without regard for immediate or long-term effects.

Revolutionary change is rarely resorted to except when situations have become so intolerable that evolutionary modifications are seen as insufficient. Alternate possibilities, if they exist, are unrecognized. Those who are deeply frustrated by the status quo are likely to champion this kind of change. Those who adhere to the status quo deeply resent it. Another motivation for revolutionary methods is the desire for speedy change. Revolution brings about a new situation rapidly when traditional assumptions and rules of conduct are overthrown. The changes may have dramatic and direct results, either positive or negative. Because underlying tensions are often based on a long period of suffering, the new action may bring more relief, despite the risks involved, than standing still or pursuing an evolutionary direction. Long-standing problems may be fundamentally resolved. However, subterranean resistances, resentments, and sabotage are likely instead of involvement, commitment, and dedication.

Both the evolutionary and revolutionary methods are deeply embedded in the assumptions that guide men. This does not necessarily mean they are sound.

Systematic development.   Systematic development does not start with acceptance or rejection of the status quo, but with an intellectual model of an ideal. The properties of the model are specified by theory, logic, empirical facts, and operating data. Its validity is pretested against probable circumstances projected over definite periods of time. In this sense, a model is a blueprint, not of what *is,* but of what *should be.* (The use of a strategic model is not equivalent to planning or to management-by-objectives. Both of these can be undertaken within status quo restraints and often entail little more than extrapolations from the past projected into the future. Rarely do they involve an active process of learning to reject the outmoded aspects of the status quo. However, both are invaluable conceptual tools in the implementation of a strategic model.)

Five specifications are important for an approach to change based on systematic development.

▪ *Design of an ideal model.* For development to occur in a systematic way, it must have clear objectives. An ideal model specifies the final state at a designated point in time. It is based on theory, fact, and logic, uncontaminated by assumptions embedded in the status quo.

The words *ideal* and *idealistic* are allied in popular thought. In our view, ideal thinking identifies what is possible according to theory, logic, fact, and data and can be tested for practicality against objective criteria. Idealistic thinking, on the other hand, is frequently rooted in self-deception and subjectiveness. It expresses what is desired without having been tested. Internal criteria that have little to do with reality are likely to be the bases of conclusions.

Ideal thinking has sometimes been rejected as idealistic. Yet several of the world's greatest change projects have come about through ideal formulations. One of the most dramatic transformations of an American business came about through the design of an ideal strategic corporate model formulated by Alfred P. Sloan in 1920 under the title "Organization Study" (Sloan 1963). The Magna Carta and the Constitution of the United States might be identified as early examples of ideal formulations. The production of the atomic bomb, the Allied strategic plan in World War II, and the United States program for the exploration of space are more recent ones.

■ *Objective appraisal of the existing situation.* To permit point-by-point paralleling between actual and ideal circumstances, it is as necessary to learn what the status quo is as to describe what it should be. When the ideal is used to spotlight the actual, the weaknesses and strengths of the present situation become clearer and objectivity is more likely. Without an ideal model, rationalization, self-deception, and second-nature habits obscure the situation. Thus, to change a situation, those responsible for perpetrating it must learn to reject it. This is not "unlearning." It is new insight into deficiencies of existing arrangements. From a technical point of view, it is a strategy of escape from corporate ethnocentrism. Learning to reject the status quo is difficult, however, and is usually left undone. For example, the Constitution was insufficient as an ideal model. Active learning was necessary in order to reject the status quo which permitted deep injustices in the American cultural scheme. Amendments and court interpretations attest to this, and we continue to identify and reject some of these deep-lying contradictions.

■ *Contrast of the actual with the ideal.* Gaps between the actual and the ideal become motivational forces. Closing those gaps gives development its character and direction. When conditions needing rejection and replacement are identified, steps of development can be planned and programmed.

A far deeper significance than might appear on the surface appears when development is built around gap production and gap closing. Two concepts of motivation, tension reduction and financial and status rewards, can be contrasted. Much industrial thinking is predicated on the notion that financial and status rewards are key motivational forces. These alone, however, appear insufficient to motivate men to search for solutions to problems. Indeed, they may do the opposite. Many organizations give raises and promotions to those who do best in conforming to outmoded models. On the other hand, psychological factors intrinsic to problem situations appear to be important in stimulating creativity and innovative problem-solving. When a clear discrepancy is recognized between what is and what should be, tensions arise that focus thought, effort, and feeling on resolving the contradiction and removing the barriers to corporate performance. These tension-based motivations may be used for harnessing energy toward the orderly production of change. Energy is at present only partially tapped in industry.

This contrast of motivational forces of tension reduction with those of financial or status rewards does not necessarily imply that they must work in opposition, though we have seen that they can. Money and status contribute to a person's feelings of acceptance by the organization. Such feelings help people become involved with the organization and committed to its objectives, thereby experiencing the tensions that are associated with discrepancies and that call forth action.

Motivational tension is unlikely to promote organization effectiveness when management and supervision are run along authority-obedience lines; it may then provoke antiorganization behavior. The conditions conducive to arousing positive motivational tension are involvement and commitment.

■ *Consideration of all identifiable forces bearing on each sub-system.* The environment in which the organization exists and by which it is influenced and also the forces under direct organizational control must be considered. Only then is the ideal model complete.

■ *Steering, correction, and control mechanisms.* Setting processes in motion does not insure the conversion from actual to ideal. Steering, control, correction mechanisms, and retrolearning involve a sequence of insight-gaining techniques with which the on-going situation or completed event is submitted to analysis, review, summary, and generalization.

When the situation can be measured before development is initiated, again at points along the way, and finally at its termination, information is available for steering action and for learning from it as well as for determining results. Unanticipated factors that impede progress can be identified. Unsuspected weaknesses and limitations in the ideal model can be found. Tendencies of drag and drift can be anticipated or corrected.

Systematic development has several advantages. One is that it relies upon theory, logic, and facts. It can produce enthusiasm for change rather than resistance to it. The only conceptual limit to possible change is in the capacity of men to think, analyze, and reason. Risk is reduced because the projected changes can be pretested for probable consequences.

There are also disadvantages in this procedure. The depth of intellectual endeavor calls for rigorous thinking which is both demanding and time-consuming. Many managers find it difficult to give up the fun and excitment of "fire-fighting" to permit the essential conceptual activity.

These three sets of assumptions about change are useful in understanding how change occurs. From our point of view, evolution and revolution are "natural" ways which have emerged through history. Systematic development, by comparison, has properties in common with scientific methods used in designing experiments and verifying results. Systematic development as an alternative to evolution and revolution is an example of the movement from a prescientific to a scientific society.

ORGANIZATION DEVELOPMENT SCIENCE PROPOSITION 1

The greater the reliance on systematic development rather than on evolutionary or revolutionary approaches, the greater the likelihood that a sound problem-solving organization will result.

To the best of our knowledge, no description of the training-group consultant approach reflects explicit agreement among consultants. They have a wide range of assumptions and tactics, thus making comparisons complex and objectivity difficult to achieve. Two widely quoted sources describe the methodology of the training-group consultant approach: *Personal and Organizational Change through Group Methods: The Laboratory Approach* by Schein and Bennis (1965) and *T-Group Theory and Laboratory Method* by Bradford, Gibb, and Benne (1964). From them we have isolated three strategic organization change elements on which training-group consultants might be expected to agree, and on these we base our evaluation.

▪ An unstructured group learning experience takes place with a trainer present (usually an applied behavioral scientist). The terms for describing this basic learning group include training group, development group, encounter group, or sensitivity-training group. The aims are described in a variety of ways, but the significant objectives are increased personal and social understanding.

▪ More than one member of the organization must engage in this kind of learning, though not necessarily simultaneously.

▪ Consultant followup is desirable.

We have found no explicit use by training-group consultants of ideal-model thinking as a conceptual strategy. Even in the behavioral area, we have been unable to find agreement on a single theory of sound managerial behavior. Neither the Schein and Bennis nor the Bradford, Gibb, and Benne book refers to the actual-ideal pattern in connection with assumptions about laboratory training. The training-group consultant approach appears to accept the existing situation and to work within it, identifying blocks to behavioral effectiveness or opportunities to increase it. This approach, then, brings evolutionary adjustment into the status quo.

In the absence of a clear-cut behavioral model, interpersonal adjustments lack consistency and clarity and have no built-in connections with organizational or systems improvements. A possible exception is that those training-group consultants who embrace Theory Y, Davis (1967) for example, might be said to advance a behavioral model. We then consider McGregor's Theory X-Y (1960). This is first of all a two-sided formulation and raises some objections. Theory X is clearly authoritarian. But are all non-authoritarian models—democartic, con-sultative, participative, laissez-faire, bureaucratic, paternalistic, Machia-vellian, "organization man"—Theory Y? If so, Y is too complex for clear interpretation. There are two other objections to Y as a behavioral model. First, if McGregor intended only to deal with two types or sets of values, more of importance to understanding is omitted than is included. Second, Davis reports that managers using Y as a behavioral model disagree about whether it is "strong" or "soft" or a combination. Thus, Y or X-Y are not very workable as behavioral models. Another fac-tor to consider about training groups is that the heavy reliance by train-ing-group consultants on here-and-now situations precludes attention to models of what should be. Finally, although extensive use is made of feedback techniques for here-and-now analysis, there is no systematic critique and control in training-group consultant programs. This may be the result of the lack of clarity; where goals and objectives are unclear, critique and control mechanisms are seen as unwieldy or useless.

Development: individual, membership, or organization? In en-couraging excellence of corporate performance, three distinctive sets of assumptions must be examined concerning the individual, the mem-bership skills, and the organization as a system. Confusion is widely evident because these have not previously been clearly differentiated.

Individual development. The individual is presumed to be more or less an autonomous, independent contributor to corporate effective-ness, and the organization is considered equal to the sum of its parts. Thus, the development of each person to his maximum potential should result in optimizing corporate performance. Individual develop-ment is implemented as needed by education or training on a one-by-one basis, with the expectation that the learning will automatically be applied to job performance. Training may be of a behavioral or tech-nical nature or a mixture of both; transfer of learning is assumed. Issues of fade-out are perhaps recognized but are disregarded. Notions such as "cultural island" and "stranger training" are accepted, as is the sending of selected executives to advanced management courses in universities.

Membership development. Membership development has been popularized in recent years as a way of dealing with transfer and the issue of fade-out. Individual development is regarded as insufficient to produce the required transfer of learning into the social system of the firm. The additional step of increasing understanding between members to improve cooperation is required. With improved interpersonal, team, or intergroup relationships, the conditions necessary for transfer of training are presumed present. Under membership development assumptions, the corporate status quo is accepted. The development problem is to help individuals use their learning more effectively while cooperating within the status quo organization. Thus, changes suggested by the logic of new technical systems are not implemented; the new systems are instead adjusted to existing practices. The result is that anticipated benefits are less than fully realized. Furthermore, the only business and operational problems submitted to analysis are issues which require cooperation of members directly and in the here-and-now.

Organization development. Organization development assumptions also stress the importance of strengthening cooperative skills; however, they do not end there. The reason is that the corporate status quo influences what individuals do when pursuing cooperative objectives. Unless the status quo is examined in the development context, change is likely to be severely limited. Thus, organizational development leads significantly beyond both individual and membership development.

The rationale for developing the organization as a system must be understood. First, individuals within an organization are significantly interdependent. The effectiveness of each one within the system is a function of the character and quality of his interdependence. This interdependence, in turn, is significantly governed by the culture of the firm, its traditions, precedents, and past practices; its rules, regulations, and policies; its norms, customs, and habits; its historically embedded ways of thinking and doing. The corporate culture can either enhance or inhibit the possibility that individuals will use their capabilities for removing barriers to corporate performance. Influences in corporate culture which act on individuals working interdependently, or even on individuals acting alone, are what make the whole more than and different from the sum of its parts in synergistic terms.

The key to organization development is to bring under control the constraints and inhibiting forces of corporate culture. In order to realistically achieve successful organization development, those who lead the organization must be willing to study it as a primary subject, investigating its fundamental tenets and beliefs at strategic, policy, operational, and tactical levels. In psychoanalytic terms, these beliefs are preconscious or so inaccessible as to constitute a corporate unconscious, comprising some of the most significant and adverse influences on corporate effectiveness. Unless organization development brings them out for scrutiny, it is unlikely that they will be brought under control. The corporation must reform its basic culture to the degree necessary for profit excellence.

What conditions are essential to cultural reformation? Two are of great importance. If either condition is absent, the endeavor might properly be classified as individual or membership development, not as culture change.

First, the entire organization membership, including the executive leadership, must engage in development endeavors that result in flexibility of thought and dedication of effort. The purpose is readiness throughout the organization to create and implement changes. The readiness to change is achieved by creating optimal values and norms under conditions of involvement and participation as opposed to authority and obedience.

The rationale for involving everyone in the organization in the development endeavor is based on the concept of critical mass. To illustrate, think of an organization as a mass in motion. Mass has inertia, and inertia must be overcome before a change in the rate or direction

TABLE 1. Financial Tenets of Corporate Thought

Implicit Assumptions Embedded in Corporate Culture Persisting Even After Individual and Membership Development	Explicit Commitments as the Basis for Culture Reformation
Do as well as possible, with dollar volume profit improvement expected from one year to the next.	The businesses operated by this company are those which within three years can yield a 15 percent minimum and a 25 percent optimum return on investment (before tax) with increases in dollar volume from the present $80 million by a compound growth factor of 15 percent. These objectives are to be reviewed on a yearly basis but not revised for at least five years.
Achieve a 5 percent profit margin on sales.	A minimum return on employed assets of 25 percent as a five-year objective, with a minimum, optimum, and dollar volume to be set on a business-by-business basis.
Double sales and keep expenses under control.	A 19.8 percent return on sales (after tax) with a five-year, 20 percent compounding of dollar volume.

of movement can occur. Setting organizational change into more rapid motion requires much more widespread participation than is possible through initiative by one or a few, as under individual development, or pockets of executives or managers, as in membership development. The greatest momentum toward excellence is realized when every one of an organization's members is personally committed in a deliberate and integrated way. There is a threshold where a critical mass change of motivational level seems to occur. Shared commitment to common values provides a strong foundation for taking actions required to achieve excellence.

Secondly, the executive leadership of the company must subject the fundamental tenets of the corporation to rigorous tests of private enterprise profit logic. The likelihood of attaining excellence is remote if a corporation has come to accept yesterday's achievements as yardsticks for today and tomorrow.

Table 1 shows the kinds of fundamental tenets and beliefs that exist throughout an organization and that must be brought to a plane of awareness if they are to be shifted in explicit directions for development. These particular tenets and beliefs concern financial objectives before organization change and after it takes place, as a result of a change strategy other than the training-group consultant approach (Blake and Mouton 1968).

ORGANIZATION DEVELOPMENT SCIENCE PROPOSITION 2

The greater the recognition of and provision for eliminating constraints to effectiveness embedded in corporate culture, the greater the likelihood that a sound problem-solving organization will result.

Evaluation of the training-group consultant approach.   The training group appears to try to eliminate constraints according to the assumptions of individual development. Research results report changes in individual behavior (Bunker 1965, Bunker and Knowles 1967, Miles 1965ab, Valiquet 1968). When conducted in a cultural island context among strangers, the research concentrates upon the individuals' here-and-now behavior. The training-group methods first used in the corporate context and reinforced by consultant followup were by Shepard and us (Peek 1960). Others, such as those of Argyris (1962, 1965), Beckhard (1966), Davis (1967), Friedlander (1966, 1967), Kuriloff and Atkins (1966), and Winn (1966), are consistent with the assumptions of membership development. Neither individual nor membership development can be expected to promote organization development, though both may contribute to its improvement.

Another study reports on a training-group consultant project (Marrow, Bowers, and Seashore 1967). It is difficult, however, to trace main effects and isolate them by intervention strategies because the study has so many variables. The organization had recently been acquired by another company; there had been leadership replacement; approximately a year-and-a-half of nontraining-group consultant intervention on technical and production problems had continued through the change project; the organization's survival was in question; a survey research project was acting on the situation. Only after all these influences had been interacting to produce a climate of change was a training-group consultant approach begun. The report is a significant study of change, and ascribing some influence to this approach may be justified. According to performance curves, however, major performance improvements had been realized before it was introduced. Thus, using it as an example of an organization development project based on a training-group-consultant model appears unjustified.

Behavior or operations development?   Two approaches are possible in pursuing development. In one view, behavior is the core problem preventing an organization from achieving effectiveness. If relationships are sound, operational problems can be dealt with more effectively. This concentration on human behavioral skills has led beyond individual development to the membership development approach. The alternate view is that limitations in operational understanding and know-how are the barriers to effectiveness. The problem is to aid managers in acquiring the needed business, technical, and management skills. Such areas as planning and scheduling, cash flow, and PERT are included. It is assumed that when management techniques are improved, behavior is no barrier to operational knowledge. This is the management science view.

Each definition leads to a different strategy and in the final analysis, neither can be isolated as "the" approach. Efforts limited to developing human effectiveness often have little constructive impact on operational results. Exposing managers to courses that focus on studying operational aspects of the business has often failed to improve performance. Likewise, good results are not achieved by pursuing both objectives separately, even in parallel.

The dilemma is subject to resolution. Faulty behavior undoubtedly produces difficulties. Efforts to treat them directly as operational problems often fail, because behavior is the barrier and it is not brought under control. No matter how sound the problem-solving behavior among managers is, if the requisite comprehension of business, management science, and operational skills is insufficient, it is unlikely that solutions to operational problems will result. A sounder approach is in recognizing that both views are valid, but that neither is fully valid by itself. When both behavioral variables of business logic and technique have been systematically dealt with, truly sound operational results become possible.

ORGANIZATION DEVELOPMENT SCIENCE PROPOSITION 3

The more explicit and deliberate the effort to insure a fusion between behavioral and operational aspects of organizational problem-solving in a sequential change process, the greater the likelihood that a sound problem-solving organization will result.

The training-group consultant approach concentrates almost exclusively on the behavioral side of the behavior-operations dilemma. While the training-group literature on individual development describes designs for behavioral learning and membership development literature describes designs for studying how faulty behavior leads to ineffective operational problem-solving, we have found no descriptions in which training-group consultants have been engaged in aiding organizations toward systematic investigation of the tenets of organization or deeper-lying implications from deliberate use of management science, problem-solving strategies. Argyris (1964) describes a "mix" model that is an excellent example of concentration upon behavioral aspects of organization. The behavioral aspects are well described from the consultant's side of the training-group consultant approach by Ferguson (1968). Bennis (1966) shows this approach and operations research as methods of change that are essentially equivalent although independent, rather than complementary or interdependent. He has expressed the following rationale for concentrating on human factors to the exclusion of operational ones (Schein and Bennis 1965, pp. 206-208):

This is the basic paradigm: Bureaucratic values tend to stress the rational, task aspects of the work and to ignore the basic human factors which relate to the task. Managers brought up in this system of values are badly cast to play the intricate human roles now required of them. Their ineptitude and anxieties lead to systems of discord and defense which interfere with the problem-solving capacity of the organization. The aims of change agents then, are (1) to effect a change in values so that *human factors and feelings come to be considered as legitimate and* (2) *to assist in developing skills among managers in order to increase interpersonal competence.*

Education or training?   Mastery of concepts and principles is central to education. A common assumption is that businessmen can apply knowledge acquired through education in solving operational problems, but this is seldom verified in practice. One need look no farther than the inadequacy of one's own academic education on entry into business to recognize the insufficiency of pure concept-learning without skill in utilizing the concepts.

An objective of training is to master the skills essential in performing an activity. The assumption is that if an individual has the know-how, it is unnecessary for him to understand the principles involved.

This split in approach has had unfortunate consequences not only in the corporate context but also in society. The disillusion with pure education has resulted in an inclination to sacrifice formal education and to emphasize skill development. However, the training emphasis which can increase a person's ability to carry out a variety of actions yields little evidence that development of the capacity to think, to analyze problems, and to see cause and effect relationships is improved very much. This deficiency in generalization may even reduce the capacity of an individual to resolve unique situations not directly involved in training. It may limit the potential of the trained specialist to become a generalist.

A sounder approach to development avoids this split. It provides for acquiring fundamentals associated with understanding concepts and principles and insures that these understandings will be applicable in operating situations.

ORGANIZATION DEVELOPMENT SCIENCE PROPOSITION 4

The closer the amalgam of education and training leading both to comprehension and utilization of concepts, the greater the likelihood that a sound problem-solving organization will result.

The training-group consultant approach can be described as training rather than education. The major component of group learning is existential and experiential, with here-and-now feedback and analysis of behavior by oneself and others. Similar encountering tactics may occur through consultant interventions in group situations within the company. Neither involves the learning or use of theory. While theory sessions are sometimes presented in group laboratories, the theory is not related intrinsically to the learning experience. Rather, it tends to be fitted to the *in situ* experiences. These theory sessions might more accurately be described as presentations of philosophy and values which have no necessary connection with operational planning, problem-solving, and implementation processes. The confusion over theory is best illustrated by a description of optimal conditions of training and learning within the training-group context by Benne, Bradford, and Lippitt (1964, p. 64):

> *Maps for understanding and organizing experiences.* Present experiences must be related to patterns which the individual has accumulated from past experiences, if learning is to occur. Effective learning requires examination and reassessment by participants of value systems, conceptual frameworks, prejudices and stereotypes, and ways of judging and deciding which they have developed before their entry into the laboratory. The laboratory provides opportunities and encouragement for such reassessments; however, the staff is obligated also to present tested and usable "theories." Theoretical materials presented are three general sorts.
>
> 1. Cognitive concepts for understanding human behavior at various levels of organization: the person, the "interperson," the group, and larger social systems.
> 2. Principles underlying various value positions, including the value of democracy.
> 3. Models for diagnosing and acting in human situations, particularly models useful to the agent of change.

A comment by Schein and Bennis (1965, pp. 46-47) uses the concept of cognitive map which in a similar way adds emphasis to the point that a unified theory of behavior is lacking:

> Much of the behavior generated by laboratory training can be characterized by the words *emotional* and *perceptual*. Equally important for learning and, in fact, the basis for the affective component is a framework for *thinking* about the experiences. The term cognitive map is frequently used in laboratory training to refer to this intellectual framework. Of course, there is not one cognitive map, but many, for linking and ordering the variegated experiences the delegates encounter. . . . In general, there is no set solution to the problem of how many or what kind of theory inputs should be given. Many staffs argue fervently on this issue and one of the main conflicts dividing staff trainers is the amount and presentation of cognitive material given. Some trainers favor practically no cognitive material, others desire a rather large portion. The decision about the quantity and type of theory material to be used is usually made on the basis of needs of the delegate population, the importance of con-

ceptualizing the experience, the need for linking the material to action steps, and the inclinations of the staff.

Thinking or emotions?   Awareness of barriers to corporate effectiveness within human behavior is reaching a peak. Here too an important dilemma is to be found. It is revealed in instructional courses which employ two quite different approaches, both of which are calculated to increase behavioral effectiveness. One approach assumes that if a person knows how to think, his feelings and emotions are of little or no consequence in influencing his behavior. The opposite assumption is that emotions and feelings get in the way of sound thinking and the solution to the thinking problem is in a person's becoming aware of his feelings and emotions. One horn of the dilemma is seen in efforts to resolve it through developmental approaches centered on thinking and logical analysis to the exclusion of feelings and emotions. The other is evident in training which centers on feelings and emotions with little regard for thinking, conduct, and performance.

Learning to understand behavior as the basis for changing it dates to the earliest philosophers. One trend, evident almost from the beginning and not significantly interrupted until perhaps Dewey, was intellectual analysis of qualities of the mind. Locke, Berkeley, and Hume are outstanding examples of men who sought to rationalize the nature of mental processes. Their studies, however, proved disappointing and had little impact on the way men used their minds in daily activities. They failed to grasp the importance of learning about one's own thought processes in specific terms and under circumstances that give rise to feelings and emotions. Investigating general laws of thought contributed little to changing the capacities of individuals to think.

Deweyism departed from intellectual analysis by emphasizing experiential learning. Its influence can be observed in sensitivity and training groups and in the emphasis on personal growth in one wing of the laboratory movement. Intellectual analysis is devalued and replaced by introspective analysis and feedback examination concerned primarily with feelings and emotions. Although this approach has had a great appeal, studying one's feelings and emotions without a broader intellectual framework does not appear to be a sound basis for changing behavior. It can now be seen why the human relations movement, as epitomized by laboratory- and training-group approaches, often is referred to as training and as an anti-intellectual endeavor rather than as education. Argyris (1967) has been outspoken in emphasizing this danger.

A dichotomy thus exists. University courses in logic or short courses in general semantics concentrate on principles of thinking. Minimum regard is placed on how feelings and emotions can divert logical thought. On the other hand, training groups, encounter groups, psychodrama, and other methods concentrate on feelings and emotions in specific situations. They do little to aid comprehension of sound principles of thought and behavior. We have found it difficult to identify examples of developmental endeavors where these two aspects of behavior have been the topics of simultaneous learning up to the most recent past. A more valid approach treats thinking and emotions as inseparable.

ORGANIZATION DEVELOPMENT SCIENCE PROPOSITION 5

Since thinking and emotions are interrelated aspects of experience, the greater the personal insight and skill in maintaining clear thought, even in the context of emotion-arousing events, the greater the individual's potential for contributing to problem-solving behavior.

The training-group consultant approach focuses learning on feelings and emotions. Indeed, anything more than secondary attention to cognitive elements is often viewed as evidence of "flight" and as a way of avoiding intimacy problems. Argyris (1962) presents findings which we interpret as demonstrating that changes as a result of group training are almost all in the direction of defining problems in emotional, as contrasted to intellectual, terms.

Consult or teach?   The emergence and rapid growth of the consultant industry—the result of managers' needs to increase their understandings in the face of advancing technologies—is a recent development in the history of the corporation.

A self-reliance/dependence paradox has arisen with the emergence of the consultant as an external influence on corporate affairs. If line managers submit to a consultant's guidance by taking what he offers as expert advice, they abdicate normal line responsibilities. Furthermore, an attitude of dependence on further assistance often develops. On the other hand, if the consultant's expert advice is rejected, the potential contribution which his specialized knowledge could have provided is sacrificed. Other alternatives are that the line manager compromises by accepting some but not all guidance, or that the consultant exercises his influence on a mutual agreement basis. Such agreement is difficult to achieve because it is likely that line managers would not have needed counsel in the first place if they were in a position to agree.

The paradox is no less obvious when viewed from the standpoint of the consultant who realizes that if his advice is given directly and taken on faith, attitudes of dependence are aroused which often result in counter-dependent hostility. Thus, many try to avoid giving advice directly. This is particularly true with respect to training-group consultants (Ferguson 1968; Lippitt, Watson, and Westley 1958).

If expert competence is withheld, then, what contribution can the consultant make? Many consultants have great difficulty in resolving this dilemma. Some avoid contribution to content and employ instead a variety of nondirective strategies, such as rephrasing, stopping an activity to inquire, "What is going on?" or simply by asking questions they see as pertinent.

Two resolutions of the dilemma are being evaluated now. One is to aid would-be consultants in acquiring consultation skills. The assumption seems to be that the problem is deficiency in such skills, and that if they are acquired, the relationship problems will disappear.

The other more radical approach questions the intrinsic validity of the consultant concept. This view holds that the problems in the client-consultant relationship are fundamentally contradictory to self-reliance and the exercise of personal responsibility. The solution is to create conditions which allow people to learn how to help themselves without even initial consultation support. This can be done by designing instruments which aid managers in diagnosing, analyzing, and planning for change, either by themselves or by teaching line managers these skills at a level of conceptual understanding and skill. The instrumentation alternative is more thoroughly explored elsewhere (Blake and Mouton 1962).

ORGANIZATION DEVELOPMENT SCIENCE PROPOSITION 6

The greater the self-reliance of line managers on their own initiative and personal responsibility for inducing change, the greater the likelihood that a problem-solving organization will result.

The training-group consultant approach relies almost exclusively on the consultant as a catalyst in learning and development situations (Ferguson 1968). The advantage is that he may be able to see and, through intervention, help organization members examine obstacles to effectiveness. The disadvantage is that there are likely to be side effects of dependence-hostility in the consultant's relationship with the organization. To the degree that an organization values the consultant's contributions, it is likely that those benefiting from his contributions feel not only affection for him because of his helpfulness, but dependence upon him for further assistance. Such dependence, unless well-worked through, often evokes counter-dependent hostilities and resistances. Likewise, those who are influenced (sometimes adversely) by the consultant's interventions, although they are not in direct contact with him, are likely to feel suspicious toward him and threatened by him.

One consequence of this situation is polarization. When those with whom the consultant is working are "for," often others who are directly involved are "against." This polarization can produce organization regression rather than development. It can also adversely affect the applied behavioral science consultant. The fact that since 1955 many have joined business firms and then moved on to others or back to university environments should not be ignored. The dilemma may be more real than illusory.

Authority-obedience or involvement-participation? The authority-obedience formula for organizing and controlling human activity has begun to crack, and a deep-lying human dynamism is appearing. People are searching for involvement, commitment, participation; they want a voice in affairs and influence over outcomes. Behavioral science contributions have had only minor effects on this desire for involvement and participation. These developments have their roots in the institutions of democratic practice, the emergence of the labor movement, the feminist activities of this century, both the ancient and modern history of civil rights, student protests, and the problems confronting religious institutions. Equally important is the advancement of education, which provides the knowledge that militates against acquiescence.

The confrontation of the involvement-participation and authority-obedience approaches is based on rising expectations, both local and worldwide. It cannot be suppressed for long by reimposing authority-obedience control, for involvement-participation roots lie deep in the thoughts and emotions of men. There seems little doubt that involvement-participation for many reasons is the sounder way to organize human activity. The behavioral science contribution is providing a systematic basis for understanding this approach and is inventing methods to bring about its orderly emergence.

Once the authority-obedience formula is rejected, however, and demands for involvement-participation are responded to, a key dilemma of this decade and probably the next will be revealed: Desire to do a thing is not the same as understanding it and having skill in carrying it through. Managing in ways that promote involvement-participation calls for leadership radically different from that required to implement patterns of authority-obedience. The incapability of subordinates to perform effectively in involvement-participation situations is equally evident. Concepts and skills for effective involvement and valid participation must be acquired, just as software skills must be required for an effective computer operation. These are far more demanding skills than those of the political democratic process, such as learning *Robert's Rules of Order,* expressing oneself on the majority-rule thesis one-man-one-vote, or carrying a placard. If the implications of the involvement-participation approach are recognized, corporate systems in the decade ahead may lead change in sound and constructive ways rather than be shaken by revolutionary upheavals, as are universities today.

How can the dilemma of the two basically different approaches be resolved? Evolution is at best a less than satisfactory way to proceed. The snail's pace from an authority to a participation basis is too slow to meet today's expectations. Revolution is equally unacceptable, because it presumes authority-obedience methods for bringing an involvement-participation situation into existence. Systematic development, however, provides a way for the orderly and controlled emergence of involvement-participation. It provides a way of learning the concepts and skills for conducting business along these lines and provides the basis for converting actual corporate conduct from where it is—whether authority-obedience, bureaucratic, or laissez-faire—to an involvement-participation basis.

ORGANIZATION DEVELOPMENT SCIENCE PROPOSITION 7

The greater the utilization of concepts and skills for bringing about involvement, participation, understanding, and agreement as the bases for communication, coordination, and control, the greater the likelihood that a sound problem-solving organization will result.

The choice between authority-obedience and involvement-participation is resolved in the training-group consultant approach, where involvement-participation is acknowledged as sounder. In this approach, the model is implied by the consultant's own behavior. Theory as a model used in the training-group context has the limitation mentioned earlier, in that it is difficult for managers to conclude whether the involvement called for is "strong" or "soft."

IMPLICATIONS AND CONCLUSIONS

The formation of a scientific basis of organization development provides a basis for the design, operation, and continuous growth and development of organizations. It is one thing to achieve conceptual clarity about the essentials of organization development; it is quite a different matter to apply these concepts to achieving organization results. In this respect, the training-group consultant approach appears to have inherent limitations as an inclusive approach, at least as regards methods of achieving organization development. (Its worth for membership or for individual development is another matter.) A brief summary of the history of the approach may suggest some reasons for this.

The training group emerged as a social learning device aimed at reducing religious tensions and as it evolved, new motivations tending more toward providing participants with an experience in group development learning became apparent. These motivations too changed. They came to be centered on helping individuals become more sensitive to themselves and others—thus the name "sensitivity training." The recent emergence of encounter groups reflects a still greater shift toward personal growth and development. The central role of the individual and his relationships, however, seems not to have been changed from the beginning. Schein and Bennis (1965, p. 4), in commenting on the difficulty of describing laboratory training, arrive at a similar conclusion:

> . . . laboratory training is new. It started as recently as 1947 in Bethel, Maine. Since then, like most intellectual movements, it has moved along in an erratic rhythm, incorporating and ejecting ideas in a topsy-turvy way. Laboratory training is not, and should not be construed as a monolithic entity. Instead, it is a rapidly growing and ever-changing enterprise, composed of ideas and procedures practiced by social scientists and professionals who share certain beliefs and values, and who, on occasion, disagree on major issues. Because of its newness and novelty, laboratory training has not truly "settled" or codified its concepts and practices, nor should it.

Group development and sensitivity motivations have relevance to the way people conduct relationships. This is so regardless of the content that relates them. Thus, the notion emerged that a training-group consultant approach might help improve organization-based management of individual and group relationships. In accordance with this belief we, along with Shepard, initiated the original organization improvement experiments in Esso Standard Oil Company in 1958 (Peek 1960).

These attempts seemed to contribute to organization improvement through increasing the membership skills of individuals, but they left much to be desired in bringing about change in the more basic dimensions of corporate performance. As a result of our own dissatisfaction with organization results obtained, we launched another series of field experiments calculated to eliminate what seemed to us, both then and now, inherent limitations in the training-group consultant approach for the induction of organization change (Blake and Mouton 1968).

In our view, little progress in modifying the training-group consultant approach to make it fit organization development specifications is likely to result from trial-and-error evolutionary discoveries. It may now be an appropriate time for adherents to the training-group consultant movement to design a systematic development model which could provide direction and guidance in identifying the kinds of fundamental changes essential if this tradition is to make significant contributions to the strengthening of organizations.

REFERENCES

Argyris, C. Interpersonal Competence and Organizational Effectiveness. Irwin-Dorsey Series in Behavioral Science in Business. Homewood, Ill.: Dorsey Press, 1962.

————. Integrating the Individual and the Organization. New York: Wiley & Sons, 1964.

————. "On the Future of Laboratory Education." Journal of Applied Behavioral Science 3, no. 2 (1967): 153-183.

————. Organization and Innovation. Homewood, Ill.: Richard D. Irwin, 1965.

Beckhard, R. "An Organizational Improvement Program in a Decentralized Organization." Journal of Applied Behavioral Science 2, no. 1 (1966): 3-26.

Benne, K. D.; Bradford, L. P.; and Lippitt, R. "The Laboratory Method." In T-Group Theory and Laboratory Method: Innovation in Re-Education edited by L. P. Bradford, J. R. Gibb, and K. D. Benne, pp. 15-44. New York: Wiley & Sons, 1964.

Bennis, W. G. Changing Organizations. New York: McGraw-Hill, 1966.

Blake, R. R. and Mouton, J. S. Corporate Excellence through Grid Organization Development: A Systems Approach. Houston: Gulf Publishing Co., 1968.

————. "Foundations of a Science of Organization Development." Paper presented to Seminar in Behavioral Sciences in Management. Cambridge, Mass.: Massachusetts Institute of Technology, March 17, 1969.

————. "The Instrumented Training Laboratory." In *Issues in Training*. Selected Readings Series Five, edited by I. R. Weschler and E. H. Schein, pp. 61-76. Washington, D.C.: NTL Institute for Applied Behavioral Science, 1962.

Bradford, L. P.; Gibb, J. R.; and Benne, K. D., eds. *T-Group Theory and Laboratory Method: Innovation in Re-Education*. New York: Wiley & Sons, 1964.

Bunker, D. R. "Individual Applications of Laboratory Training." *Journal of Applied Behavioral Science* 1, no. 2 (1965): 131-148.

Bunker, D. R. and Knowles, E. "Comparison of Behavioral Changes Resulting from Human Relations Training Laboratories of Different Lengths." *Journal of Applied Behavioral Science* 3, no. 4 (1967): 505-524.

Davis, S. A. "An Organic Problem-Solving Method of Organizational Change." *Journal of Applied Behavioral Science* 3, no. 1 (1967): 3-21.

Ferguson, C. K. "Concerning the Nature of Human Systems and the Consultant's Role." *Journal of Applied Behavioral Science* 4, no. 2 (1968): 179-193.

Friedlander, F. "The Impact of Organizational Training Laboratories upon the Effectiveness and Interaction of Ongoing Work Groups." *Personnel Psychology* 20 (1967): 289-308.

————. "Performance and Interactional Dimensions of Organizational Work Groups." *Journal of Applied Psychology* 50 (1966): 257-265.

Kuriloff, A. and Atkins, S. "T-Group for a Work Team." *Journal of Applied Behavioral Science* 2, no. 1 (1966): 63-94.

Lippitt, R.; Watson, J.; and Westley, B. *The Dynamics of Planned Change*. New York: Harcourt, Brace and Co., 1958.

Marrow, A. J.; Bowers, D. G.; and Seashore, S. E. *Management by Participation* New York: Harper & Row, Publishers, 1967.

McGregor, D. *The Human Side of Enterprise*. New York: McGraw-Hill, 1960.

Miles, M. B. "Changes During and Following Laboratory Training: A Clinical-Experimental Study." *Journal of Applied Behavioral Science* 1, no. 3 (1965): 215-242. (a)

————. "Learning Processes and Outcomes in Human Relations Training." In *Personal and Organizational Change through Group Methods: The Laboratory Approach*, edited by E. H. Schein and W. G. Bennis, pp. 244-254. New York: Wiley & Sons, 1965. (b)

Peek, B. N., ed. *An Action Research Program for Organization Improvement (in Esso Standard Oil Company)*. Ann Arbor, Mich.: Foundation for Research on Human Behavior, 1960.

Schein, E. H. and Bennis, W. G., eds. *Personal and Organizational Change through Group Methods: The Laboratory Approach*. New York: Wiley & Sons, 1965.

Sloan, A. P., Jr. *My Years with General Motors*. New York: Doubleday & Co., 1963.

Valiquet, M. I. "Individual Change in a Management Development Program." *Journal of Applied Behavioral Science* 4, no. 3 (1968): 313-325.

Winn, A. "Social Change in Industry: From Insight to Implementation." *Journal of Applied Behavioral Science* 2, no. 2 (1966): 170-184.

Ethical Issues
in Group
Training

Some Ethical Issues in Sensitivity Training*

MARTIN LAKIN
Duke University
Durham, North Carolina

S ENSITIVITY training in its various forms has developed over the past two decades as an obviously significant contribution to American psychology, a powerful form of experiential learning which includes organizational, interactional, and self-understanding. Moreover, with the evolution and growing popularity of mutant forms of training, especially those emphasizing expressive behaviors, scrutiny of the aspects of sensitivity training that affect public welfare and reflect on professional standards has become an urgent necessity. The ethical problems which are relevant to setting up and conducting a group experience and which follow its termination must be examined with these issues in mind.

Sensitivity training had its origins in the study of change and conflict resolution, giving attention to underlying as well as to overt interactional processes. It has been widely used to reexamine managerial, pedagogic, and helping relationships from factory to classroom, community to home. Typically, small groups of participants under the guidance of a trainer use data from their own spontaneous reactions and interactions to effect change of one kind or another. The trainer

---

*The ideas presented here have been advanced in part in Lakin, M. "Group Sensitivity Training and Encounter, Uses and Abuses of a Method," *The Counseling Psychologist* 2, no. 2 (1971): 66-71; ——. "Some Ethical Issues in Sensitivity Training," *American Psychologist* 24 (1969): 923-928.

facilitates communication, indicates underlying problems of relating, and models constructive feedback. He keeps the group moving and learning about processes and persons and helps avoid counter-productive conflict or unnecessary damage to participants.

The number of persons who have experienced some form of training is rapidly growing. However named—training, encounter, human relations groups—the experience invariably involves emotional confrontations and an implicit injunction to reconsider if not actually to change personal behavior patterns. Because participants are not in psychotherapy but are "normal," and because trainers are presumably not concerned with "curing" but with the educational objectives of learning or personal growth, it is difficult to draw a firm line between training and psychotherapeutic forms.

Comparison, however, forces itself upon us. The distinction between normal and pathological behavior is hazy at best, and this realization compels us to consider the ethical implications of the differences between the contractual relationships—between participant and trainer on the one hand and between patient and therapist on the other. Mere statements of differences between training and therapeutic goals and definitions of themselves as "patient" or "participants" by those taking part only partially meet concerns about contractual implications.

Formerly it could be argued that the trainer had little therapeutic responsibility because he initiated little; interactions of the group were the result of collective interchange and give-and-take and did not occur at his insistence. Thus, a participant disclosed intimate details of his life or revised his behavior patterns as a result of personal commitment or collective experience rather than because a trainer directed him to do so.

Training groups evolved from a tradition of concern with democratic processes and democratic change. The generally accepted hypothesis was that individual and collective awareness could forestall insidious manipulation by dominant leaders or conformist tyranny by a group and thus provide psychological protection against unwarranted influence.

Many people currently involved in the various forms of training are not as psychologically sophisticated or as able to evaluate training processes as were the mainly professional trainers of some years ago. Many trainers now seek cathartic emotional experiences rather than intellectual understanding.

Moreover, a strongly positive reaction to training frequently impels the gratified participants to seek further training experiences. Unfortunately, almost as frequently, he seeks to do training himself. It appears relatively easy; the apparent power and emotional gratifications of the trainer seem very attractive. If steps in professional preparation are not better articulated and closely wedded to the traditional helping professions, we shall soon add vastly to the numbers of already inadequate trainers who practice their newly discovered insights on others, in the naïve conviction that they have mastered group-process skills and their application to personal and social problems. Because training is increasingly used as a vehicle for social change, it is important to explore its ethical implications, notwithstanding our as yet incomplete understanding of its special processes.

PRE-GROUP CONCERNS

In contrast with the training intention, the psychotherapeutic intention is clear. Sophisticated therapists know that this clarity is not absolute; complex issues of values and commitment to specific procedures cannot really be shared with patients, despite the best intentions of the therapist to be candid. Nevertheless, the therapist's mandate is relatively clear: to provide a corrective experience for someone who presents himself as psychologically impaired. The trainer's mandate is ambiguous. Some trainers view the group experience primarily as a vehicle to produce increased awareness of interactional processes in social or organizational settings. Others dismiss this goal as trivial and favor an expressive or "existential" experience. Both approaches are similar in postulating a participant-observer role for the trainee, but the emphasis on rational and emotional elements differs, and this difference makes for divergent experiences for participants.

Participant expectations and fantasies about training vary widely. The problem is that there is no way for a participant to know in advance, much less to appraise, the intentions of trainers, the processes of groups, or their consequences for him. It is not feasible to explain these because training, like psychotherapy, depends on events which, to have maximum impact, must counter the participants' habitual expectations. Since it is inimical to training to pre-program participant or process, the nature of the training experience depends almost entirely on the translations, intentions, and interventions of the trainer. It is therefore imperative for the trainer to be clear first of all about his own intentions and goals.

In recent years, training has begun to attract more psychologically disturbed persons. As a higher proportion of individuals seeking personal release or solutions come into the field, a larger number of inadequately prepared persons become trainers. To my knowledge, only the NTL Institute of Applied Behavioral Science (formerly National Training Laboratories) has given systematic consideration to the training of leaders, but even its accredited trainers are not all prepared to deal with the range of expectations and pathologies currently exhibited by some participants. The many programs offered by individuals and organizations inevitably include trainers who are inadequately prepared either to help others to identify and to express feeling or to interpret how others respond to their actions. Others, equally poorly prepared, apply training to social action and to institutions. Recently it has come to my attention that there are inadequately prepared trainers who lead student groups on college campuses without supervision. Eyewitness accounts of these groups suggest that the highest value is placed on intensity of emotionality and on dramatic confrontations. Screening of participants is virtually unknown and follow-up investigation of the effects of these groups is unheard-of. Their leaders are usually individuals who have themselves participated in one or two sensitivity-training groups. Most disturbing, these leaders show no awareness of or concern about their professional limitations. Unfortunately, competent, accredited trainers have done little to counter the belief that training requires little preparation and is universally applicable. I do not exempt the NTL Institute from responsibility in this regard.

It will be difficult to restrain poorly prepared individuals from practicing training in the absence of a clear statement of training standards, trainer preparation, and a code of training ethics. (An antiprofessional bias is very popular just now, and training fits nicely the image of "participative decision-making.")

"Adequate preparation" should be spelled out. While it is desirable to avoid jurisdictional protectionism, a degree in a recognized educative or therapeutic discipline is certainly one index of responsible preparation. For work with the public, trainers should have, in addition to an advanced degree in one of the helping professions, background in personality dynamics, a knowledge of psychopathology, and preparation in group dynamics, social psychology, and sociology. An internship and extensive supervised experience are other requisites.

It is almost impossible to effectively screen out participants for whom training is inappropriate because it is almost impossible to prevent false assertions about mental status on application forms. There is also difficulty in assessing the precise effects of training on an individual. Some trainers explain away apparent negative results by arguing that short-term discomfort or stress is often followed by long-range benefits. Eliminating the promotional literature which implies that training is psychotherapy and can produce immediate results would help greatly in reducing both unrealistic expectations and unfair evaluations.

Why has such a step not been taken? One reason is that many trainers do indeed view training as a form of therapy even though they do not explicitly invite psychologically troubled applicants. They do not wish to screen out those who seek psychotherapy. Reluctance to exclude such persons makes it almost certain that psychologically impaired individuals will be attracted in large numbers to training as a therapy.

More serious is the fact that there is little evidence on which to base a claim of therapeutic effectiveness. It seems indefensible that advertising for training should be as seductive as it is in offering hope for in-depth changes of personality (or, for instance solutions to marital problems); evidence that such changes or solutions do occur is inadequate. Greater candor is necessary about the needs which are met by the newer training forms. A legitimate case can perhaps be made that training at least temporarily alleviates the loneliness so widespread in contemporary urban and industrial life, but the training experience as a palliative is neither learning about group processes nor is it profound personal change. Such candor is obviously requisite when one sees the brochures used in some promotions. I suggest that immediate steps be taken to investigate these claims, to reconsider the implementation of screening procedures, to set up and publicize accreditation standards, and to monitor promotional methods in order to safeguard the public's interest and the profession's integrity.

PROCESSES OF TRAINING GROUPS

Being a trainer now is exciting. Being looked to for leadership and being depended upon for guidance are very heady. In its beginnings, however, training was based on the idea that participation and involvement of all the members of the group would lead to the development of a democratic society in which personal autonomy and group responsibility were important goals. The trainer had only to facilitate this evolution. Personal exertion of power and influence, overt or covert, was naturally a significant issue for study and learning. Evaluation of the trainer's influence attempts was crucial for participant learning about responses to authority. The trainer was indeed an influence, but the generally accepted commitment to objectification of his function made his behavior accessible to inquiry and even to modification.

Experienced trainers have almost always been aware that the degree of influence they wield is disproportionately large; therefore, they have tried to help the group understand the need for continual assessment of this factor. Awareness of this transference element has stimulated trainers in the past to emphasize group processes which would reveal its operations and effects. However, with the advent of a more active and directing training function—including trainer-based pressures on participants to behave in specific ways, but without provision for monitoring of trainer practices—the democratic nature of the group interaction is subverted. There is less possibility for participants overtly to evaluate the influences exerted upon them by the trainer. In some groups which emphasize emotional expressiveness, there are trainers who purposely elicit aggressive and/or affectionate behaviors by modeling them and then inviting imitation. Some trainers even insist that members engage one another in physically agressive or affectionate acts. Others provide music to create an emotional experience. Such leadership intends to create certain emotional effects. It does so, however, without sufficient opportunity to work them through. Moreover, trainers sometimes view analytic or critical evaluation of such experiences as subversive of their aims.

Although it will be argued that participants willingly agree to these practices, the fact that the "consumer" seeks or agrees to these experiences does not justify them as psychologically sound or ethically defensible. It should be remembered that the contract is not between persons who have an equal understanding of the processes involved. It cannot be assumed that the participant really knows what he is letting himself in for. At the insistence of the trainer and under pressure of group approval, some displays (slapping or hugging, for instance) are later viewed by some participants as iniquities.

The question of group acquiescence involves a related point. A crucial element in the history of training was its stress on genuine consensus. It acted as a deterrent to the domination of any single power figure or to the establishment of arbitrary group norms. Action and decision were painstakingly arrived at by means of increasingly candid exchanges in the group; influence could be exerted only under continuing group scrutiny and evaluation. Kelman (1965) has suggested that a group leader has the responsibility for making group members aware of his own operations and values. I find no fault with that suggestion; however, it is very difficult to accomplish. It is made even more difficult when (or if) trainers want the group to remain unaware of their manipulations in order to sustain the illusion that it is the group's rather than the trainer's decision which results in a particular emotional process. The intention may not be consciously to deceive.

It is difficult for trainers to practice complete candor with their participants and yet to facilitate the processes of training.

Some trainers whose primary goal is to elicit expressiveness are also committed to democratic values. But there is danger that their primary commitment will lead them to use subtle or even covert methods to achieve it, that what is promoted as group decision is really the trainer's, and that his function will be obscured while he tries to get participants to experience and express strong emotions.

In the light of these issues, trainers should reexamine their own activities. It may be that aroused concern will lead established trainers to take the necessary steps to educate aspirants for professional status to a new awareness of these issues.

LEARNING AND EXPERIENTIAL FOCUSES

Genuine differences in point of view and in emphasis exist between trainers. Some regard the emotional-experiential as of primary value. Others uphold a more cognitive emphasis, while recognizing that a high degree of emotional engagement is a vital part of training.

Participants are more often than not so emotionally involved as to be confused about just what it is that they are doing, feeling, or thinking at a given time; we know that they slide back and forth between cognitive and affective experiencing of training. The participant must depend partially on external sources for confirmation or lack of it for his perceptions. He looks for clarification to other members, but most of all to the trainer. Dependency plays a huge role, of course but it will not be destroyed by fiat.

It is the responsibility of the trainer to make as clear as he can his own activities, his own view of what is significant, and to encourage exchanges of views among participants so that all can have the possibility of differential self-definition and orientation during the training process. This would help prevent a situation in which inchoate and inarticulated pressures push individual participants beyond their comprehension.

In a training "society" as in any other, there are pressures of the majority on the minority, of the many on the one. Scapegoating, where recognized, would be objected to as demeaning whether it occurred as a means of inducing conformity or of building self-esteem. When the focus is upon group processes, it is often brought into the open, discussed, and countered. Where the emphasis is purely on personal expressiveness, however, scapegoating may be used as a pressure. The implicit demand for emotionality and emphasis upon nonverbal communication even makes it more difficult to identify scapegoating when it occurs in such groups.

EVALUATIONS

The ethical issues relating to evaluation, participation, and confidentiality have not been sufficiently studied, nor sufficiently stressed in the training of trainers, and the growing numbers of unaccredited and marginally prepared trainers increases concern in these areas.

Participants sometimes come to training under the threat of evaluation. Their concern about this aspect of the training situation is unavoidable, despite professional reassurances and protestations. After all, it is difficult for most people to monitor tendencies to gossip or inform—and how does one separate informing from evaluating? The fact is that if the trainer is also an evaluator of participants, he cannot really separate the impression he gets of behavior in training from other data about the participants. Perhaps it would help to make everyone aware of this. At least the risk would become explicit from everyone's point of view.

Nor can we ignore the implications of a refusal to participate by an employee, a subordinate, or a student. I recall an instance in which an employee of a highly sensitive security agency was sent for training. His anxious, conflicted, disturbed response to training norms of openness and trust were not only understandable, but predictable. The commitment to maintain confidentiality was honored; nevertheless, should his participation have been solicited or even permitted?

The problem of confidentiality has another aspect. A diminution of risk was considered one of the major advantages of "stranger" groups; time-limited contact was thought to encourage a degree of candor and interpersonal experiment that was nominally proscribed. Obviously, this cannot be the case in groups where participants are relatives, classmates, or employees of the same company or agency. It is almost impossible to assure confidentiality under such circumstances or to prevent "out-of-school" reports. Trainers must be especially sensitive to this factor in preparing other trainers and must grasp all opportunities to teach the importance of professional detachment. Trainers should learn how important it is to avoid irresponsible behavior in order to maintain the confidence of participants, how vital it is to inhibit a desire for personal contact when there is a professional role to play. Essentially, student trainers have the same problem as the fledging psychotherapist who must inhibit his own curiosity and social impulses to perform a professional function. The detachment emphasized here is yet another significant and ethically relevant area that is not articulated by emotional expressiveness as an end in itself. Responsibility is taught and modeled. It should be as consciously done in training as in any other helping relationships.

POST-TRAINING CONCERNS

A final issue is that of post-training contact with the participant. Participants are often dramatically affected by training. In some cases, trainer and group are mutually reluctant to end the group. In a recent case which came to my attention, the trainer was seduced, as it were, by the group's responsiveness to him. In turn, the participants were delighted by the trainer's continuing interest. Trainers must be aware of the participants' powerful desire to sustain relationships with them and, therefore, must be certain at the outset what limits they propose for training. It is as important to be clear about the termination point of training as about any other aspect of its conduct. Under the conditions of ambiguity and abivalence of an indeterminate relationship, participants appear to be caught midstream, uncertain as to the definition or possibilities of a relationship with this presumed expert upon whom they depend for guidance and limit-setting.

Sensitivity training is one of the most compelling and significant psychological experiences and vehicles for learning as well as a promising laboratory for the study of human relationships, dyadic and group. It may be a superior device for personal and social change, even for amelioration or resolution of social conflict. However, it may also be abused or subverted into an instrument of unwarranted influence and ill-considered—even harmful—practices. The immediate attention of the profession is necessary to maintain its positive potential and correspondingly respectable standards of practice.

The questions which I have raised do not admit of quick solution. They are ethical dilemmas. Steps to eliminate or ameliorate the grossest of them can be taken through awareness and self-monitoring. One practical step which I propose is the immediate creation of a commission by our professional organization to investigate training practices and standards of training preparation, and to recommend a code of ethics for accredited trainers. Research may help, but I doubt that it can come quickly enough to affect the increasing danger of the current and potentially still greater excesses in this area.

REFERENCES

Kelman, H. C. "Manipulation of Human Behavior: An Ethical Dilemma for the Social Scientist." *Journal of Social Issues* 21, no. 2 (1965): 31-36.

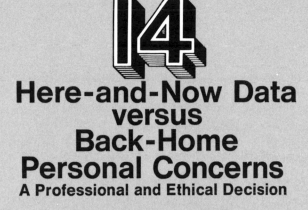

Here-and-Now Data versus Back-Home Personal Concerns
A Professional and Ethical Decision

WILLIAM G. DYER
Brigham Young University
Provo, Utah

AT a management laboratory at which I was a staff member, a participant in my training group asked one day, "When are we going to start talking about our sex problems and our marital problems as they are doing in some of the other groups?" Later at a staff meeting, I mentioned that my group had heard that such material was being discussed, and two staff members reported that these topics had become the focus of much attention in their groups. This led to a lively argument about the legitimacy of such topics in a management laboratory.

When a person comes to a training laboratory, he brings with him concerns that affect his functioning both in his back-home situation and in the laboratory setting. Included are certain job-related problems, interpersonal concerns both with family and work, and such personal worries as health, values and goals, fears and anxieties, and personality.

How do we deal with these back-home or there-and-then data? I had answered my group by saying that there was no plan at all to talk about marital or sexual problems, that our focus would be on behaviors of group members as experienced in the group, and that we would examine our development as a group and learn about our group processes. My answer reflects a way of thinking: the major concern of training is to help people understand how a group forms, functions, and develops (or does not develop) appropriate processes for dealing with group concerns. Focus on back-home issues moves the group away from this goal and the training group becomes a form of personal therapy.

Yet cogent arguments can be advanced for viewing the laboratory as a means of helping members become more aware of the forces that tie up emotional energy and restrict the ability to engage fully and freely in effective work with others. In this case, there-and-then concerns cannot be divorced from here-and-now issues, and the training group is seen as releasing, cathartic, and therapeutic.

ARGUMENTS AGAINST THERE-AND-THEN DATA

Certain arguments against introducing there-and-then, back-home data have become virtually traditional.

1. The introduction of there-and-then data represents a safe position, a flight from what is happening in the group. The back-home situation may be interesting, even absorbing, but it keeps the group from dealing with problems and issues that are present in the group.

2. Back-home situations provide insufficient data for problem-solving; the participant's view of his position is one-sided. Only data the group shares in the here-and-now can be dealt with without the risk of moving in inappropriate directions. A person ought to think about his back-home situation, perhaps with the help of group members, but only after the training group has helped him see how he has functioned in the group. With this new perspective he may be able to reexamine back-home conditions in a new light.

3. Group members who expect to develop new leadership or management skills may feel that a group dealing primarily with individual problems, while interesting and involving, is not what they came for. An additional danger is that the sponsoring organization may expect participants to receive certain kinds of learning not consonant with an individually oriented group.

4. Apart from the catharsis that may be provided, it is doubtful that a training group can be really helpful with personal problems in a one- or two-week period. It may even be irresponsible to open areas

for examination without adequate follow-up opportunities. When we focus on here-and-now data, we can at least be responsible for what is happening in the group, even though we cannot be sure what will happen when the person tries to apply his learning back home.

5. Unless the trainer is careful, personal emphasis may lead to a group norm of exposure, pressuring the participant to reveal problems he had no intention of sharing. This may lead him to feel uneasy, anxious, fearful, or even resentful when he goes home.

6. Dealing with personal problems requires certain clinical skills, for often personality disorders and malfunctions surface in the discussions. Many trainers have neither the training nor the experience to deal effectively with such problems.

ARGUMENTS FOR THERE-AND-THEN DATA

Those who favor allowing there-and-then data in training groups have three major rationales.

1. The proper place to start any training group is the point at which the participant finds himself right now. If "right now" includes job problems or disruptive relationships, the group should listen and try to learn how to be helpful. An important purpose of the laboratory is to help the participant connect his laboratory learning to the back-home setting, and this goal cannot be met if there-and-then data are proscribed. A group familiar with the participant's back-home concerns helps him look at his behavior—as it is observed by the group—and assess its effect in the back-home situation.

2. Management- or group-process learning and skills will not be useful until the person is functioning at the best possible personal level. A training-group experience is sometimes called therapy for normals, since the opportunity to work on the concerns normal people have is unique to the training group. If people who are expending emotional and psychic energy can release it in more creative and productive ways, this is surely the best contribution a training experience can make to the organization (or the individual).

3. The training group is an unstructured learning setting, and as in a projective test, the individual will respond to the situation in terms of what is important to him. If the setting inspires him to deal with deeply personal problems like sexual or marital relations, the group should listen. We live in a closed, impersonal, non-communicative, feeling-deprived culture. The training group should provide an atmosphere in which one can experience deep trust of and deep con-

cern for others. If we deny the back-home data, we deny the group the chance to share deep intimacy.

DISCUSSION OF ISSUES

In deciding which training focus to use, the trainer may examine the following issues.

Nature of the contract.   In responsible training, the general purpose of the laboratory contract—the advertised statement of content that provides the basis for participant expectations—ought to be met in specific fashion. Following is an advertisement for a widely known set of management laboratories (NTL 1968).

> Working with a qualified trainer, participants create a productive work group out of an unstructured situation. They develop leadership and membership functions from their own resources. In the process, they get a clearer view of their own ways of coping with human problems in organizations. They have an opportunity to learn, often for the first time, how their ways of working with people are seen by and affect others.
> This work group (typically called a T Group) provides the participant with a macrocosm for studying the problems he faces in his own organization. As he learns to deal more effectively with human problems arising in the work group, he also learns to work more effectively in his managerial position. . . .
> Participants tend to derive benefit to themselves and their organizations when they come with an interest in self-development, a willingness to invest themselves in an intensive learning experience, a potential for growth, and an opportunity to contribute to organizational improvements following the conference.
> Participation in the conference is not recommended for individuals with deep emotional problems. Although the laboratory experience is an intense and involving one, it is not intended as a substitute in any way for individual or group psychotherapy.

This is a carefully worded statement about laboratory training. It is, however, open to a variety of interpretations. A trainer emphasizing back-home concerns and oriented to helping participants release their own potential could point to the statement "an interest in self-development, a willingness to invest themselves in an intensive learning experience, a potential for growth" as justifying his approach. The here-and-now trainer would point out that the contract says the participant "learns to deal more effectively with human problems arising in the work group," and that participants will create a productive work group from an unstructured situation.

The total statement clearly implies that the laboratory as a whole is concerned with the manager in his organization and that training is offered which will make some difference in organizational functioning. It also points out that the laboratory is not a substitute for group psychotherapy. It would seem a breach of the implicit contract if the work of the training group were not clearly related to the work of the manager in the organization.

A trainer should probably not contract to do a laboratory if he feels his training and experience will lead the group away from those issues for which they came to the laboratory. A group-process trainer should refuse a laboratory with major emphasis on intrapersonal behavior, and vice versa.

The overlapping of the here-and-now and the there-and-then. In dealing with group process, a participant may get a great deal of feedback from group members about his style of working with the group. This feedback may cause the participant to want to examine his back-home life, to talk about how he developed this particular behavior pattern, and to discuss the problems the behavior has created. Most trainers, I think, would see this type of examination—back-home factors viewed in the light of here-and-now data—as legitimate and desirable activity, useful in stimulating thought about post-laboratory applications of learning.

In dealing with a participant who is beginning to explore the back-home implications of his laboratory learning, the trainer has certain options. He can limit the focus to the world of work. He can encourage the participant to see applications in various systems and relationships; he can ask the participant not to take group time but rather to explore such applications in private; or he can suggest that the participant review back-home concerns more extensively and intensively. Any combination is possible, of course.

How far the group moves depends on the orientation of the trainer, the intensity of the participants' feelings, the perceived legitimacy of the back-home issue in regard to the contractual focus of the laboratory, and the skill of trainer and group in refraining from verbal voyeurism and instead using the experience for learning purposes.

The trainer must be alert to the seductive quality of the there-and-then discussions, which do of course deal with deep, personal, important matters. If this factor is not considered, the group might move from one disclosure to another with increasing feelings of intimacy and concern without ever generating firsthand data about each member that can be shared, evaluated, and discussed in terms of applications.

Personal disclosure does have cathartic value. Participants experience the processes of sharing and of accepting others and see the binding values to the group when people learn to be more open, to allow others into previously closed areas of their lives. This is learning of a different dimension from, let us say, examining one's ability to deal with difference and conflict in a group and experimenting with new ways of handling conflict situations. Both learnings are valuable, and which—if either—is to be emphasized depends on the trainer. There are trainers who claim to be able to focus on both group-related, here-and-now factors and personal, back-home concerns, but research on training style is inadequate to show what participants learn under such conditions or if, in fact, the trainer moves readily from one level to the other.

Trainer competence.   Some trainers do not work with group processes such as the forming of goals, the effects of norms, climate, problem-solving and decision-making, task and maintenance functions, control mechanisms, leadership attempts, or communication patterns —all of which are part of the emphasis on group dynamics in traditional group training.

Others are insensitive to personal anxiety, threat, or fear, or to feelings of inferiority or inadequacy, deep-seated authority concerns, feelings about sexual attraction or repulsion, guilt, or alienation. All these are feeling responses that often occur in a training group. They are usually (although not always entirely) related to back-home conditions and relationships, or at least have been experienced in back-home situations. Pointing out such responses in the group is likely to cause the participant to examine back-home factors.

It is possible that the trainer feels competent to deal with the emotional dynamics that stem from the group process, but when participants talk about similar problems with a spouse, parent, child, or colleague, that trainer may be uneasy because he does not have access to data or responses from all concerned parties. Other trainers with some clinical training, used in dealing with such reported problems, may be inclined to pursue such discussions.

At present, there are no clear criteria for determining competence to deal with the various phenomena in a training group. We must rely on the trainer for the integrity and honesty to recognize his own strengths and weaknesses and to stay within the limits of his competence.

Training versus therapy. Training and therapy are difficult to define in terms of laboratory education and even more difficult in actual practice. Generally speaking, training is a process of trying to modify, usually to improve, certain behaviors that characterize a person's style or strategy in coping with his interpersonal world. In this context we are looking for proficiency or skill in engaging in interpersonal behaviors to produce desired outcomes. Therapy, as thought of in the laboratory setting, is a process of trying to help a person reduce personal anxieties and fears that restrict his ability to function in ways that have satisfying consequences.

It is obvious that the two are very similar and seem to be differentiated primarily on the basis of the degree of emotional stress, anxiety, or trauma associated with the area of concern. The neurotic person who could use therapy is so concerned about the area of stress that he almost compulsively protects himself from examination and experimentation. It may also be the case that emotional upsets are located in early relationships or are concerned with practices or experiences that are very personal, private, and individual. Therapy is legitimately concerned with these factors. The neurotic may indeed need training, but the first concerns may be to reduce anxiety and fear so that training may occur.

Training is primarily directed toward the public, shared part of one's interpersonal world. The trainer tends to restrict himself to those behaviors that all can see and commonly experience and share with the group. There is no question that some therapists feel that the best therapy deals almost entirely with the here-and-now behavior. In this case there is really no difference between therapy and training.

A problem comes in the laboratory when participants attend with a mixture of expectations. Some may come expecting "pure" training, while others expect help with some personal concern. Sometimes the two jibe, as when a man concerned with his function as a boss is helped by seeing the way he treats people in the group. On the other hand, a man worried about his impotency and his wife's frigidity will find very little data generated in the ordinary group to help with such a personal matter.

The function of the trainer would seem to be to define explicitly— and very early—the purposes of the program and to identify his own skills. Participants should be allowed to leave if the focus seems unlikely to meet their needs.

This does not mean that there will be no training in a therapy-oriented group, or that a training-focused group will not have therapeutic value. The two are too closely entwined to be separated. But it does mean that the advertised purpose of the laboratory is recognized and followed, that participants know the general direction it will take, and that the trainer will have skills consistent with the nature of the program and will feel obliged to keep the group moving in the general direction indicated by the contract.

Experience versus application. For some trainers, the goal of laboratory activity is to help develop new attitudes, insights, and behaviors that participants take with them to the back-home situation. An important part of the laboratory design involves looking for ways of transferring the learnings.

Others regard the training-group experience as a positive one regardless of back-home applications. If the participant has felt relationships of trust and openness and has experienced the conditions of acceptance of others, there will be beneficial effects in the long run. In fact, if such feeling components are absent, there is unlikely to be motivation to make any kind of subsequent change.

Paul Bindrim (1969) describes a laboratory in which it seems that the emotional is the major emphasis.

> Most of the participants felt that the periods of sensory-saturation, fantasy and eye-centered meditation were the most profound experiences of the marathon. The general outlines of this experience are not those of drug-induced, hypnotic or Zen-mediational trips. Many members reported a sense of going out, a traveling through and beyond the boundaries of ordinary experience and an approach to something variously called 'God,' 'warm,' 'white light,' 'birth,' 'the beauty of the whole thing,' 'the stream of the universe,' 'in a white nirvana,' and so on. These experiences seemed to have a lasting effect on the post-marathon attitudes and behavior of many of the participants. An increased sense of inner worth, a sense of having completed a crucial psychic or spiritual cycle, helped some to a better understanding of their marriage partners.

The trainer concerned with here-and-now, group-process issues would probably never find a group moving to that level of feeling, for such an experience would probably not be a part of his learning goals. A person who wants that type of experience should choose (and be helped to choose) the type of laboratory and trainer that will maximize the possibilities of achieving it.

It is an interesting paradox that those trainers who concentrate on the here-and-now are often the ones who try hardest to have participants concern themselves with there-and-then, back-home applications. A commonly reported consequence of more feeling-oriented groups is that participants, feeling differently about themselves and others following an intense laboratory experience, want to behave differently. Thus, often much less time is spent on conscious planning for the back-home situation than is necessary in groups with heavier emphasis on rational, cognitive processes.

Stress on back-home application seems to fit into a general schema concerned with training or skill development. The participant tries to understand performances and strategies that will improve consequences both in the training group and back home. The training group that begins with personal, there-and-then concerns often tries to release feelings, and the intense emotional response is perhaps a more important laboratory goal than going through activities concerned with the transfer of learnings.

However, the two orientations are not mutually exclusive, and many trainers want to achieve both. They hope participants have a deep, personal, involving, emotional experience with enough cognitional learning to try to improve certain conditions back home.

CONCLUSION

As training programs of various kinds are developed, those who are planning these activities have a professional and ethical responsibility that should regulate their performance. One element is to plan a program consistent with the advertised content. A participant has a right to be assured that what he has signed for is indeed the focus of the program. There is also the consideration that should be given the employer who is footing the bill (if this is other than the participant himself), who may have agreed to finance a participant's attendance at a program because of the program description. He has some right that should be respected even if the participant agrees to a change in training format.

As a program continues, a trainer has certain options that are presented to him at points of intervention in the group process. Even though the overall design of a program is in one direction, the trainer can continually intervene in the group process in such a way that the basic concern of the group is in a different direction. The trainer should be aware of his own style, theory of training, experience base, and personal preference when he accepts a position in a training program. A professional orientation would regulate his accepting positions in training programs that were not consistent with his own experience and personal qualifications.

There are no hard and fast divisions between here-and-now data and back-home data that can always differentiate nicely for a given program. Certain back-home concerns may be relevant for the most highly here-and-now oriented program. It would be impossible at this point in training methodology to establish definitive rules for trainer behavior. Reliance must continually be placed on the judgment of the trainer to keep the general direction of the training consistent with the agreed goals and expectations of all those who are participating in, sponsoring, and conducting the program.

REFERENCES

Bindrim, P. "Nudity As a Quick Grab for Intimacy in Group Therapy," *Psychology Today* 3, no. 1 (1969): 28.

NTL Institute for Applied Behavioral Science. "NTL Management Laboratories Brochure." Washington, D.C., 1968.

Index